Dedication

This memoir is dedicated to people instrumental to my immigration, education, family and friends: Each redirected the course of my life.

[Since 1965] Wayne Kooy changed the course and direction of my life. We fell in love, married, raised a family. For the most part, we have worked as a team. He transformed a profound tragedy into an opportunity by vowing to care for every household/family thing each day his schedule allowed so I could venture on my odyssey. Unbelievably, that's exactly what he did.

[1951] Pa Appel announced after soup one Sunday: "We are immigrating to Australia." My mother immediately objected saying, "Too far, Australia. We are immigrating to Canada." "Ja," Pa agreed, "Canada." He set to work and successfully organized and prepared for our large (8 children) family's departure in February, 1952.

[1959] Mr. Colenbrander drove up our country road one evening and announced: "We just opened a new Christian High School, bought a bus and have one seat left for Mary." "I already took her out of school," mother replied. "She's going to work." Mr. C. stayed till midnight until, my exhausted mother, relented. "If she pays for it herself,' she finally conceded.

[1959 – 1961] Rev. Wiebe Van Dijk, the Christian high school principal, stopped me in the hall: "I see you have not applied to Calvin. Is there a reason for that, Mary?" I responded: "Yes. I just finished the last two unexpected years. I graduated high school—the first in my family. She would never allow such a thing," to which he replied, "Well then, we won't tell them. I will submit your application and drive to St. Catharines to inform your parents two weeks before you leave." I kept the secret. He kept his promise. Off I went.

[1978] Winnie Prins Medema, spontaneous adventurer, lover of all things green and growing, school librarian friend who introduced me to English children's books, plants, baking, and canning. We picked fruit with our kids, and visited each other, all the while, enjoying endless cups of black coffee. Winnie taken too soon from this life; gone, but never forgotten

How did I get here?

AN IMMIGRANT'S ODYSSEY

Mary Appel Kooy

a memoir

ISBNs: 978-1-989707-31-9 (Paperback)
978-1-989707-32-6 (eBook)

In collaboration with:

Carnelian Moon
PUBLISHING

Table of Contents

"In the beginning I was so young and such a stranger to myself I hardly existed. I had to go out into the world and see it and hear it and react to it, before I knew at all who I was, what I was, what I wanted to be."

— MARY OLIVER, UPSTREAM: SELECTED ESSAYS

Acknowledgments

"To appreciate others is to unveil the hidden gems within the tapestry of humanity." – Anonymous

In thankfulness and gratitude to:

~ My loving husband Wayne, and our amazing children Tracey, Kent and Kurt, whose overarching love, interest and support have kept the momentum of my writing alive;

~ My sister Tina, whose book, *A Basket Full of Appels; Baskets Full of Stories*, revealed her storytelling strengths, her joy of writing, and her love of music. She inspired me to write this memoir;

~ My dearest longstanding BC friends, Alida, Sue and Tony, Alice and Jack, my family, listeners whose interest never flagged;

~ Sylvia Van Poolen reminded me with each telephone call: "I'm 89, I'm 90; I'm 91, I'm 92, I'm 93.. ." Where is that book? I need to read that book." I delivered the manuscript to Sylvia in March of 2024, just in time for her to read it from beginning to end – sadly, she passed in 2024. She will be in my heart forever.

~ My book club friends who read each selection with candor and brought a unique slant that encouraged us to become a wonderful community of readers and learners.

~ James Korf, professor emeritus of Drama, created over 40 posters for the plays he directed over the years at Calvin University in Grand Rapids, Michigan. His cover artwork clearly paints a picture of the uncertainties of place in this memoir entitled: *How did I get here? An Immigrant's Odyssey.*

~ My former student, Ed, who, twenty years after the class, sent a letter that captures the pointed essence of teaching and learning in schools. I learned, he taught.

~ Judith Richardson Schroeder at Carnelian Moon Publishing, Inc. guided, listened to, and supported me in the creation of my first memoir. She so artfully designed the layout and worked with the artist on the cover. The result is a luminous book that, as one reviewer said: "You will feel as if you are walking beside Mary, feeling her emotions, as she navigates the unchartered paths to discovering her greatness in a strange place.

Reader Reviews

Love this book...

How Did I Get Here: An Immigrant's Odyssey takes you on a journey alongside Mary Appel. You will feel as if you are walking beside her, feeling her emotions, as she navigates the unchartered paths to discovering her greatness in a strange place. You will laugh with her, cry with her and feel compassion for the child who felt invisible. Her victories, both personal and professional, are remarkable achievements we can all relate to and feel proud to have been invited to share the experiences with. Faith, luck and hard work come into play for Mary, not to mention her indomitable strength and perseverance. For myself, and all other children of immigrants, who didn't understand what that journey was like, this is a perfect example of the hardships and complexities that arise when starting a new life in a new country. Love this book.

— *Kateryna Bohn Reid, Toronto, Ontario*

Master storyteller...

How Did I Get Here is a deeply engaging story of the dreams, disappointments, joys and challenges of immigration, and the implications of the culture shock the author felt landing into a strange, new country. The soul-agonizing longing to simply belong and often feeling and experiencing lack of acceptance for who she is as a person, is a theme that shapes this heart-warming memoir. The tensions involved in a conflicted family system, combined with a clash of generational, religious and cultural values is told with honesty, humour and pain.

Mary Appel Kooy is a master storyteller who pulls the reader into her continually changing world. She is aware that the tension between the culture she is trying to escape and culture she is wanting to embrace is not easily resolved. She looks back in amazement and truly wonders, "how did I get here?"

— *Martin Contant*

An excellent story...

In reading this memoir, I hear the author's voice, I feel her pain at the continued rejection that she experienced, and I ache with her about the outrage she felt at always being considered an outsider. The pain and angst of the early years through high school and college that she so eloquently describes become less prominent as she finds her way in the world through her return to academia all the way to earning her Ph D.

As a Dutch immigrant myself, her description of the ollieballen, the crinkle of the roll of King peppermints in church, and the routine of the 10 am coffee came alive on the page for me and I could almost taste each of them.

All in all, an excellent story that describes brilliantly the difficulty of the Dutch immigrant experience in the early fifties and the triumph of finally accepting her Dutch heritage, embracing her new land and finding her place in both the land of her birth and in her adopted land.

— *Dian H. Toronto, Ontario*

Inspiring book...

As the child of Dutch immigrants I read this book with intense interest. This is a story of growth, in which the character of the author blooms like the proverbial dandelion. Torn from her native soil, she survives a harsh transplanting and long periods of drought, during which she struggles to find nourishment in hostile ground. It is in the field of education – the community of learning, teaching and writing – where she flourishes and bears fruit. Along the way are individuals who see what she could be, even when she cannot, providing stories of grace that contribute to the overall theme of wonder and gratitude that shines from this inspiring book.

— *Laura Peetoom, Toronto, Ontario*

Story of empowerment...

Mary courageously invites the reader into her personal story as an immigrant in an unfamiliar world, facing many challenges as she discovers where she belongs. Her voice comes through strongly as she candidly describes the characters and events that have shaped her life and identity. Delightful anecdotes enrich the memoir, drawing readers in and making them feel as if they were there alongside her. Mary's story of empowerment is inspiring.

— *Arlene Stegeman, British Columbia, Canada*

The current era of global migration makes this book all the more relevant...

This beautiful narrative about the search for a sense of belonging is told from the perspective of Mary, a post-war Dutch immigrant girl who moved to Canada with her family at the age of eight. After the war, many people fled from grief and poverty and hoped for a better life in Canada or the US. For an eight-year-old, this means she has no choice but to come along and undergo the incredible transformation of her life. Mary takes us with her when describing her life and evolving self, with powerful themes such as loneliness, love, loss, and the power of education. "Dig in and see what happens" becomes her way of taking life into her own hands, leading to a life in academia. Finally embracing her dual identity at the age of 65, she feels at home at last. Anyone dealing with or trying to understand the impact of immigration on people's lives and identity will recognize the themes Mary deals with. The current era of global migration makes this book all the more relevant and leads us to question how we can support immigrant children to find their way in a world that is confusing and to develop their dual identity. It leads to a fresh pair of eyes on immigration and appeals to a more understanding way of approaching immigrants, in which a warm welcome is included.

— *Paulien M. PhD, Radboud University*
Nijmegen, the Netherlands

Mary's story is for "such a time as this"...

Immigration is a very real event in peoples' lives worldwide today!

This book has affected me personally. I am an immigrant child. My memory is not as vivid as the author's, but her words refreshed my emotional memory. The writer's recall and odyssey are authentic and honest.

The reflections of the days prior to the departure from the Netherlands and on the ship are somber, emotional, foreboding, and intense. The sense of fear, adventure, and anticipation is felt throughout this life-changing event for the Appel family.

The author has taken us with her throughout this journey of pain, rejection, acceptance, love and hope.

— *Alice VanDyke*

Dear Mary…

I read your book – started yesterday and finished today. I couldn't put it down. Last night your childhood was my last thought before going to sleep and this morning, on waking up, it was the first thing I thought of.   I understand why Wayne cried reading it.

Your story touched me and made me sad and angry for the undeserved treatment you received from your family, teachers, and classmates. It also brought to life the immigrant story and the horrors and abuse associated with the immigrants arriving in the early 1950's.

I relate to your constant Dutch vs Canadian struggle. I loved the ending and how you came to a resolve being Dutch and Canadian. I'm not there yet, finding myself too Dutch for Canada and too Canadian for the Netherlands but I hope in time I can find that as well.

Mary, an amazing story of your life. I have always admired and respected you but reading how you arrived to where you are is beyond words. Thank you for sharing your story.

— *Corrie Mulder*

I have just finished your memoir. It's terrific. I devoured it. It's wrenching in so many ways. A young girl finding her way in a strange, often indifferent, and even hostile world. . . . And so well told. Your memory for details is, well, incredible. Thanks so much . . .

— *Dr. Nick Wolterstorff, Emeritus*
Yale University

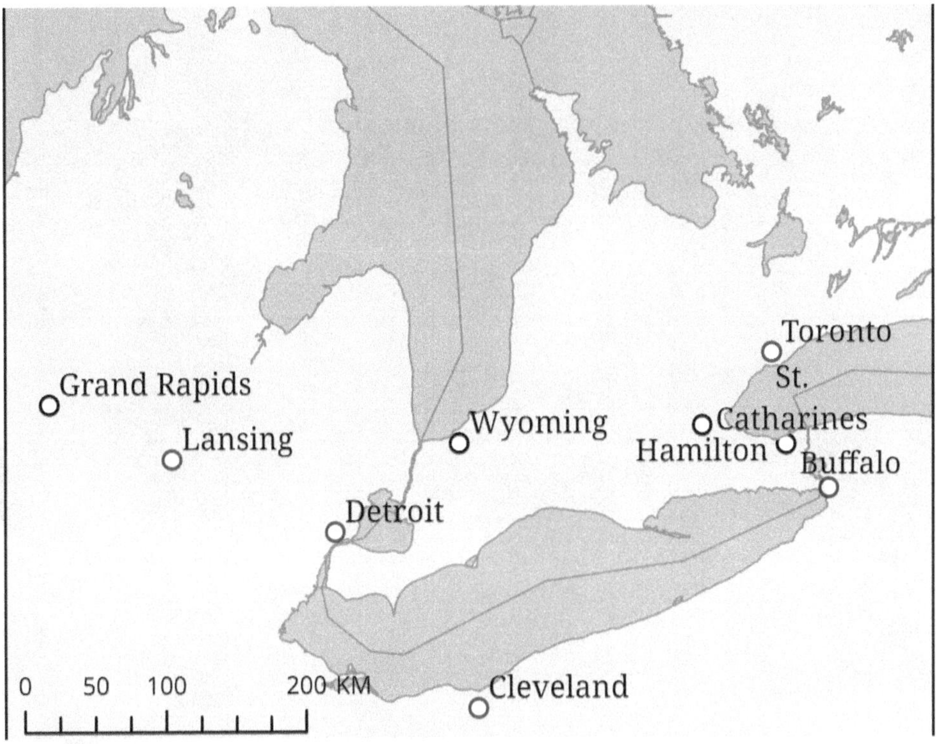

Ontario Map

BC Map

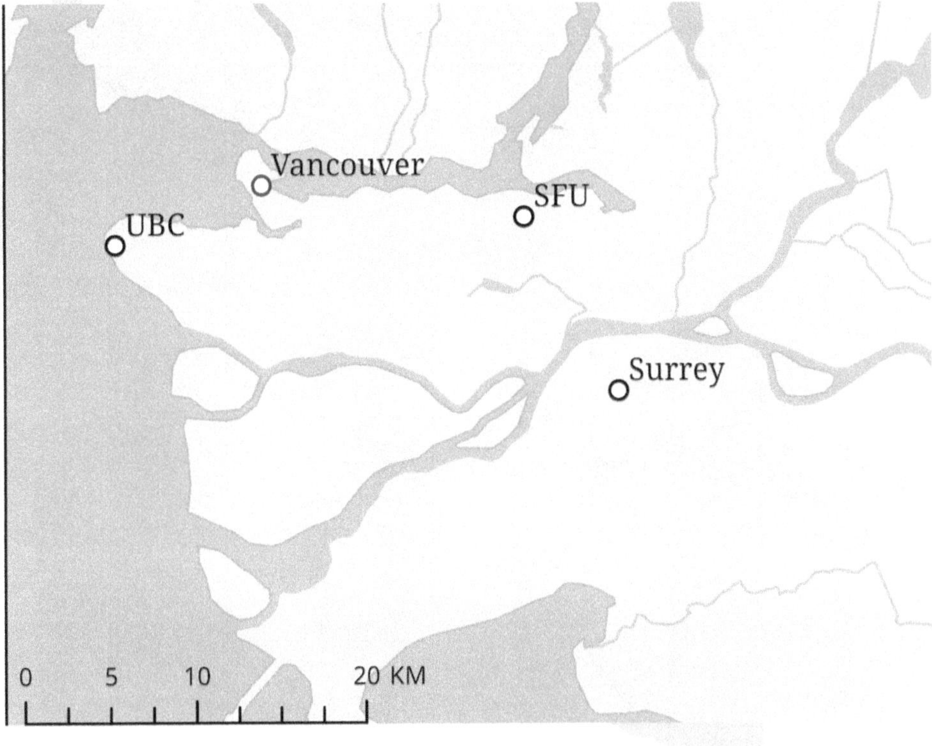

Pa
1903-1966

Moe
1907-1991

Siaak/Jack
1927-1999

Dick
1929-1937

Tinie/Tina
1931-2018

Leny/Elaine
1935

Gre/Margaret
1932-2004

Hugh
1933

Alie/Alice
1938

Ria/Mary
1943

Anneke/Anne
1947

Tracey (Jim)
1970

Kent (Vicky)
1975

Kurt (Shelly)
1975

Brett
2003

Ayla
2016

Caleb
2004

Addison
2009

Ria
2019

Mya
2006

Leah
2009

Family Tree

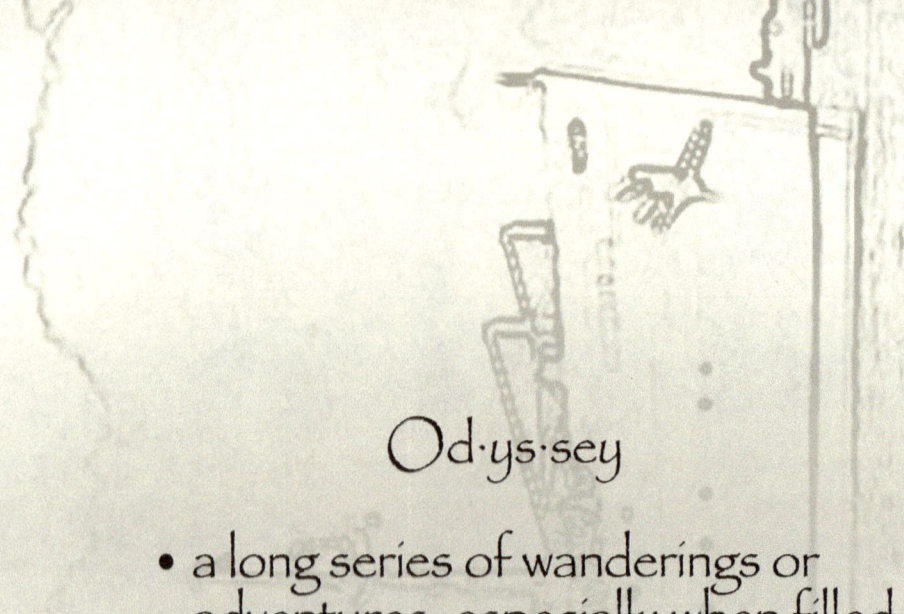

Od·ys·sey

- a long series of wanderings or adventures, especially when filled with notable experiences, hardships, etc.;

- a long, exciting journey;

- a series of experiences that teach you something about yourself or about life a spiritual odyssey;

- a long journey with a lot of adventures and difficulties.

Chapter One

~∞~

The Crossing
February, 1952

Rotterdam. Husky train whistle blows, as high-pitched screeching brake slows down the train. We disembarked – nine of us, including my Pa and Moe – stand and grab our bags and exit in single file. No laughter. Many tears. Somber silence. In the frigid February air, our breaths made little bursts of puffy clouds in the cold air. The older ones lugged the heavy bags toward the ship.

Small groups, people of all ages, gathered on the quay, saying tearful good-byes. Tearful because they never expected to return – to family, neighbours, friends, church. The somber scene soon grew into pods of families and friends. Electricity in the air. A low buzz increased in pitch and variety as the quay loaded. An orchestra of sounds. Rotterdam Quay gave me a fright.

All around me like a cloud, the noises, the ship's moaning whistles, the talking and sobbing drowned out my childish voice: "Where do we go, Pa?" I shouted.

Pa said only, "Stay close by." He pointed to a massive ship that

1

would be our home for the next eight days. The horizon disappeared.

A bewildering cacophony of random noises and loud whistles met people as they entered the quay. Mingling on the deck, crying, and talking produced a relentless buzz. I pushed against the masses of bodies all around me.

De Zuiderkruis stood docked and ready to take in over eight hundred passengers dreaming of a new life in Canada. The ship dwarfed everything around it. Its sheer size took up most of the horizon. I placed both hands over my ears and waited, teeth clenched. I wanted to get into the ship, away from the confusion.

A long, snaking line now headed toward the ship. Final family, friends, and neighbour goodbyes. Brother Sjaak followed us as long as he could, gathering extra hugs. Plans for him to immigrate to North Carolina in the US were in process. Why didn't he come with us? How long would it be before we would see him again? Sjaak lifted Anneke into the air and kissed her goodbye, tears spilling down his cheeks. Wiping his eyes with his sleeve, he turned, head down, to exit through the station door.

Finally, the ship signaled a warning, "The time has come," the rest joined the long climb up the wide wooden stairs and onto the ship's deck. Pa gave me his pocket handkerchief – white, of course, and perfectly ironed – so I could wave and wipe my tears. I found a small place at the handrail, just big enough to squeeze in.

"Clear the deck. Only passengers may remain," the loudspeaker announced.

The dock cleared. Fewer and fewer people remained. Waving handkerchiefs stopped.

The massive ship's chimney moaned. Clouds of grey smoke poured out skyward. The ship creaked and screeched as it began its exit from the dock. I balanced myself, holding on to whatever was solid and close. We were on the North Sea now, moving away, farther from the quay. The dock stood empty. Butterflies danced wildly in my stomach – excitement at the adventure, mesmerized by all things large, the commanding scenes, my family. I felt so small, because, of course, I was.

I stood with Pa at the railing, watching Holland get smaller and smaller until it disappeared altogether. Only water, as far as the eye could see, remained.

On board, crew members got to work, dividing us into two groups: men to one dormitory and women and children to another. Each dormitory held at least sixty beds, Tinie told me.

Moe entered the large room filled with bunk beds. No wardrobes, no table space. Close quarters. A sink on the wall stood at the end of each bunk bed row. A space under each lower bunk bed would store our clothing and necessities. Beds in the air? Ladders?

"Can I sleep up there, Moe?" I begged.

"Ja," she responded. "I'll sleep on the lower bed with Anneke beside me."

My sisters bustled around and organized their space under each bunk bed as Moe tucked away our belongings. I had difficulty sorting it all out. Sitting on the edge of the bed, I listened to the stories my sisters told. They put on brave faces. Much nervous laughter.

In the crowded and noisy dormitory, people cried, sobbed softly, looked frightened, and trembled in fear; all around us was the bustle of children being put down to nap, diaper changing, lots of crying, washing up under the tap. Ready for our water journey.

Tinie writes: "I'll never forget one woman with pure white hair - and she wasn't that old either! Someone told me her hair had turned white overnight because one of her daughters had run away the day before.

She did not want to go to Canada."

AFTER AN EXHAUSTING DAY FILLED WITH FEAR AND DOUBT, THE DAY ended. Without complaint, I put on my pajamas and climbed the stairs to bed. A bed in the air, high enough to see through a porthole and hear the ever-stretching, spectacular water gently lapping against the ship. The water calmed and soothed me, though everything was strangely unfamiliar. I comforted myself with daydreams: home, school, church, friends and playing games on the street. Barely en route, I daydreamed about returning to Holland.

Tinie observed in a letter to Jan, her fiancé: "Mornings are hectic!
People have to wash up, and the washrooms are a beehive of activities. After our wash, brush, and comb, we divided into groups.
We are Group A, which means we go to breakfast first."

Quickly moving up on the deck, the others followed Tinie. She cleared a large space for the choir, stacking chairs along the wall.

My family, like the Dutch in general, were singers. Singing in church, school, at royal birthdays, Sinterklaas, Christmas, and New Year's Eve. Singing at celebrations, parades, and every kind of feast had a shared musical repertoire for each occasion. Lyrics and music stayed alive by sharing. Led by Moe, we continued the tradition that marked our family as "the Singing Appels" on board.

Outside, young adults stood in a protected area following Tinie's lead. "There by the Windmill" (*Daar bij die molen*) she sang, quickly linking arms with Gré. Others followed, and so did the singing. With arms hooked, they started the familiar sway from left to right. Tinie called, "C'mon, Ria. Stand here with me."

Me, join? This was my chance! I edged closer to my family and their growing collection of new singing friends. I couldn't get there fast enough. Oh, what a glorious grownup feeling. Belonging. So I joined the singing.

The music drew a growing audience, some to listen and most to join the singing. I sang until my throat felt dry. I was a choir member.

An interruption: *"Lunch begins in the dining room in 15 minutes, precisely at 12:00."* Our first onboard announcement. The first meal.

The choir unhooked their arms. All the Appels made their way to our table in the dining room where food fragrances wafted over the tables.

We were Group A, the first line in. People poured out of the dormitories. I looked around for my name, Appel, on the tables. "There it is," I said. I counted. Just the right number of chairs for our family.

Our silence broke only for munching and spilt drinks. After the prayer, noise filled the air. Hearing people speak, even at our own tables, proved challenging.

But oh, I loved the food.

Anneke and I stayed with Moe till our plates were clean. No surprise here. Moe's less-than-stellar cooking capacities were common after-dinner stories, erupting as soon as Moe was out of sight. She covered everything in a bland white sauce, regardless of what lay under it: cauliflower, carrots, peas – you name it, she had it covered.

After every meal, the announcement came: *"Please finish up and bring your plates and silverware to the window before leaving. The next group will be here in five minutes."*

Women and children returned to the dorms to prepare young ones for bed. Limited bathroom facilities made washing chaotic and challenging.

Moe pointed to my pajamas laid out on the lower bed. "Your pajamas are on your bag under the bed. Leave your other clothes there for tomorrow," she instructed.

I stood in my underwear and searched and found my flannel nightgown, proud to get ready by myself.

Tentatively, I climbed the wooden steps that gently swayed as I moved from one step to the other. The nightgown pulled over my head; I snuggled under the blankets. Picking up a storybook, I puffed up my pillow, pulled back the blankets, and looked around in the dimming light.

"Don't forget to say your prayers," Moe reminded me.

On my knees in the bed, I recited, "I'm going to sleep. I'm tired now." ("*Ik ga slapen, ik ben moe.*")

Everything around me grew quiet. Calm seas lulled me, and after such an exhausting day, sleep came with little effort, though not before visiting my life before this ship, picturing my friends, my school, my church, our street, our house.

BY MORNING, DAY THREE, THE OCEAN WATER SLAPPED MORE insistently against the ship, rocking it back and forth. I stayed in bed to read my book.

A sharp knock silenced the chatter in the room. Several voices chimed simultaneously, "Ja?"

In walked a crew member with a basket of yellow fruit piled high in a brown willow basket.

"What is that?" I asked politely.

"Bananas."

I had never seen a banana, let alone tasted one. A feast for my eyes: bunches of yellow bananas.

A crew member demonstrated. "To eat this banana, you tug at the top," he said, "and pull down the other side. If you do that only halfway, you can start eating the banana from the top. When you reach the peel, you pull down again. See?"

I followed instructions, taking one exotic bite, chewing oh so slowly. A whole banana to myself. Never had I tasted anything like it. I eagerly accepted all further banana offers.

NEXT DAY, BY NOON, AN UNRELENTING SWING AND SWAY OF THE SHIP changed the calm of the previous days. A storm coming. The sky was filled with ominous clouds. A darkness descended. The dorm shook, my bed shook, I shook. What was happening? What should I do? Afraid to leave my bed.

Moe said: "Ria, climb down. Your clothes are somewhere on the floor. Look for them and get dressed so we can go to breakfast. I will help Anneke."

I found my clothes and somehow got dressed. My knit knee socks matched.

Moe, Anneke, and I made our way, reeling between one wall and the next in the roiling waters, to our table in the dining room.

The talk was all about the storm and the dangers. Many got up, covering their mouths.

Moe said, "They're seasick."

"What's that?" I asked.

"The waves roll around and the ship rocks, so people get sick."

"Will I get sick?" I asked Moe.

"Probably."

Pa and Tinie were the only ones spared of any sea sickness. I was sick for only one of the three days of the storm. Just a small part of the ship's population did *not* get seasick.

Pa took me to the ship's library. He walked in; I followed behind. The book lady helped me find some I had not yet read. New stories. Pa returned shortly with two books to take to the dormitory for Moe and one for him. I neatly put my library books under the bed and settled in on Moe's bed. Propped up on my pillow, I opened the first book. Before long, the book slipped from my hands, and I was drifting away from the ship, sailing back to my familiar world.

Troubled Waters
February, 1952

W ild, ship-rocking wind had kicked up massive swells of freezing salt water over the deck as the Dutch immigrant ship laboriously plowed its way through the dark and stormy North Atlantic. Anything not tied down sailed around the rooms and along the deck. Fearing the vessel would sustain damage, the captain repeatedly announced, "In these extreme wind and sea conditions, please return to your cabins."

Ocean water had pooled in every imaginable crack and crevice. Relentless cascading waves kept the deck slippery. Crew shouted warnings: "Caution. Watch where you walk!" as if anyone could possibly be unaware.

I backed up against the wall. Mothers walked up and down the halls as their babies and toddlers, without warning, threw up. A terrible sight. A putrid smell saturated the air.

Some passengers bucked the wind to get to the ship's railing, their rubbery legs moving as though drunk, grasping at anything solid enough to prevent them from sailing across the deck, unhinged. They slid along the boards, crashing into anything tied down. At the railing, they leaned overboard for the inelegant retching of their seasickness.

TODAY, THOUGH, WAS DIFFERENT — TODAY, A BRIGHT LIGHT IN THE porthole awakened me. A brilliant sunshine and an azure blue sky greeted me. Only a slight breeze tickled the deck. Swish, swish, swish. The waves rhythmically moved the ship forward. Calm descended.

Today, the deck filled with passengers, young and old, eager to bask in their renewed world.

A crackling loudspeaker message interrupted the celebration: "This is your captain speaking…"

We snapped to attention, frozen in place.

"Mr. Gerard Appel. . . report to the ship's office for an important message."

Pa's back straightened, a puzzled look appeared on his face, and he stepped briskly to the office. The door opened and shut.

Eerily hushed, our family circled Moe, waiting for Pa to return. A worried look clouded Moe's face. Dread of the "might be" made Moe restless, skittish. Nervously, she waited, wondered, and worried.

Pa returned and slowly settled next to trembling Moe, whose feet uncontrollably click-click-clicked on the deck. She looked over to Pa and whispered hoarsely, "What? What? What did they say?"

Pa took a big breath and, just loud enough for the family to hear, said: "Our sponsor backed out. We can't go to Windsor."

Moe's already-pale face turned ashen. My siblings and I stood frozen in place, silently expecting, hoping for some alternative, some better news.

Pa pulled a document from an official-looking envelope – our identification:

Appel, Gerard Cornelis
Spouse: Oosterwijk, Lena
Family size: 7
Religion: Christian Reformed
Origin: Baarn, Utrecht
Arrival year: 1952
Destination: Windsor, Ontario

"What is this?" Moe hissed. Yanking the paper from Pa's hand, she quickly scanned it. "What is this?" she repeated, waving the paper in Pa's face. Hand on forehead, shoulders drooped, she looked forlornly at Pa and groaned, "What are we going to do? Do we have to go back to Holland?"

The day that had begun with such promise crashed into pieces around us, changing everything. We were together; yet we were alone. It was up to Pa to lead us, to seek resolution. To what? Where?

My eyes darted from one sibling to the other. No explanations, comfort, or assurances.

I stood by, on the fringes, wondering, what's going to happen to us? Why is no one telling me anything? I am scared. I need help, I thought, but did not say. With a little shuffle, I moved to stand unnoticed beside Pa. I saw doubts and concerns on all their faces – doubting all could be, would be, well. Tears on their faces, fear in their eyes.

Slowly, Pa rose from the chair, stood erect, and turned his gaze to the vast Atlantic Ocean that sparkled and danced and glinted with diamonds as far as we all could see. Shading his eyes to avert the glare, he turned up his hands and said, with a faint surprising smugness: "Well – " [dramatic pause] "… it's too far to swim home now!"

The older ones snickered, though they knew the situation was dire, anything but humorous. Moe, slumped over and utterly despondent, jaw trembling, tried valiantly to avoid exposing her worries to others on the deck. One by one, the siblings left to join those already gathered in their singing corner. Once her singing Appels were on the way, Moe lifted herself up, grabbed Anneke's hand, and returned to the dormitory room, mumbling repeatedly, "What now? What now?"

Moe complained of a piercing migraine headache as she dabbed her forehead lightly with a crisp white hankie sprinkled with *eau de cologne* – a habit she usually reserved only for church. The migraine kept Moe in bed during the day. I felt anything but calm. I was confused. A pain settled in the pit of my stomach. "I wish I could turn this ship around and go home. Why can't we go home?" I cried.

Unaware of my family's plight, the deck passengers continued creating a festive atmosphere on the deck. Crowds milled around or stopped to talk in a group. Tinie and the others joined the growing choir. Better to sing than to cry in moments of crisis. Singing soothed the soul.

THE DAY BEFORE OUR EXPECTED ARRIVAL IN HALIFAX, THE CREW distributed cards with name tags, identifying destination information. Ours still said *Windsor, Ontario*.

The cards included sponsor information, the name of the train terminal, and the number of the train. The head of the household was required to telegram his sponsor to inform him of arrival details (Raska, Jan. *Pier 21, A History, 2020*).

For my family, that was a non-starter.

Calm waters, brilliant sun. Breakfast was extraordinarily noisy with anticipation and planning for the exit of the ship for our long-awaited entrance to Canada. On a chair next to Pa, I listened to my frustrated and angry siblings fretting, "What's going on? Is this the dream of Canada open for business? Canada ready to welcome the Dutch? Dreams of economic opportunities? Rainbows and pots of gold? For the others on the ship, maybe, but not for us."

Pa bundled up on his deck chair to enjoy the calm winter waterscape. My siblings nattered and grumbled.

By mid-morning coffee time, another message arrived for Pa:

Due to the unexpected withdrawal of your sponsor in Canada, Field Man, Mr. J. will meet you at Union Station, Toronto, Ontario on 23 February 1952. Please remain on the train when it stops in Montreal, Quebec.

Some relief and less trepidation – a flicker of hope, despite unanswered questions, left the older ones no alternative but to keep singing. Even calm waters and a shining sun, however, couldn't wipe out the peril of the unknown and uncertainties facing my family.

Chapter Two

Pier 21, Halifax
19 February, 1952

All packed after eight days on the vast North Atlantic, we prepared to disembark from *De Zuiderkruis* at Pier 21 in Halifax, Nova Scotia, in the middle of a brutal Canadian winter. Noise, excitement, and fear mingled as the throngs descended the gangplank to the Halifax port that welcomed new immigrants from many Western European countries.

The deluge entering Pier 21 overwhelmed me. Throngs of people filled every space.

First tentative steps onto Canadian soil – make that snow – took us into a large red brick warehouse building where Red Cross volunteers offered cookies, milk, and coffee as we took our place on hard wooden benches lined up against the walls to wait for our document inspections.

The large room soon filled with groups of families, all awaiting processing to move to Canada, their new home. Crowded, noisy. The room, with not nearly enough space to accommodate the endless rush of disembarking immigrants, delivered a tediously exhausting wait. Babies cried, toddlers ran loose, and parents lost small children in the milling, massive crowd. The cacophony of languages created a virtual Tower of Babel.

THE OFFICIALS ARRIVED TO PROCESS THE REGISTRATION. FOLLOWING orders and whistle blows, Pa learned where to go, what line to join, what papers to have ready. Pa and Moe successfully completed the forms for our landed immigrant status. I was officially a Dutch emigrant.

Awaiting our train's evening departure, Pa and Moe went into the city to buy bread, jam, and butter for the train ride to Toronto. The cost of food on the train was higher than in the city, so like good Dutch people, Pa and Moe looked for cheaper food in Halifax.

I heard little about the grim side of immigrants landing at Pier 21, who had nowhere to go, but many had frightful or dismal experiences. The facilities, as someone noted, were "fit for criminals."

One almost implausible story involved sixteen-year-old Dori, who "spent six weeks at Pier 21 when her father's sponsor backed out of his labour contract." Dori relates how she and her father received a glass of water and a bottle of ketchup on their way to Pier 21's kitchen for lunch. Neither knew what to do with the items and thought, "maybe we have to make our own tomato juice, so we stirred the ketchup in the water." (Raska, Jan. Pier 21: A History).

We could have been in a similar situation. Dreadful.

Smoky steam whisked past the train windows as it whistled and approached the station, covered and blotched in patches of dirt and snow. Pa and the older ones carried their luggage to the train car labelled *A* (for Appel). Like the vast hall of Pier 21, the hot, dirty train was outfitted with hard slatted wooden benches. Accumulated dirt and snow on shoes and coats were deposited in the aisles and on the windows.

"This is not Holland," I thought. "This is not a 'cleanliness is next to godliness' country. Godliness, maybe, but not cleanliness." We were Dutch.

My family took up three train benches. Personal items and bags went under the seats in front of us or under our feet. There was no place to get comfortable, sleep, or even get up and walk about. Though midwinter in Canada, the hot train brought discomfort and sweat. A dismal picture of our new home.

The first leg of the train trip to Montreal took twenty-one hours.

Our view of a wintry Canadian countryside came through dirty, sooty windows on the train from Halifax. In places, pristine white covered the landscape. Trees sparkled.

Moe ran out of food for our large family. Figuring out non-metric measurements and quantities required a robust rethink. With not enough food to eat, not enough room to sleep, non-stop noise, babies crying, it seemed an interminable clickety-click ride to Central Station in Montreal, all twenty-one hours of it.

The train squealed on the tracks as it came to a grinding halt at Central Station in Montreal. Windows thick with frost kept the outside world hidden from view until I put a little spittle on a hanky and rubbed hard.

Some passengers reached their destination and busily gathered their belongings to exit the train.

I was afraid of getting lost without him by my side; Pa was my guiding light. Inside the station. Moe bought some sandwiches for the last leg to Toronto.

Loudspeakers announced departure times for Toronto, and Tinie translated: "The train for Toronto leaves in 15 minutes!"

Still, we hung back to enjoy the warmth of the station. As the crowd dwindled, we exited. Once outside, an official pointed to a line for the train. How would the Field Man meet us in the Toronto station? There were so many people.

"Trust," Pa said. "He'll find us a place to live."

But what if he could not find us? We stayed close together so Mr. Field Man could identify us at Union Station in Toronto.

It paid off. He found us.

Off to Cainsville
22 February, 1952

A gain, ice formed in delicate lacy patterns, decorating the windows, preventing me from seeing much of the landscape in icy February. Soon the lace became thick and dirty black from smoke and soot. The train rambled on, noisily clicking along the rails.

Settling back on unforgiving wooden benches, we tried to sleep after the train left the station. Sleep? Some succeeded, most not.

At Union Station in Toronto, my aunt and uncle, who also immigrated earlier from Den Haag in the Netherlands, met us at the station, waving their arms wildly. Puffs like icy clouds exited their mouths. How had they known when we would arrive? I hid behind Pa. I didn't want their attention.

They hugged Pa and Moe and my reluctant siblings. We had no time for family visits. Where was the Field Man? Time to go. The station filled with people milling, connecting, heading back to the train, collecting their bags, each connecting with their assigned Field Man.

I wished so hard; I prayed with folded hands and uttered an earnest child's plea: "Bring us a Field Man, too, God!" Of course, I did not know what a Field Man was. Miraculously, the Field Man found us and shook Pa's hand, introducing himself as Mr. J.

He welcomed us to Canada and herded us away into a large white van with wooden benches and windows on each side.

My parents and siblings waved good-bye to the relatives. I did not.

The back door of the van opened. Hugh helped Pa place our belongings in the back, and then Pa climbed into the front seat, while the rest of us found places on the benches along the sides of the van.

"I will search for a permanent house and work," the Field Man said in Dutch. He assured Pa he would find a house and promised agency-sponsored jobs. First order of business, though, was housing to accommodate nine people. Four different families in Toronto (all Christian Reformed and Dutch) agreed to take in two or three family members. Off we went.

All was new. A big city, lots of cars on the roads. Nothing familiar greeted us. Exhausted, I slept through most of the Ontario sights and sounds.

A FEW DAYS LATER, MR. J. ARRIVED AT OUR TEMPORARY HOSTS' HOMES and told us, "I found a temporary house. You can stay there until I find something more permanent." For some three hours, over the snow and gravel of Canadian roads, we huddled together on cold, hard benches in the back of the white van. We bumped along until we arrived in the small rural village of Cainsville, Ontario, where the van stopped in front of an imposing, large red brick square house. Snow everywhere.

The Field Man got out and plowed through the snow to open the front door, placing some groceries on the wood floor. "Plenty of wood at the back," he said, pointing out the window to the woodpile, neatly stacked.

"Hugh," Pa said, "get wood from the pile outside and stoke a fire in the wood stove."

The others emptied the van of our belongings for what would be a temporary stay.

The Winter family from church had prepared and collected winter clothing, including boots, coats, hats, mitts, and wool scarves, all laid out on the floor to prepare for our arrival in categories: men, women, girls. Generous families from the local CRC delivered essentials to eat and extra warm clothes to wear. Others left groceries, a hot plate, and two pans stocking the small kitchen.

We ate quickly, sitting on the cold wood floor. The black

potbelly stove roared with a flame I could see through the stove window. It mesmerized.

THE HOUSE STOOD BARE. NOTHING ON THE WOOD FLOOR. NO furniture, no beds, no table. Mr. Jongbloed delivered a load of two-by-four lumber. Pa took the hammer and nails provided and nailed them into bed boxes, large rectangles. A local farmer donated straw and church members brought sheets, blankets, pillows, and other essentials for sleeping. This dormitory paled in comparison with the ship's fully equipped rooms with actual beds, beds in the sky.

Pa spread straw evenly in each bed frame and lined up the "beds" in a long row along the floor, one hooked to the next. My sisters placed flannel sheets atop the straw. It was a story in the making.

"Where's my bed, Pa?" I asked.

Pa pointed to a bed in the middle of the row. The others followed, each nestling under the blankets. Moe piled our coats on top of us. Hugh had loaded the wood stove to keep us warm during the night, and we tried to sleep.

This world had little to recommend it: raw, basic, yet a place to sleep besides a ship, a train, or a van.

LOST AND UNMOORED, PA AND MOE HAD HAPPILY ACCEPTED THE invitation of the Field Man, who told them as he waved a friendly goodbye, "The Winter family will come by tomorrow morning to take you to church. Be ready by the front door by 9:30 AM."

After a fitful night of sleep, we climbed out of straw beds, itching all over. Scratching. Getting dressed proved challenging. The cold house in the morning left me shivering and shaking. Time to load the stove. Hugh filled it with wood that soon roared to life. We cleaned up at a pump in the little kitchen. Picking through the piles of winter clothes took some time.

"I guess this is what they wear in Canada," Tinie said with a grin on her face. We all got dressed, and Moe prepared breakfast.

TIME FOR CHURCH

One by one we peeked through the front window, waiting, ready for pickup. The van plowing through the snow arrived, and Mr. Winter climbed out. We were ready. We piled into *another* large white van, found our seats on the hard benches, and headed to our first church service in Canada.

A plain, unadorned country church borrowed from a Canadian congregation would be our church. The snow on the path to the door had been shoveled, leaving a narrow path to the church doors. Carefully finding our way out of the van, we walked into church single file. Small church with well-worn pews.

Our family, as usual, took up an entire pew. At least that was familiar.

I recognized familiar rituals: sermon in Dutch, song numbers on two boards on either side of the pulpit. When the organist began playing, others in the pews opened the hymnals from the racks on the back of each pew – all in English. We found the number on the sign in the front and sang (at least we tried to), "The Old Rugged Cross."

Tinie's powerful alto voice rang out.

A smile crossed Moe's face. The smile got broader. She raised her hand and covered her mouth, trying desperately to suppress the laughter. Alas, in vain. Instead, she released little explosive spurts of laughter.

One look at Moe set the others off.

"What is so funny?" I asked.

"A *cross*?" Moe whispered back: "They sing about a *cross*. In Dutch, that's an old jalopy car. Why would they sing about an old jalopy car in church?"

Once we got outside, gales of loud laughter rang all the way back to our temporary home. Church had started off with a bang.

Off to School I go
25 February, 1952

On Monday morning, Pa opened the front door of our first real Canadian house. We would begin our Canadian life here.

"Come here and look, Alie and Ria..." Pa motioned for us to come to the open door to look to the left: "Keep walking on this same road till you see a school on your left side. It is a bright red small building," he said.

Two days after arriving in Cainsville, Alie and I walked along a never-before-seen road in the never-before-experienced freezing weather, to a never-before-seen sight: an apple red wooden building, a one-room schoolhouse far out into the country, smoke billowing from the chimney.

The bell clanged noisily. The teacher pumped it and motioned for all to come in. Guardedly, we followed students into the school. What we saw confused us. Rows of single seats. Only one room for an entire school? One teacher and all grades?

A potbelly stove stood at the back of the room, a large stack of wood drying next to it. A fire burned behind the small stove window. Those who sat close kept warm. Desks stood in eight rows, one for each grade. A piano stood in one corner. The front wall had blackboards with chalk and board erasers. I could read the numbers. I wondered, where am I? This is school?

Hesitantly, I looked at the teacher, who pegged us as immigrants, probably without a word of English. She found two small desks for Grade 1 students and, without speaking, pointed to Alie and me.

Alie looked over at me with fear. She tried squeezing into the little desk, twisting to and fro. She finally succeeded – but she was stuck. Trapped. How would she ever get out? It was in the first row! Had the teacher just put her back to grade 1? Alie looked ready to cry. Failure in school in the Netherlands deepened her misery. Alie started school a year late because of the World War II occupation. She spent two years in Grade 4. She hated school. To make matters worse, we spoke no English, obviously – and the teacher spoke no Dutch, also obviously. We felt lost.

The teacher pointed to books, the blackboards at the front and our two small desks. Alie did not cry. She set her jaw.

My brief school experiences in the Netherlands had not prepared me for this, but certainly did not compare to Alie's experiences. The gobbledygook of the language made things considerably worse. I could not explain: "I am in Grade 2 and my sister is in Grade 5."

"This is not school. I want to go back to my school. Here, big kids and small kids all sit in the same class. I don't like Canada. I am in a foreign land and observed: things are different here."

A Grade 1 reader appeared on our desks. While the teacher worked with the other grades, Alie scanned the first three pages, slammed the book shut, folded her arms on the tiny table and waited.

I did not. Examining every page, puzzled by the picture style of the characters, I tried to read, but took no meaning from the words, "Run, Dick, run," even though the pictures told a story.

These books were stiff and uninteresting, not like my beautiful proper story books. "I want my Dutch books," I whispered to myself.

It's difficult to explain the muddled, strange, unknown world I now occupied – curious to see books but not understanding them, people smiling but unable to respond, other than with hand gestures or another smile.

The teacher clearly had no notion of where to begin, and clearly, neither did we. We knew, however, that we were not in Grade 1.

When the teacher handed out arithmetic books, Alie and I looked at each other and grinned. Finished in record time, we closed the arithmetic books and folded our hands on the desk to show we had finished.

We looked on as the teacher wandered around, stopping by each grade row to assign and listen to the other students – all able to speak English fluently and for us, mysteriously. We tried following instructions by watching other students, though not the Grade 1 students.

Lunch at school was another new phenomenon. Moe found a paper bag for our sandwiches and handed it to Alie at the door. Some children stayed inside to avoid the bitter cold outside, another first. Others ate and quickly put on coats, hats, and mittens to play outside. Alie and I watched at the windows as snowballs whizzed by and, to our amazement, a snowman grew. All foreign, unknown phenomena.

After lunch, singing time. The teacher sat on the piano bench. This was promising. We knew how to sing. The teacher sang in her clear, loud voice: *"D'ye ken John Peel?"* Students limply joined along.

Alie stared at the teacher in disbelief. Her mouth dropped.

I whispered, "What's the matter?"

She shook her head, her cheeks blazing. She was too outraged to explain.

At 4 p.m., with the ringing of the teacher's bell, school was officially declared over for the day. With our hats, mittens, boots, and coats back on, we began our walk back to the house.

"Alie, what happened when the kids sang that song with the teacher? Why did you look so mad?"

Alie said, "I'll tell you when we get home." As we walked, she complained and grumbled all the way back to our temporary house. Alie flew up the steps, opened the front door, and hollered loudly, "Hallo!"

Catching our parents' attention, Alie announced loudly and without hesitation, "I will never, ever go to school in Canada again. They sing dirty songs here. They sang about a *piel*."

Shock appeared on all the faces.

That word, Alie understood, did not belong in school: the word

Peel in the song was pronounced exactly like the word *piel* in Dutch, a slang word for penis.

Alie was having none of it.

SO HERE WE WERE IN A CANADIAN SCHOOL WITH DESKS THAT DID NOT fit, a foreign language we could neither speak nor understand, baby worksheets in arithmetic, and a dirty song that convinced Alie to vow she had no intention of ever returning to school.

"I want to go to work," Alie repeated over and over.

Moe agreed. Nobody objected.

Alie joyfully abandoned school. She had completed Grade 4 back home; one day of school in Canada turned out to be more than enough. Like me in kindergarten in the Netherlands, Alie was a one-day dropout. She joined her older siblings, none of whom had completed secondary school. School, obviously, did not hold rank or importance – jobs, work and money were most important in this land of opportunity.

Chapter Three

Fenwick, Canada
1952

From the window of the van, slowing to make a turn, we saw a yellow brick house with a large front porch and the classic yellow gingerbread trim on the roof edges. The house, unlike any we saw at home, sat far back on the property of Prudhomme's nursery, a scrubby lawn stretching from the house to the road, curving at the house, an arc.

Our family pitched in, setting up the house with the belongings in hand. Bed setup required additional lumber, this time to build separate single beds. A borrowed table and chairs for the kitchen, with a wooden bench along the wall. Firewood stacked at the front door fueled the black stove.

Work at the Prudhomme Nursery began when the weather warmed enough to plant and work the fields. Each sibling worked fifty-nine hours per week at forty cents an hour and received $1.00 spending money per week.

Too young to work, I set out alone each morning with a lunch bucket to walk to the one-room school.

The first morning, Moe handed me my lunch; Pa took me to the road and pointed to another red brick school. I concentrated on his directions along the gravel road. Off I went.

Still unable to speak English, having been in Canada only slightly more than a week, I panicked. How will I tell the teacher who I am? How will I say, "I am in Grade 2"? How will I know what to do? What if they sing dirty songs?

My body tensed as I plodded along the road. I wanted to turn back and tell Moe I needed my real school, where I could speak Dutch and play with my friends. I moaned, feeling sorry for myself, not impressed with this muddled, strange, unknown world.

At school, once again, I followed students who confidently walked inside.

The teacher, looking up, saw me hesitantly inching toward the front of the room where she stood at her desk. She smiled and welcomed me. At least that's what I assumed – in English, of course – and pointed to a desk. In the first row. Back to Grade 1.

A copy of *Dick and Jane* landed on my little desk. Again, I opened the book and looked at the beginning, slowly turning the pages of the frozen images, little stock characters, few words: "See Dick. See Jane."

I examined every page and tried to read. Reading, I thought, is different here. Nobody laughs, cries, or worries about the characters, who are just puppets. Fake. They don't have adventures.

Another arithmetic workbook fell on my school desk. I knew these simple forms of arithmetic! Finished first, I set the workbook on my desk and folded my hands to show I had completed the assignment. I looked over at the Grade 2 work. Easy.

I was in the wrong grade. Bored, I took up the Arithmetic book again and found the next lesson, and the next. Easy. How would I tell the teacher? I wanted to talk to her, even if I could only point.

The teacher walked up and down, stopping by each row to

assign and listen to the other students – barely keeping up with the assigned work for all eight grades, let alone able to address language instruction for a young girl who spoke no English.

I felt so alone. I wanted to go home to my family.

In a strange land, with a strange new language, in a strange school, in the wrong grade, I recognized little of my former life. Everything around me was awkward and unfamiliar. I wanted to go back to my real home. But, I had to cope. I had to learn English.

When the others in my Grade 1 class read aloud, they followed a singsong halting drone, with hesitations, stumbles, even full stops after words along the way. My pointer finger followed carefully along as the others turned the pages and took their turns. It was confusing, but I listened and looked. In the *Dick and Jane* book, I discovered my first two-syllable English word: *something!*

I was excited – I didn't know what it meant, but I knew it was bigger than most of the words in the reader. Mental clicks occurred. Before long, I zipped along, easily following the texts.

Already knowing how to read, having finished Grade 1 in the Netherlands, provided a link for this new Canadian learning. I did not know English, but I knew reading. I understood what reading *did*! Reading made me laugh, cry, hold my breath, be afraid, sprout tears, and hope for happy endings. Stories in books were my companions. Would Dick and Jane ever feel like my companions? Stiff, boring. "No comparison," I said to myself.

THE ROUTE TO SCHOOL IN FENWICK BECAME FAMILIAR AS EACH DAY I managed it. English made sense at times. It took real concentration to focus on a foreign language and make it my own, but bit by bit, phrase by phrase, meaning developed. The breakthrough was exhilarating.

Truth be told, most desperately, I wanted to know English to fit in, to be included. School had been my refuge at home, and I set out to reclaim it – this time in English. Near the end of that school year, in late June 1952, I came home with my report card and my sister

Tinie read it aloud, nodding affirmatively. She turned the card over, with a big smile on her face, and said: "You have been promoted to Grade 3."

"But I haven't finished Grade 2," I argued internally. "How does this work in Canada?"

Ironically, however, those simple, one-syllable word texts most likely were instrumental in improving my English. Fed by my determination to engage fully in the school experience, and having what Moe called a gift for language, I processed and began to understand English. By the end of the first school year, five months after our arrival, I could perform a basic translation for my parents at the bakery and the bank.

Education in Canada Style
1950 - 1951

B ack in Holland, my Grade 1 teacher announced to the class: "Soon it will be the Queen's birthday. Since the palace is nearby, we are going to walk to the palace together. Queen Juliana has invited all school children to come and wish her our congratulations."

Go to the palace? Electric excitement! Walking to the palace was an annual event at my school, seeing it was close enough for us all to walk together. For me, this was the first time, and the last time, to walk to the palace, given we were moving to Canada. I knew about the Palace in Soestdijk. Moe bragged to the neighbours about her brother Gerard, the royal baker who lived in the palace. I wondered if I would see him.

On the appointed day, the sun shone brightly on the school's asphalt playground, students noisy and excitedly waited for teachers to organize us and get going. We fell into pairs, and our line snaked around my classroom window that faced the street. The line continued along the sides of the street with water-filled ditches. I could hardly breathe.

The long snaking line of schoolteachers and all the students of the school arrived at the massive black spears of the wrought-iron gates. Perfectly still, guards were on watch on either side. Quietly, respectfully, we entered the royal grounds and the path leading to the palace. Each step crunched my way toward the palace that stood stark and white, stretched across the landscape.

The royal family sat on the massive patio on regal chairs with Queen Juliana in the middle, Prince Bernhard on the left, and Princess Beatrix, heir apparent, on the right. On either side were Princesses Margriet, Irene, and Christina.

As we filed down the gravel walk, the space behind the royal family filled with the brilliant array of flowers the Dutch are famous for, especially tulips in the myriad of colours of early May. Teachers stopped their charges in front of the Queen to allow one girl or boy from the class to extend a bouquet. My classmate handed the bouquet to the Queen, who acknowledged the colourful spray and smiled. I imagined myself handing the flowers to the Queen. Oh, how I wished the teacher had picked me!

We walked in pairs around the other side of the immaculately graveled arc and out through the gate and into the street. Nothing for the rest of my school years even remotely compared.

Princess Margriet and I were born the same year, though not surprisingly, under vastly different circumstances. Our teacher explained Princess Margriet was born in Ottawa, Canada, where her mother Princess Juliana, the designated Queen, took refuge during the war. The Ottawa Civic Hospital was declared Dutch soil so the princess could hold Dutch nationality.

Celebrations for her birth started with a waving a Dutch flag on the Peace Tower and Dutch music playing in the tower carillon. After Canadians liberated the Netherlands and Princess Juliana returned home, she sent gifts – including 20,000 tulip bulbs. Tulips still arrive in Ottawa annually inspiring tulip festivals.

My own ill-timed birth, on the other hand, came midway through World War II, and Moe, severely undernourished, could not nurse me. Pa was a long way away in France, conscripted to dig up cadavers of soldiers to send back to Germany for proper burials. Macabre task.

Black shades covered every window as darkness approached. No light in the dark. No milk. Seven children. No school. The Hunger Winter (1944-1945) lurked just around the corner. It would not get better. Life was a series of crises.

Occupation of the Netherlands by Nazi Germany affected every aspect of life. My sister Tina, just thirteen years old at the time, told me a story of a painful experience she had in 1945:

"A crisis happened on April 26, 1945, when a girl named Alie, who lived one street over, and Hugh and I went to a farming area to get some milk for Ria, my younger sister, who was a half year old at the time. Hugh and I each had (I think) a glass bottle and some money, a few coins. We arrived at an intersection in Baarn barricaded by the Germans to keep Canadian soldiers from advancing to that area. So we snuck through someone's garden and went on our way. The place was about 15 km from our house.

When we got to the first farm, I said to Hugh (9 years old): 'Try to get some milk here and if you get some, go straight back home. Use the coins I gave you. Don't follow us. Go straight back home!'

When we arrived back at the Baarn intersection, we heard whistling, piercing sounds - enormous explosions. One after the other. Not knowing what they were, we stood under a tree, trying to decide what to do. The explosions continued around us.

Two men stood a little way away. I said to my friend, Alie: "Let's go stay with them." They told us: "It's not safe here for you." They were some kind of air wardens. Instead, they told us, "Every time you hear the whistling sound (more like a screaming sound), press yourselves against a tree trunk (thank goodness for trees!), and after the explosion, run and find shelter in a house in the area."

We approached the first house we encountered. The

woman answered the door and said: "You can stand inside our front door!" Moe always warned us to never ever stand inside a door or by a window. Get under a table, if you have one. Go to a cellar. We quietly snuck out of that house and soon found another where the people took us downstairs to their basement. They even gave us some soup!

The attack lasted until 7 in the morning. We thanked our gracious hosts, took our half liter of milk and started for home. The road was littered with shards from the exploding grenades. We obviously survived. In looking around at the devastation, I thought it might be interesting to take some grenade shards home for souvenirs.

When I arrived home, Mother just stood there, speechless! I guess she thought I could not still be alive. The shards I carried along, however, did not impress her. In her estimation, if you could not put an item to good use, it wasn't worth keeping. So much for storing the shards."

The days got warmer, and we used more items in our carry-on baggage. In the little town of Fenwick, Moe bought work clothes in the local general store for the six family workers. The General Store was, as it said, General. They carried groceries, clothing, footwear, and furnishings, all things needed to get us started in our new immigrant lives. We had to be creative with the clothing – Anneke and I had the most trouble; we grew taller and quickly outgrew the clothes Moe packed for us in the Netherlands.

Living in Canada was different. We lived far out in the country, not in town with access to groceries and markets. Now, every Saturday, Pa and Moe got a ride to the General Store, where they filled big paper bags full of food and basics. Moe's delight included white bread. She marveled at the purity of the bleached white slices, assuming pure white meant better, though it really meant bleached, which doesn't sound better.

Canadian raisin bread, though, could not compare. Real raisin bread, we knew, had to be filled with small black dried currants. We didn't want *raisin* bread; we wanted currant bread. Raisin bread included only a smattering of raisins that landed only here and there on each slice. My sisters said, "This Canadian raisin bread had only a raisin here and there. You need a bike to get from one raisin to the other." Uproarious laughter always followed. Every time I heard that, I laughed, picturing the bike traversing the bread.

Pure white margarine came in a sturdy plastic pouch, and its small orange-colour pellet amazed Moe. At home, she broke the orange pellet and squashed and squeezed till the margarine looked orangey-yellow, supposedly resembling butter. I shudder at the thought. Moe, however, found the orange "butter" and pure white bread magically miraculous and, of course, cheaper than real butter or Dutch currant bread.

To great fanfare, some four weeks after we arrived in Canada, the long-awaited crate, the size of a single-car garage (the kist) that held our worldly goods, arrived! Cheers! Enough towels, bed sheets, linen tea towels, real tablecloths, clothes, books, and dishes, pots and pans, and actual beds and bedding for everyone. No more straw mattresses or endless itching when we got up.

Everybody helped unpack the crate, made their claims, and set things in their proper places. Another piece of settling. My earthly goods had been packed. I sat on the floor, surrounded by my long-lost treasures. A touch of my real Dutch home.

Wedding preparations for Tinie went into full swing. Her fiancé arrived, and by law, they had only thirty days to be married. Tinie shopped for a wedding dress. She complained that none suited her. Mrs. Haist, our new neighbour, came to the rescue, offering her own wedding dress that miraculously fit Tinie perfectly.

Invitations went out to family members in Toronto. Anneke and I had new matching dresses. Mr. Glasbergen made a bouquet from weeds and field flowers, perfect for a new bride in a new country filled with fields of wildflowers. Moe, Gré, and Tinie prepared the food the day before. A large fresh block of ice in the icebox kept everything fresh.

So, on a sunny summer Sunday in August, after the second church service, Rev. Persenaire married Tinie and John. The entire congregation, eager for shared celebrations, stayed and witnessed the ceremony. Toronto relatives drove in. Celebration began in earnest with family and neighbours and lots of food, stories, pictures and, of course, singing. Faded black-and-white photos still show the bride and groom posing at various places on the front deck and the lawn. Anneke and I flanked them on either side. I was so proud of my new yellow nylon dress with flocking.

WELL INTO SPRING, PA AND SIBLINGS WORKED IN PRUDHOMME'S fields, planting vegetable seedlings – scooping away dirt, planting the tiny plants, and covering each one. The plants needed daily watering. Later, the plants established, they pulled weeds and cleaned dried-up weeds out of the straight rows. They perspired in the scorching sun; they got badly sunburned, but their pleasure in being together, telling stories and jokes, even singing while they worked, could be heard across the fields.

In the sweltering heat of July, Tinie got heat stroke and had to take three days off with fever before returning to the field – after that, Moe found a way into town and got wide-brimmed straw hats for everyone.

With Tinie married, Gré was alone. Her best sister-friend married and left. Gré's chance to return to the Netherlands and be reunited with her lost love, Henk, faded, and ultimately, disappeared. She wrote:

"The hard part about leaving Holland was that I had a boyfriend who would not go to Canada. Just before we were ready to leave, he had an idea to go to Spakenburg to people he knew. I was to stay there until my family was gone. So we took the bike, but to go there, we had to go through this open and flat country road; the wind was so strong that we had to give up, and we went back home... At the train station, Henk and I said good-bye. He asked me not to cry, which I didn't, but sitting on the train, I did. I remember really missing everything that we had left behind. Quite a few times, I walked out in the back of the field bawling my eyes out, saying to myself: 'I am not staying in this Wild West country. I want to *go back home.' I have to say this, that I never really knew that the first years in Canada had bothered me so much - thinking about it made me bawl! I have always said I would never do that to my kids."*

CANADA PROVED TOO HARSH FOR GRÉ, WHO SUFFERED SEVERE homesickness. She probably should have returned to the Netherlands. But where would she go when she got there? Where would she get the money? It began to sink in: she was in Canada to stay and she was unhappy.

The Haist family welcomed us to Canada, offering help wherever needed. Tinie connected our families, translating, asking questions and expressing sentiments. Our first Canadian friends. Grateful for their generosity, we gladly accepted the offers of help. The Haists even took my parents along to town to get groceries and supplies and taught them how to find and use the bank.

DUTCH IMMIGRANTS LIVED IN THE OTHER HALF OF OUR FARMHOUSE – the Zwier family, Mr. Zwier, his wife and daughter. They lived and worked for Prudhomme's like we did, but were sponsored by them, unlike us. The Zwiers suffered a tragedy when, shortly after they arrived, their five-year-old son wandered into the horse barn, saw an open container, ate rat poison, and died. It's beyond imagining the pain that brought to the family, who had no relatives in Canada.

My parents understood mourning a child. Oddly enough, brother Dick never emerged in the stories and conversations around the table. He died when he was nine, shortly before my sister Alie was born. I never asked: "Who is in that picture?" because no picture hung on the wall. I met my brother in death, not in life, and again when Tina introduced Dick in a book she wrote years later.

In Grade 2, several sad things happened in my life. During the beginning of the year, my Oma Oosterwijk passed away at age 52. Soon after, on March 27, my brother Dick, aged 9, passed away from meningitis. In writing, the memories came back. One memory is seeing the small coffin on the two chairs in the living room. Neighbours and family came in and out to comfort our family. I remember Dick wore a light-blue shirt. I also remember the drapes stayed closed during the time the coffin remained in the house. Because my mother was expecting Alice, she felt unable to go to the cemetery. After the burial, my parents opened the drapes in the living room once again. This was very difficult for my mother, I can imagine.

The deaths of their children bonded our two families. The Zwiers became good friends, in part because of their shared trauma of leaving our Dutch homeland, but particularly through the loss of their young son. Their friendship lasted long beyond our stay in Fenwick.

STORIES CAPTURED IN OUR FAMILY'S 40-YEAR IMMIGRATION anniversary booklet documented how immigration affected us. We were swallowed up in adjusting and work, or in my case, school. Immigration left its marks on my young life. Homesickness and yearnings for home preoccupied me. It was my first thought in the morning and that last picture in bed.

I learned to stand by as the world moved on. The dense heat of the summer and the freezing cold of the long, long winter proved challenging. But, I was also a child who lived in hope of a return, long after the unattainable would have expired. My friend, who immigrated the same time and age I did, told me her bedtime ritual for several years involved a short scene that showed her running to her Oma's house in Amsterdam, shouting, "I'm back, Oma! I'm here!"

Immigrating, adjusting, finding work, the unrelenting heat of summer, and being new to Canada became the stuff of stories. Like a sponge, I took it in. Stories often told of hilarious language errors and confusions: making a Dutch word sound English or using the Dutch reading to pronounce. For instance, my Pa would ask for "lemon pie" that he pronounced, "*lemoen pea*." The oddities grew as one man said, "*M'n bek ligt op m'n rug and me rug ligt op de vloer*" (Translation: My mouth [*bek*] is on my back [*rug*] and my back [*rug*] is on the floor.)

THE MOST NOTABLE OF THESE FOR ME HAD TO BE STORIES OF SKUNKS – for the Dutch, these were an unheard of, never-smelled species. Skunk stories grew into urban legends: if a skunk sprayed under your car, you had to burn it. If a skunk got under your porch and sprayed, the smell would never leave your house, no matter how much you cleaned it.

Mr. Van der Steen, the story went, found an enormous cat near his house and approached it, thinking it would be a beautiful kitty for his family. He picked it up and took it home. When he put the skunk down on the floor to the utter shock and surprise of the whole family, its putrid spray saturated the air. They hastily ran outside, leaving the skunk inside. It was funny when I heard it, but I became terrified of skunks.

One sunny day on my way to school, in broad daylight, in the middle of the road, lay a fat black skunk prominently displaying the white stripe on its black back. Lounging, stretching, downright comfortable. It was not to be disrupted. I panicked. How would I get to school? Should I turn around and go home? What if it sprayed me? My breath came out in rapid whisks; my heart pounded. I do not know how long I stood and waited – it seemed forever. At some point, the skunk arose and, to my absolute relief, sauntered off into the fields without a spray. I went on my way, hoping another skunk did not find its way to the road.

MOE, CHARGED WITH SAVING MONEY TO BUY A CAR, TOOK ALL THOSE weekly pay envelopes. With so many earners' contributions, it took no time to reach an amount that started Pa on the hunt for a car. As Hugh, my youngest brother, described it, Pa settled on "a 1939 Plymouth, repainted the brightest green you have ever seen. To us, it was a limo. We were all nine packed in it, no seatbelts, and went to church." Pa was in his glory!

Chapter Four

Pa and Moe
Boskoop, 1927

To understand our family requires looking back, extending the context of the people and events with a bit of history. What happened in my family emerged from a multitude of influences and experiences. War and occupation, hunger, death of a child, dangers and death all around. This fostered a rich source for storytelling. Fortunately, my oldest sister Tina was a born storyteller with a sharp, quick wit and a quirky sense of humour. She loved to laugh. Over time, when I heard multiple versions, her stories became my own. I could not separate the knowledge from being a bystander to the lived experiences.

MOE

The eldest daughter born and raised in Boskoop, the Netherlands, Moe's family consisted of ten boys and three girls, with Moe the oldest girl. Her home-life included strict adherence to the family and church policies and practices, spoken and unspoken. Her brothers were loud; Moe and her two sisters were not. A family that largely relied on traditions, rituals, and practices to maintain order.

In a highly class-conscious country, Moe had privilege – at least from the outside looking in. Opa was a well-to-do plant nursery owner in Boskoop, the centre for growing nursery stock in the Netherlands. They lived in a large house with a thatched roof and a canal running along the side of the house to move the nursery stock.

Moe's powerful musical gifts led her parents to arrange for organ lessons. She became highly proficient and could play any melody she heard. Leading the Oosterwijk nightly chorus by age ten, she learned the tradition of after-supper singing. Nightly family choirs became a much-loved tradition.

When Moe was just eleven, in Grade 6, her mother took her out of school. Moe deeply resented her involuntary withdrawal. She loved school and saw her family had the means to keep on their household helpers.

Moe was charged with no small project: laundry for fifteen people, for instance, all by hand. Boiling enough water through the night in light of the absence of the luxuries of an electric washing machine or wringer to squeeze the water out of the heavy clothing and the large bed sheets in the canal that lay alongside their house. Oma gave up her hired house help. Hard to imagine, but somebody had to do it.

PA

Pa, on the other hand, looked and acted differently than Moe's boisterous brothers. Classic Dutch tall boys and men were blond and blue-eyed. In sharp contrast, Pa was handsome, dark, ebony-coloured hair, brown-eyed, tawny skin, aquiline nose. In one word: handsome. He grew up in a family of seventeen children; he was the second youngest and his big sisters spoiled him. Despite family poverty and tragedy, Pa's warm, caring family bonded. In that context, it seems implausible to imagine they lost seven children, all before adulthood. One, aged nine, knowing his death was approaching, planned his own funeral. Another, aged seventeen, was buried at sea. Despite the sorrow that regularly visited the family, they did not bend to grief. Instead, their strong faith allowed them to say, *"The Lord giveth and the Lord taketh . . ."*

Pa finished Grade 3. Though he attended school only three years, it was just long enough to become not only a reader, but an avid reader. Sunday afternoons were spent reading books from the church library in his smoke chair (rook stoel). He tried hard to fit in some reading daily in addition to the bible readings after each meal. His calm and loving nature came from his family, but he carried it with him all his life.

THE WEDDING

Moe's search for an escape from a troubled home life led to her pregnancy at nineteen, a situation that triggered the strict judgment of her church. Publicly shamed, she stood trembling in front of the congregation. The weight of her coerced confession scarred her deeply, it never left her. Lingering like an invisible anchor, her experience isolated her in silent suffering. Forced into marriage with Pa, their union began under a heavy shadow. The lifelong repercussions of the "sin" overtook the joy of her youth.

REGARDLESS, A GLOW OF WARMTH PERVADED PA'S HOME, AND HE never relinquished it. With him hand in hand, I felt secure and surer of myself, comfortably happy even when I was not at home. He was guileless and generous in his love. Though he never openly said, "I love you," I knew he loved me. I believed my Pa was perfect.

Pa was a calm, quiet presence in our lives, not so much a peace*maker* as a peace*keeper*. By handing critical family and finance decisions over to Moe, he remained our loving Pa, who made no negative decisions. Logically, he could never make bad ones since he usually made none. Moe, in stark contrast, had a sharp tongue seemingly unable to show love to her family. She looked like the classic Dutch woman, though shorter: blonde hair, clear blue eyes, fair skin, plump.

Moe never let Pa forget she came from a rich family (class consciousness). She wanted to be seen and known as highly capable, clean, and competitive – and ideally, richer and above her neighbours. Needing to be first in anything that could be seen (new curtains, for instance), she strove to be first with her laundry flapping in the wind on wash-day Monday morning; the first to scrub the lane for all the neighbours to see.

Pa never reacted. He loved us, though not enough to challenge Moe's domineering, self-serving ways. That never occurred to me. He was perfect. Moe was not.

Moe's unhappiness grew. Headaches came every single day. She took aspirins like candy! Small wonder she grew grumpy so often. Music relieved Moe like nothing else could; it made her happy. Whenever she sat at the organ, she sang lustily. Others automatically joined in. We had a choir, four-part harmony. The organ was no small thing to sustain Moe.

Moe sometimes told stories, and one in particular stuck with me. I was probably thirteen or fourteen when she first told it: "On a freezing cold day in Boskoop," she began, "I had to wash the clothes and the linens for my entire family (fifteen people) in the cold, unheated washing room of the house, with only a large steel tub, no washing machine. My hands got so red and chafed. I wrung out the sheets, put them in a willow basket and took them to the canal, where, shivering with the cold, I doused the sheets with water, wrung them out again, and headed back to the shed. As I continued the washing, I looked down and there I stood, blood dripping down my legs, standing in a pool of my own blood. My ignorance added to the horror of the situation while my mother saw it and grumbled. My first period. I thought I was dying."

The gruesome story upset me. I felt sorry for Moe. I could not imagine myself in that experience. Moe, however, did not feel sorry for herself. She never criticized her mother; always upholding and honouring her – even so; she sought a way out. Pa appealed to her. Being boys, thanks to Opa, the boys were trained and had skills to count on as they grew older. Not the girls, though. My father, of course, had no such opportunity. He was a hard worker who absolutely did what he could to support his family as an unskilled labourer.

To School, Highway 20, St. Anne's, Ontario
1952

E arly in September 1952, I prepared to go back to school (without Alie now). Work at the Prudhomme farm suddenly ended. What now? Tina was married and settled in an unheated one-room cabin. In short order, Gré and Leny became housemaids in Burlington; Alie got short-term work in a chicken factory, though that ended with the end of the slaughter season. Pa and Hugh scoured unsuccessfully for work.

The next order of the day involved a search for another house. The promised year of support from the Christian Immigration Society fell short. We were on our own. Pa managed to find a house in St. Anne's on Highway 20 – at least half a house. Packing again. Unpacking again. Everything new again: different house, school, church. The only similarity: this house was isolated, also in the country.

I became increasingly lonely, always in strange, unfamiliar territory. Maybe, I dreamed, I would find a new, good friend here. A young family lived in the other half of the house. Their children, however, were tiny and would not make great friends.

The unpacking began. Trucks whizzed by the front window. Pa and Hugh found temporary work cutting down trees for a farmer. When they knocked on the front door to pick up their promised pay, the farmer shouted and pointed and kicked them off the property. They came home without a penny.

Moe fumed. "Go back. He has to pay you! Take Hugh with you."

Pa repeatedly pleaded with the farmer to get his money, but to no avail. Life on Highway 20 was dark and disappointing. Poverty lurked. Only the very small incomes from Gré, Leny, and Alice kept us from hunger.

On the first morning, I stepped out the front door and walked down Highway 20 to yet another school – my third in seven or eight months out of the Netherlands. Instead of growing accustomed, I now missed my real Dutch school more than ever – my best teacher, my friends, Baarn. Barely nine still, I had no choice. I could dream, though. No wonder it's called "homesick." I was sick of Canada and wanted desperately to return home to the Netherlands.

On the first day of this school, I arrived and told the man teacher: "I am in Grade 3."

He pulled a desk into the Grade 3 row, handed me a reader and an arithmetic book. I could speak some English now, but taking one look at my non-Canadian clothes, he assumed I could not understand English, so he gestured and smiled.

I didn't belong. This was not my home.

Approaching the school one morning some days later, I stood at the fence and watched, entranced, as a snowman emerged. Rolling one giant ball, then another a bit smaller, one smaller yet, the kids dug around in the snow for sticks to serve as arms, and rocks that became eyes and a curved mouth. In the far corner of the playground, another group used their hands to dig up snow and pat and push the snow into bricks, building up a dome with an opening, a door.

Kids took turns sitting inside the igloo in the schoolyard. I stood outside the fence in wonder. I would draw a picture to show Moe. My actual school in the Netherlands looked nothing like this, but for the first time in my brief life, I saw an igloo and snowmen of all sizes, from giant to dwarf size, scattered across the playground.

Then the teacher came out, clanging the school bell, calling everyone into school.

I hated school – as much as I hated the cod liver oil Moe forced on me each morning. I would wither at the taunting on the playground, the freezing cold weather, the unfriendly reception. I walked along the highway each morning, burping up the cod liver oil, pain beginning in my stomach. Every day I debated: "Should I go back home, or should I stay on the road?" Most days, I turned back, rehearsing and polishing my excuses for Moe.

In school, most students ignored me. On the playground, I stood and watched. One bully stands out. He gave me lots of looks and attention. I saw him at church. He taunted me. He came close to my face, fists poised to punch. Fortunately, he did not follow through.

To our great dismay, Moe's rheumatoid arthritis flared up again. I saw the signs. Memories flooded back as Moe became increasingly ill. The slow walk, the wincing, the obvious pain. Once again, she needed hospitalization. Tante now lived in Toronto, Canada, and could come and get me, like a bogeyman. Would I be sent there again? I never spoke her name, hoping Moe would not think of sending me there.

Somehow, to her credit, Moe coped for six long weeks before Pa took her, very sick, to the hospital. With no English, she used hand gestures and pointed to make herself understood.

The bright green Plymouth went to the hospital to visit Moe. Without Moe, Pa drove to Burlington to pick up Gré, who quit her job on the spot to take over the household: cooking, cleaning, sewing, laundry, mending, and playing the mouth organ to lead us in singing.

This time, on Sunday nights, it was Gré who worked with Pa to fill the massive washtub and set it to heat overnight on the stove.

Six weeks into her hospital stay, thankfully, Moe came home. She needed rest, but with Gré's help and care, she recuperated. As winter set in, the old stone house remained very cold. During the day, Moe lay on a sofa with a heater fan blowing, making her back too hot and her front too cold.

"I'm burning and freezing at the same time," she complained.

Stoking the kitchen stove and the wood furnace took considerable time and effort, and did little to balance the hot and cold of the house.

Several times every day, Gré rubbed Moe down with wintergreen (I am not sure why). The smell filled the air in the house, infused everything everywhere. Every room smelled of wintergreen. I swore off wintergreen forever.

Slowly, Moe's health improved. Her colour returned.

My oldest brother, now settled in the US and known as Jack, lived and worked on a farm in North Carolina. He visited during that harsh winter, probably because of Moe's illness – though it had been less than a year since we left, the Netherlands, and we missed him.

Jack came like Sinterklaas, handing out gifts: I got a colouring book, Anneke got a colouring book and a pair of white Canadian lace-up skates. I was nine years old and keenly felt the inequity. Anneke, just five, was his favourite. I knew that. A week later, with Moe on the mend, Jack returned to North Carolina.

With no work in sight and a still-missing pay envelope from tree-cutting, Pa still found us another house. Far out in the country again, at the end of a long gravel driveway that sliced through grapevines on either side. A true pastoral scene.

A classic red brick Ontario farmhouse stood at the end of a driveway that ran along one side of the house. The side door led directly into the kitchen with a large black stove with four burners and the curved legs at the bottom. A large living room, a small dining room, and a grand staircase led to four bedrooms upstairs. Leny remembered, "We even had a telephone – what a luxury!"

That telephone, on a party line, opened communication with new Dutch friends from church or other Dutch friends not from church. Anne learned to lift the horn (as the speaker part was called) and dial the number. When the operator signed on, we would say: "2020 (two-o, two-o) Stoney Creek, please." We then waited until our friends picked up the phone.

Extra rooms allowed Tina and John to move, reuniting our family. John worked at the Zeller's warehouse in St. Catharines. With all the rest unemployed, he supported the whole family with his small income. His English was good. Unable to work in the fields because of childhood rheumatic fever, this position suited him. Tina stayed home to help Moe. That's what women did. Marriage meant the end of work and, for most, marriage became a sought-after relief.

Nevertheless, jobs were urgently needed. Gré, Leny, and Alie found housekeeping jobs. Pa and Hugh looked further afield for jobs and a more permanent home.

I went to yet another one-room school out in the country. On the first morning, with yet another set of directions, I crunched down the interminably long driveway to the gravel road. The fourth school in a bit more than a year.

I was careful to smile at the kids on the concrete steps of the school. They did not smile back. They stared.

I felt uncomfortable, strained, scared.

Inside, I walked to the front of the class to speak to the teacher at his desk. "I am Ria Appel, in Grade 3," I said.

He kindly walked ahead of me to a desk in the Grade 3 row and brought the appropriate books to tuck under the small table. I pushed my lunch alongside the books, put a pencil on the groove at the top of the desk and waited for school to begin.

Like the other teachers in Canada, this teacher strode down one row and up the next, assigning work for each of the eight grades. I quickly completed the Arithmetic worksheet and set it on the corner of my desk, placed my folded hands on the desktop, and waited.

When the teacher got to Grade 3, I found my reader; I read aloud when it was my turn. It got very quiet. When I looked up, I saw the students frowning and staring. I spoke English now, but I probably still had a real Dutch accent – which, of course, I could not detect myself.

At lunch, comments about "funny" clothes reached my ears. Moe had painstakingly knit the knee socks that fit into my gleaming Dutch leather school shoes.

Out of the teacher's sight on the playground, one boy asked, "Can I see what's in your lunch bag?"

When I removed the wax paper and showed him two slices of bread with a piece of honey cake between them, he grabbed the sandwich out of my hand, took one look at and whiff of the honey cake on the bread, threw it on the concrete and stomped on it until it was pancake flat.

My cheeks burned with anger, but I dared not say a word. Why did he do that? Why did the others laugh? Perhaps the worst part was the wasted food, which was unacceptable to my family who lived through war and the hunger winter.

With no lunch, I went back into the school, slunk into my desk seat, and picked up my reader. I listened carefully, completed my work, and stayed quiet – hoping against hope that I would not be noticed. After school, I walked home dejected, not knowing what to do or how I would face them again tomorrow.

Tomorrow came, of course. In time, the teacher recognized me as a most capable student whose skills exceeded my assigned Grade 3 work. The teacher appointed me his helper, and he assigned me Grade 4 work. Soon he asked me to lead a small group of Grade 4 students who needed extra help in reading. I wanted to say, "But I am only in Grade 3!" but of course, I did not, though by now I was comfortable in English.

The teacher sent us off to the small side room where I explained, listened, and reported progress. He sent me to listen to the Grade 5 students. The children must also have wondered how that was possible. I sure did.

"What a strange country," I mused.

Although the teacher did his best to keep me busy and occupied, the other students increasingly resented the Dutch immigrant kid who thought she was so smart. They ignored me until the teacher left the room and outside at recess and after lunch. The students, all boys – the girls watched from the side – taunted, mocked, and teased me. They laughed and pointed at my clothes. I wore the same clothes every day of the week. They wore a different outfit every day.

On my walks home and in bed at night, I longed for my own school and Juffrouw Kok in the Netherlands. I did not belong in Canada. Still desperately homesick, I missed Willie and her mother, Juffouw Kok, and my other friends on the street and in school. I wanted to play on Heuveloordtstraat. At night, I lulled myself to sleep, picturing *De Zuiderkruis*, the immigration ship slowly turning, facing east, and taking me back to my real home where I would not be lonely, not be afraid.

I NEEDED SOMEONE TO TALK TO AND PLAY WITH AT RECESS. IT DID NOT happen. I asked the teacher: "Could I bring my little sister to school with me? She's only five, but she's smart."

Without hesitation, he said, "Bring her tomorrow."

The bell rang. School was out. I ran all the way home, up the driveway, threw open the door and yelled, "Teacher said Anneke could come to school with me tomorrow."

Surprised, Moe agreed to let me take her.

The next day, Moe packed up lunch bags for both of us. I helped an excited Anneke put her sweater on and we headed out the door, down the driveway, and along the dirt path beside the road. Anneke wore her best clothes. Hand in hand, we went along the country road to school.

I introduced the teacher to Anneke, and he took her to a desk with the Grade 1 students, and gave her a pencil and a notebook. She was spellbound by all the activities and books. I had been her only "teacher" and now everything – including the language – was new. We sat together at lunch and talked (in Dutch) and laughed.

The day was relatively uneventful until school let out. Without warning, a group of boys on bicycles circled around us. One got off his bike, came over to me, and clasped my hands behind my back. I started to cry when the group of boys moved towards Anneke.

By her facial scowl and little fist motioning trouble ahead, they understood enough to know she would not back down. She looked straight into their faces, repeating in Dutch, "Go away. Leave me alone."

A big boy pulled Anneke over, pushed her to the ground and held her there, his knee on her back. Two more boys on bicycles sped over and as Anneke lay in the dirt and rode their bicycles over my sister. I yelled in protest. I cried, but could not free myself. Anneke screamed. Hot tears burned down my face.

Then, as quickly as they had appeared, the hooligans rode off.

I picked Anneke up off the dirt path, brushed her off, wiped her tears and mine. We walked home. Terrified the boys would return, I didn't dare turn back to tell the teacher. I feared what the boys might do if I tattled.

It was all my fault. I should never have asked for Anneke to come to school with me.

Somehow, we made it home, and I told Moe the whole story. Like she'd said to me after my first day in kindergarten in the Netherlands, she told Anneke, "You don't have to go back. You can stay home with me."

And she did, of course.

I, however, had no choice. I returned to school.

The next morning, petrified as I approached the school, the boys averted their eyes. Had the teacher heard the story of the terror they inflicted? I ate my lunch alone, undisturbed. I looked up and saw a girl who walked over and sat right down beside me.

"My mother asked if you would like to come to play and eat supper at my house," she said.

Disbelief. Tears welled up, and I said, "Thank you. I will ask my mother and tell you tomorrow." Perhaps she had witnessed the events of the day before. Waves of gratitude washed over me. I smiled.

My first real Canadian meal – food I had never seen or experienced. For the first time, I ate fried chicken and mashed potatoes. It was delicious beyond telling, though still not as good as the warmth I felt, sharing a meal, feeling included and accepted. A real friend?

Happy Moe said "yes," and it certainly was a different era. I went with complete strangers. No background checks required. The girl and her dad took me home in their shiny truck. I glowed.

Chapter Five

~∞~

It all began one Sunday. . .
August, 1951

After a Sunday noon dinner of meatball soup, just before the closing prayer, Pa rose from his chair at the head of the large dining table and stood erect, calmly waiting for silence. A hush fell. He announced to the nine of us and Moe: "We are immigrating to Australia!"

Moe, wide-eyed, jumped up, and boldly shouted: "No, no, no. I am *not* doing that. Australia is too far away. We are immigrating to Canada."

"*Ja*, Canada." Pa nodded his head. And, that's exactly what we did.

The announcement sent shock waves through the family. They sat like pillars of salt (think Lot's wife in the Bible), dumbstruck until the silence shattered. Questions, one after the other, shot through the air. The war that ended only six years before left cataclysmic lingering consequences on our lives. Just when new normal lives were slowly being restored, this bombshell.

ONLY THREE MONTHS EARLIER, TINA, GRÉ, AND HUGH HAD simultaneously found ill-timed love. Their first concern?

Tinie: "What about Jan?"

Gré: "What about Henk?"

Hugh: "What about Henny?"

Pa, unruffled, responded: "The decision has been made. We move ahead. A lot must happen."

I wanted *nothing* to happen, but nobody asked me. Leaving everything familiar – my home, my school, my street, friends, the park – was unfathomable. What about my magnificent Juffrouw Kok, my teacher, who, in short order, etched a permanent imprint on my life? She had extended an invitation: "Come with me; I'm a reader." I jumped at the chance. She initiated a transformative journey that brought me to reading and building the imagination that became a part of my life.

Supper over, Pa took the Children's Bible, opened it, and sat down in his chair.

A reverent silence descended. The reading began. I listened to every word, looked at the small, detailed black-and-white etchings. Pa finished and looked at me. "What was the last word, Ria?"

He knew I knew. I said the word. He smiled and bowed his head to pray aloud.

Every day after supper, Gré and Tinie cleared the table and did the dishes in the small kitchen, boiling water on the stove. Their talk and laughter echoed through the house until the organ sounds reached their ears. Then everything stopped except the singing.

Moe had made her way to the organ, opened the hymnal, found a song, and played the first line while those remaining left the table got up and circled Moe. Hymns accompanied me up the stairs and into my bed.

Pa pushed aside his chair and moved to his reading chair (rook stoel, meaning smoke chair), lit a cigarette, picked up his book, and began reading. He never joined the singing at home.

I THOUGHT AND THOUGHT ABOUT IMMIGRATION, TRYING TO FIGURE things out with only a child's knowledge. The more I thought, the more I worried. The more I worried, the more I cried. Sometimes, my legs shook. Sometimes, Pa's vision pointed me to a colossal ship, a grand adventure, and new places to explore. I wanted to know things. I needed to get ready.

Wheels turned. Pa took things in hand. The newly established Christian Emigration Organization persuaded him that Canada, the country that rescued the Netherlands from the war, was open for business, ready to welcome the Dutch who dreamed of economic opportunities, though most said, "We came for our children." That may have been true for a few, but most often older children lost out on the opportunities to stay in school and went to work, leaving their weekly pay cheques on the table and any chance of further schooling behind.

Those who left Holland with all their dreams often experienced poverty. Scarce resources became a reality during the war and long after. It's not hard to imagine that the lure of a better life was seductive. For the most part, immigrants brought few skills other than farm work, exactly as advertised. My Pa had never worked on a farm; he worked in a factory.

Pa faithfully attended every meeting of the Christian Emigration Organization. After supper, he would give a detailed report of what he learned, heard – and particularly, details about what remained. The family talked of little else; the older ones raised questions. What would happen next?

His excitement and strong leadership surprised me. I believed him, but the pieces of the puzzle did not easily fit. Each day was a rollercoaster in my mind.

Questions kept coming. Some challenged Pa; some debated the value of leaving their lives behind to go to a great unknown. Others grumbled and complained at the enormous impending change to their lives. They asked: "What if we don't like it? What if we can't adjust? What if we want to go back?"

A mystery. I had questions I did not ask, though I wanted the answers to the questions I heard my siblings ask.

Tinie despaired. She wanted to marry and settle down in Baarn.

Hugh loudly protested every discussion and step of immigration.

Alie demanded answers to questions not yet asked. "I don't want to go," she repeated each time the subject came up.

Gré seemed to take it all in, but never argued aloud.

Silently, I agreed. I didn't want to go either.

"Why are we going?" Pa asked rhetorically, voice rising as in a question. "There's not enough work here! The war's destruction makes it impossible. Employment will be a big problem for some time to come. We need a way out of poverty. Canada needs help. They want us to come. It's unlikely we will have a chance like this again."

Canada was the land of milk and honey, the pot of gold at the end of the rainbow, Pa and Moe believed. Every step of the process had to be conducted and completed on a tight schedule. Early in the process, there was the matter of English: only Tinie spoke English, though with a decidedly British accent. She had studied English at school and worked as a nanny for a year in England, enjoying the change of scenery, job, and the opportunity to connect with our aunt who immigrated to England a few years earlier. Finding her stride, a church, and new friends, Tinie was forced to leave it all when she fell on the tennis court and broke both wrists. Completely unable to care for herself, she was not happy with this turn of events, but not yet twenty-one, she had no choice. Aunt Tonia took her back to the Netherlands.

Hugh and Gré registered for English lessons.

Tinie tells a story:

"I can still hear Gré one night when she came home -
"Well," says Gré, "I can speak some English! [Ik
kan al wat Engels, hoor!] Trim my moustache."
"I thought to myself," said Tinie, "that would be a
very good thing to know, especially if you are a girl!"

Tinie helped Gré and Hugh in their English exercises. Even I got caught up in the fervor of learning English, creating my own version. I began speaking my "English", though only to my sister Anneke, who must have wondered, "What is this?" In her company, and without fail, I boldly used hand gestures and spoke in my new tongue. I was moving to Canada, after all.

Tinie, twenty-one, Gré, nineteen, and Hugh, eighteen, had all found love, and were reluctant to abandon their romantic connections, though no one was in any position to say, "no thank you. I am staying put here."

Tinie writes:

"It was a genuine struggle for me, too. I was
caught in the middle. I was not quite 21 years old, so
I had to obey my parents legally. Come to think of it,
I guess I did not have the nerve to stay in Holland
and go against my parents."

Knowing that she would have to leave for Canada, Tinie got engaged to John Wynia just before we left the Netherlands. In good Dutch form and in quick order, we celebrated the event with an engagement party.

Sitting in a large circle with John's family, friends and neighbours, the adults enjoyed coffee with Dutch pastries (gebakjes), and small dishes of rich, creamy custard-like *advocaat* (a traditional beverage made from eggs, sugar, and brandy), eaten with a traditional miniature teaspoon. Given its high alcohol content (15-20%), these drinks were reserved for adults. Alie, Anneke, and I enjoyed drinks made with orange syrup. Laughter, loud singing, stories, and music with Moe at the organ resonated throughout the house.

Jan's heart history of rheumatoid arthritis offered little hope he would be eligible for immigrating to Canada. If he failed the test, Moe assured Tinie, she could return to the Netherlands to get married. Tinie was skeptical for good reason. While Moe pulled her out of school too early, she also gave Tinie the gift of music. Tinie could not decide which form of her mother to trust.

Gré and Hugh, both lovesick, grumbled about the move and were ready to pack in the immigration plans, but Moe tolerated no such talk. The three often talked of staying in the Netherlands together, or maybe going to Canada and then all coming back to pick up where they left off. I worried that Moe would hear them, or that they really would stay behind.

At twenty-four, Jack did not take part in the problems and protocols of immigration. He had dreams of becoming a farmer and decided on immigration to the United States.

Moe contacted her two brothers, who lived in North Carolina, to inquire about farming possibilities for Sjaak, and both brothers volunteered to sponsor and introduce him to dairy farming in America. He accepted their offer and made plans to go his own way.

I WANTED A CHOICE, A VOICE. I GOT NEITHER. TARA WESTOVER (*Educated*) captured my young self: "It happens sometimes in families: one child who doesn't fit, whose rhythm is off, whose meter is set to the wrong tune. (p. 43)." In my family, that was me. Caught between a younger sister (four years) and an older, needy sister (by five years), I assume Moe found me strong and capable. She needed the time to nurture my sisters.

Nobody asked for my opinion, my concerns, or questions. I did not fit; I did not belong in this family. I learned to listen and create a world of my own.

P a arranged for the required passports and inoculations, medical exams, bicycle rentals, and for departure announcements to school and factory, church, and neighbours.

The process began in earnest when Moe, an expert knitter, made sure we would look the part, and make her proud when we got on the ship. Matching outfits for Anneke and me composed of delicate, short-sleeved, off-white sweaters and green skirts with a white apron on the front and knit suspenders. I watched in awe as the green skirt grew and the small white apron began to appear on the front. Gré's best friend, Joop, took the skirt home, and embroidered the little apron with beautiful multi-colored flowers along the three edges. In our immigration family picture, both Anneke and I wore the matching outfits. I wore my knit set with such pride.

Medical examinations and inoculations for the whole family were scheduled early in December 1951. We travelled to Amersfoort, disembarked from the bikes and walked them to the official building, where Pa found a bicycle rack for all the bikes. Streets in Amersfoort had shops and bakeries and grand, immense homes. I felt excited to be in the big city.

Inside the massive official building, we found the sign for the medical division and were sent into separate cubicles to wait until our names were called.

I stood and waited and waited. Someone called out names. I did not hear mine.

I stood or sat on a bench in the cubicle, in only my little knit undershirt and underwear (Moe knit everything, including our underwear). I got cold, shivery, and bored with waiting. On all fours, I peeked under the divider at Alie, who saw me, jumped, and hollered so loudly Moe and everyone around could hear: "Ria is peeking under the walls of the cubicle!" Moe did not respond. I presume she avoided identifying herself as my Moe.

At last, my name: "Ria Appel." I opened my door and followed the doctor, who proceeded with the examination. When that was complete, he took me to a place where I had to roll up my sleeve to receive the required inoculations – diphtheria, tetanus, pertussis, and smallpox – on my upper left arm (I was right-handed). Good news: the whole family passed the test! Oh joy! The bliss was short-lived, however, when one after the other grew red, crusty, oozing scabs from infections on their left arms. It was painful, but I said not a word to anyone. The Salvation Army Christmas dinner and program came just in time for the scab to bloom at its most painful.

Hugh and I were invited to a Salvation Army Christmas dinner early in December 1951. I have no idea how we got this invitation. Maybe I told them we were moving to Canada. I could not wait. I pestered Hugh – who knew all the details – until the day finally arrived. Hugh found the way to the hall.

Nobody knew about my painful swelling inoculation. My cheeks burned hot and flushed, and my arm felt too small for my skin, about to burst like casing on a sausage. Revealing the truth, however, would prevent me from attending the celebration. I stayed quiet, taking no chances.

In the grand decorated hall, I sat next to Hugh at one of the long tables laden with special Christmas foods. We filled our plates fuller than anything I had ever seen and began eating.

My spoon felt like a lead weight; I could hardly lift the spoon to my mouth. Why did I not feel like eating? Why was Hugh picking at his food?

Hugh slumped in his chair.

"I feel sick," I said.

"Me, too. Time to go home, Ria."

Completely dejected and fever-blazing sick, we left together.

At home, Moe put her hand to our foreheads and declared us officially sick. The inoculations had already begun oozing, with crusts forming.

I had to miss the dinner and the program and the music. I cried myself to sleep. My arm still bears the three scars.

The 1952 New Year's Eve celebrations signaled that our departure was getting closer.

All the inoculations had healed.

AS AN EIGHT-YEAR-OLD, I WAS THE ONLY FAMILY MEMBER COMPLETELY and eagerly swept up with the fifth of December: *Sinterklaas Dag* (Santa Claus Day). This celebration gripped the children of the Netherlands. Sinterklaas, on his white horse, jumped from one roof to the other, delivering gifts for the small children. All day long we sang Sinterklaas songs. Children learned the rites and passages of Sinterklaas before they entered school.

I dove in to the celebrations. Anneke was too young and Alie already too old for Sinterklaas, but I was in Sinterklaas prime-time, picturing him coming down the gangplank of his great ship mounted on his white horse, ready to fly over my roof, stop, and deliver a gift to my wooden shoe. In return, I filled a wooden shoe with some strands of hay from the dove cage in the backyard.

I prepared early – at least two days early, on December 3. He was expected on the night of December 5. Wondering if Sinterklaas might get a head start, I took one wooden shoe from the back entry and set out to find some straw. In the backyard, Hugh had two pigeon cages with fresh straw. I grabbed a handful out of a cage and headed back indoors, stuffing the straw deeply into the wooden shoe.

"Moe, can I have a carrot and a glass of milk for Sinterklaas?" I pleaded to no avail. A carrot and a glass of milk, I reasoned, would increase my chances of getting a splendid gift. Moe, however, did not bend. To make up for the missing items, I wrote a little poem for *Sinterklaas* using the words of a familiar Dutch *Sinterklaas* song and placed it neatly on top of the straw.

Early in the morning, the house was silent with my sleeping family. I crept out of bed. Overcome with excitement, quietly sneaking into the living room, I expected to see what Sinterklaas brought.

In the living room, I found an untouched wooden shoe with the hay still on top. No gift was cradled in the straw or right beside the wooden shoe. It had remained untouched.

"Too early," I reasoned.

For the next three nights, I repeatedly placed my straw-stuffed shoe by the fireplace. Each morning, I came away empty-handed. My disappointment left no choice but to transfer my hope for Sinterklaas Dag festivities on the night of the fifth, for a present to arrive later that day.

Sinterklaas Dag celebrations arrived. Everyone celebrated, particularly since this would be our last one in the Netherlands. Everyone seated around the room anticipated the arrival.

Knock! Knock! Knock! All eyes turned toward the door.

It swung open and a cascade of small, rounded ginger cookies (*pepernootjes*) flew in. We ran and gathered them off the floor. Ready to pop one into my mouth, I looked closely and, to my complete amazement, I recognized Sinterklaas.

"That's not Sinterklaas!" I cried, "It's Henk! It's our neighbour, Henk!" This Sinterklaas was an imposter.

Moe stood up, gathered Anneke, covered her ears, and spirited her out of the room. I sat on the floor, dejected, while the others continued their laughter and stories. With all the pepernootjes eaten, we awaited Sinterklaas. Anneke received gifts from both my brother, Sjaak and Sinterklaas. I received only one present — a box of paints. Anneke got two presents; I got one. Envious, I stomped up the stairs. I kicked the box of paints under my bed, reluctantly pulled back the covers, crawled in, whispered goodnight, and settled into bed. No prayers for me today.

NEW YEAR'S WAS THE BIGGEST TRADITIONAL FEAST IN THE Netherlands. The day began with making the oliebollen (Dutch fritters) dough. Moe would add currents and apple pieces before allowing it to rise. You could smell its aroma throughout the house. Time to cook! All day and evening long, Moe worked at the stove and kept the hot oil bubbling. She dipped a big spoon in the water to ensure the dough wouldn't stick to the spoon, scooped the oliebollen dough up, then dropped it into the sizzling oil. She waited for each to float to the top, then flipped each one over. When the other side turned a golden brown, Moe gingerly lifted each one with a slotted ladle and added it to the washtub set beside the stove. She made dozens and dozens of oliebollen.

With oliebollen complete, Moe made thin apple slices to dip in the batter (*appelflappen*). They plopped in the hot sizzling oil until they floated gracefully to the top. Moe skimmed them with a ladle as well, lifting them delicately out of the hot oil, and added them, one by one, to the growing mound in the washtub.

Moe filled small containers with pure white icing sugar and set them about the living and dining rooms. Guests dipped the oliebollen and appelflappen in the powdered sugar, enjoying their sweetness.

The atmosphere was pure magic, a perfect moment. Doors up and down the street stood open. Neighbours and friends entered each house. Everywhere, happy singing and talking filled the air. We walked from one house to another greeting and wishing all a Happy New Year, while eating, sharing stories, offering wishes of "Happy New Year," and lots of laughter. A grand feast and for me, an unforgettably delicious memory – especially because for the first time, I stayed up till just after midnight.

ONLY A MONTH BEFORE PA AND MOE'S 25TH WEDDING ANNIVERSARY, Moe organized an early party to celebrate with relatives and friends to say our good-byes. Aunts and uncles, some older cousins, and my Opa Oosterwijk filled our small living and dining rooms.

A traditional family celebration ensued, with food, drink, and much merriment. Moe played the organ. The outstanding singing included a much larger choir than our standard after- supper one.

Moe herself came from a singing family. The choir rang out. Everyone sang lustily.

A massive wooden crate stood in the alley, ready for packing. With limited room, what to take, what to leave behind, and what to give away became shared issues. Pa made containers for each person; Moe took care of Anneke's and mine. Packing the crate with everything neatly folded, tucked, and pushed until the box was filled to the brim, jostling, jiggling the items, squeezing every inch of space occupied the family for some time.

The organ, the centerpiece of the family, took up too much room in the crate and could not accompany us to Canada. It had to be sold. Moe cried inconsolably when someone came to take it away. Everyone cried along with her.

Moe loved her pump organ, her necessary accessory, her psychological support, and her way of bringing us all together in our nightly hymn singing. To assuage her sadness, Pa promised another organ would be the first thing they'd purchase in Canada.

Before long into the process of immigration, I realized I could not bring the things I loved: my house, street, school, teacher, or church. I had to leave behind the only place and people I ever knew. At the end of the lane, I stood and took it all in. Immaculate red brick houses separated by narrow brick lanes lined my street. The same townhouse windows faced the street. Every house had the same classic Dutch lace curtains in the two large front windows. Every house had the same immaculate front garden with short black wrought-iron fences. Neat and tidy. I made mind pictures of the street. Wanting to see Het Bosje Park one last time, I walked to the woods on my own and dreamed about belonging to the royal family.

I had no choice, of course, but my siblings didn't either. Immigration was the uncertain certainty. I listened to stories and instructions and pulled it all together in my own way as an eight-year-old.

Chapter Six

Grade 2 in Baarn
1951-1952

I n Baarn, I could hardly wait for school to start. On the first day of Grade 2, I met my teacher, Juffouw Kok, tall and willowy, smartly dressed. She had a kind face and a welcoming spirit. Her hair was neatly cut, short and curled with a perm (probably done at the Mannifarges hair salon) in the centre of Baarn, where Moe and my older sisters got their hair cut and permed. She wore a crisp white blouse and a long pencil skirt. Traditional lace-up shoes, the same ones every day, neatly polished, finished the picture.

Juff introduced me to the wonders of reading and the magic of books. It's not that I was now learning to read (I was in Grade 2, remember); I already *knew* how to read. I accepted my teacher's invitations into new worlds. Hungry for more, I hurried through each assigned reading, and when called on, read sections aloud with expression and meaning. A simple look brought Juff to my table with a new book while others finished their assigned books. Juffrouw Kok expected me to succeed, and I did not disappoint. In my head, I heard her say, "You are smart, Ria." My seven-year-old heart unreservedly believed her.

Our books came primarily from the prodigious Dutch children's author, W. G. Van de Hulst, a Christian writer whose books were a staple in all Christian schools in the Netherlands. For me, they opened new story worlds with titles like *Pig under the Pew, The Little Wooden Shoe.*

They included an angry janitor, a black kitten, three children lost in the snow. My ultimate favourite, *Bruun the Bear*, the story of a sick young girl in bed on the third floor of a grand house with a canal running right past it. Her brothers took her favourite teddy bear and tied a string around its neck. They moved to the windowsill and unwound the string, dangling the fuzzy bear precariously from the third story, over the canal below while its owner, a poor sick girl lying in her bed, was helpless to rescue it.

The girl was horrified and, frankly, so was I. My heart raced. I didn't dare turn the page. I became so anxious I *had* to turn the page.

Finally, cautiously, ever so slowly, I lifted the bottom corner of the page, closed my eyes and lifted a little farther. I peeked and saw the brothers. Hearing their sister cry, they ran down to the canal. To their shock and dismay, the beautiful bear sat atop a pole sticking upright out of the water. The boys rounded the corner to the canal. The bear was gone. Disappeared. A glance sideways found two bigger boys tossing Bear around. Of course, the boys cut a deal, and much to her relief, Bear was returned safely to Rosie.

Juffrouw Kok recognized my abilities and fed them richly. She opened new worlds, connecting me with new books and new friends. She opened doors I didn't know existed. New and magical. She saw there was more. The powerful feelings gave me a sense of self, of being important. Belonging. Fitting in. I felt more at home here; I belonged at school. My Juff sparked a fire for learning and reading that has never been extinguished despite moving so far away to Canada.

After school, friends called. Some lived close to us on our local street; others lived in large, stately homes. Mansions with large green spaces and matte black wrought-iron fences surrounded the large mansions of Baarn. Sometimes, nannies picked me up on their bicycles so I could play with their charges. Moe became friendly and greeted them ever so warmly.

Outside, the nanny lifted me onto the back seat of her bike, making sure I sat securely. She rode out of the lane and biked speedily off to the house with both my arms wrapped tightly around her waist. Sometimes, I sang a song to the nanny, who usually said, "I like that song. Can you sing it again?" We entered the long driveway to the front door. The nanny popped me off the bike and took me indoors, where my friend and her mother greeted me warmly.

For some strange reason, the houses, in all their splendor, remain an enigma. We played in the playroom. Toys – mostly wooden – sat neatly on the shelves. A doll buggy, dolls. An entire bookcase filled with books. In our play, we read, we built, we had a cup of tea and a good Dutch cookie.

"Time for you to go home, Ria. I will take you," the nanny said. I said goodbye to my friend's mother and my friend. When the wind outside howled or it poured down rain, the nanny made sure my coat was buttoned. She struggled to get on a rain cape. On the back of her bicycle, though it was growing dark, she whizzed us down the streets. She pulled into our lane, passed the door, halted, leaned her bike against her, propped me up and set me down. She knocked on the door. I waved goodbye—time for supper. Nobody ever asked me about my visit with my friend.

Despite the silence around my visit, Moe informed the neighbours that I played with rich girls who lived in mansions with nannies who picked me up to play and delivered me back home before supper. Moe was a peacock, and I was her crest, flamboyant, ostentatious – the unmissable spread of feathers.

Sundays in the Netherlands
1951

Without a doubt, Sunday was the most important day of the week. Early in the day, all ten of us – parents, young adults, adolescents, and younger kids – got ready using the single tiny bathroom one at a time. The lineup went from oldest (Pa and Moe) to youngest (Anneke). Urgings of "hurry" and "my turn" rang out repeatedly around the dining room. We could not eat till all were seated around the table and Pa had prayed.

Sunday's special breakfast included rusk, Gouda cheese, bread thick with currants, butter, *koek*, *hagelslag* (milk chocolate shavings), and strawberry jam.

Sunday clothes and polished shoes – at last everyone was ready. No one did *not* get ready. No one said: "I don't think I'll go to church today." That brief sentence crossed no one's lips –

except for Moe, still weak, who often stayed home with Anneke.

The rest of the Appel family went to church twice every Sunday. No options allowed.

Our neighbours, the Van Surksums, never attended church, which marked them as "heathen." Heathens, sadly, would never enter Heaven – especially Willie's older brothers, who got up early every Sunday morning to prepare the ice cream cart. They drove it up and down the streets of Baarn, shouting, "Ice cream! Ice cream in the cone!" They worked on Sundays, even in the rain.

When the weather got warmer, I asked Moe after church, "Can I have an ice cream cone? The Surksums have their cart ready."

"It's Sunday," she said, brusquely. That meant, "Not a chance. We don't work on Sunday. We don't shop on Sunday. And we don't force other people to work on Sunday just so we can have an ice cream cone."

End of story.

We worshiped in a classic large Dutch Reformed Church: red brick, grand arched double- entry doors. Inside, on one end, was a large balcony. The front of the church had a pipe organ with brass pipes spreading across the front. The organist climbed the high stairs and sat down to play. He played the Psalms and Hymns listed as *Ps. 42: 1, 2, 6*, displayed on two wooden boards in the shape of church windows on either side of the pulpit. A small Psalm book came along to church with us each Sunday.

Dominee, the minister in his flowing black-velvet gown, walked regally to the front, followed by the elders, and shook hands with the last elder. He climbed the stairs to the pulpit, opened his Bible, blessed the people, and spoke out the number and verses of the first song. The majestic swell of the organ filled the air. Voices chimed in and blended like a choir. Everyone knew the melody and most knew the words. I knew many too, through our daily singing at home. I sang along lustily.

Moe's purse sat on her knees, carrying our Sunday treasure: King peppermints distributed at precisely the same two intervals during the sermon. Moe started by quietly peeling the King peppermint paper down the roll, took one out for herself and passed the roll on to Pa. The peppermint role traveled to the end of the bench and then returned – no one would dare take a second, not yet – to Pa and then me. We each got two.

Frequently, Moe reached into her purse for her Eau de Cologne bottle, sprinkled some on her perfectly starched white Sunday handkerchief, dabbed her forehead, and sniffed the hanky, taking in its fragrance. Another headache.

The sermon droned on. Bored, I counted the organ pipes. There were a lot of them so it took a while, but passed the time. The final prayer countered any idea of finishing off church because it lasted for such a long time. It's very serious in church. Inevitably, as the sermon proceeded, one sibling (probably Tina, sometimes Hugh, never Jack) whispered a joke or an observation, passed it on and the suppressed chuckling began, heads down to hide the laughing. They never passed it on to me. I sat quietly and endured.

Dominee Zegers pronounced loudly, "Amen!" The organ playing signaled time to leave. In a beat, the congregants rose and shuffled out the rows to the door where Dominee Zeegers shook every adult hand, sending each out the doors and on to the street.

TIME FOR THE BEST MEAL OF THE WEEK! BUT FIRST, DESSERT. AFTER church, the adults drank coffee with hot milk and sugar and a special almond-filled cookie or a Dutch pastry. We all got the cookies, but the young ones, including me, did not get coffee. Two cups of coffee for everyone over fifteen. Pastry with the first cup on a little plate the size of a saucer; a regular cookie with the second cup. A tiny coffee spoon to stir it all up.

Dessert before the meal. People laughed when they heard about it.

At home, the family sat in the living room while Saturday's soup warmed up on the stove (no unnecessary work on the Sabbath). Sunday soup, filled with vermicelli noodles, vegetables, and best of all, nutmeg-spiced meatballs. The aroma wafted throughout the house.

Before dinner, Moe took the meatballs for Anneke's and my soup, cut them in half and placed them in our soup bowls. Yum! A bottle of Maggi (soya sauce) went around the table, stopping alongside Tina, Gré, Hugh, Leny, Alie, Anneke, and me. The grinding sound of moving chairs indicated my siblings took their seats at the table – I took mine, too. Each older sibling shook four shots of Maggi into each bowl.

Bread and butter and the Dutch staples for Sunday dinners sat on the long dining table: Gouda cheese, lunch meats, liverwurst, sugar, appel stroop (thick apple butter for spreading on bread). The Gouda block had the Dutch cheese knife lying beside it, a razor-thin blade that cut slices for the sandwiches – I can almost taste the cheese now! While the soup was still too hot, the older ones made sandwiches, and Moe sounded out the warning – one slice of Gouda *or* lunchmeat, not both.

Sometimes in the old days in Holland, Pa invited me on an afternoon walk. He took my hand, and we'd head out to the country fields close to Baarn to search for stork nests on the high, white poles that stood in large fields. The always-empty nests stood out starkly on the landscape.

I scoured the sky from one end to the other. "Where are the storks?" I asked Pa.

"Wait a while and see what happens."

We wandered up and down the street in the countryside as I remained hopeful, believing. Each time, I set out with the conviction that I would see a stork deliver a baby to its nest on a sky-high pole; a baby, cradled in a small white hammock with the ends firmly held in the stork's beak, a baby gently rocking back and forth as the stork headed for the high, massive nest. It never happened. The special time with Pa did happen. We walked hand in hand; I talked, and Pa listened. In his unflappable manner, Pa loved me, and I loved him back.

SOMETIMES AFTER SUNDAY SUPPER THE SOUNDS OF TUNING BRASS instruments came in through the windows of our street. Men and women readied to play and sing. Dressed in black uniforms – skirts and jackets for the ladies, a black bow and red band on their hats and the words Salvation Army written at the top of their uniform jackets. Band members in dark hose and matching, shiny black shoes began the *oompapa, oompapa*. They drew observers from up and down the street that lingered close enough to enjoy the music. The tunes were catchy, sometimes familiar. Moe's music ear went into high gear, listening to any new songs that caught her fancy. She would go into the house, sit at the organ, and play the tunes she just heard. Tinie, Hugh, and Margaret stood with her and all together added to Moe's songbook.

Shortly after Anneke's birth in 1947, Moe began to walk awkwardly, holding on to the walls as she made her way. She complained of pain in her knees. She shuffled ever more slowly, dragging her feet along the floor, wincing with every step. Huffing, she paused at the wall along the way, or when climbing the stairs became too much. On each step, she placed both feet firmly on each tread, took a big breath, and rested momentarily before proceeding.

Pa jumped on his bike and sped to the doctor's office. The doctor followed him home, examined Moe and said, "Rheumatic fever." He demonstrated a series of procedures for Gré and left, saying, "I will be back in two days to check and see if you have done your homework."

Pa and Sjaak dismantled the bed on the second floor and carried the pieces to the living room, so Moe could either face the dining room or look out the windows at the street. Gré made the bed with clean sheets and put the heavy Dutch blanket on the bed. From there, Moe could direct life at our house.

Gré, Leny, and Alie went to work and school; I was too young for either. Tinie, the oldest girl, had neither interest nor skill in housework. She preferred school, choir, and friends, and was a very good student. Gré, 17, less than two years younger, completed a home economics program in school, and joyfully quit her job as a housekeeper to come home and lead the household.

A born homemaker and seamstress extraordinaire, Gré took over the sewing, the cooking, the mending, the washing, and the cleaning. On Sunday nights, she worked with Pa to fill the massive washtub and set it to heat overnight on the stove, so that she could, with his help, start doing the laundry at 5 a.m. Before Pa went off to work on Monday mornings, the wash hung, perfectly aligned and pinned, on the line.

Leny, though only 11 years old, was pulled out of school to help Gré with the daily errands: early every morning Gré gave Leny orders to pick up food for dinner and supper meals. She also looked after Anneke and me, and though Moe promised, Leny never made it back to school. Her schooling ended at Grade 6.

Despite Gré's diligent efforts – cold presses for the fevers, back massages, salve on the rashes – Moe's condition deteriorated. The doctor returned. In a low voice, he spoke at length to Pa.

We stood, silent, in front of the large picture window as an ambulance arrived. Two men lifted Moe out of bed, carried her outdoors, and slid her into the back. It drove away. Where was my Moe going? No one explained. Moe did not come home.

Peace reigned in our house while Moe was hospitalized. Pa paid all the bills and did the bookkeeping – apparently very successfully. Bills were paid and paid off. The house ran with an unfamiliar ease and calm.

Throughout the day, before and after work, the older family members visited Moe in the hospital. In the three months she was hospitalized, Pa even took me to visit once. We entered the stark white building with its massive doors and white walls and went down a long corridor to a room Moe shared with seven others, four patients on each side.

Moe sat up in her bed, bolstered by pillows. Her face, still drawn, was a pasty cream colour. She looked tired but happy to see us.

"Hallo, Moe," I said, gazing around the room in wonder.

As Moe spoke to Pa, I walked around the ward, stopping at each bed without visitors. The patients were eager to tell me stories. At the end of visiting hours, Pa and I left, but I took with me the picture of the room and each of the patients.

Big sister Leny cared for Anneke and me. She talked to us and took us out for long walks. We accompanied her to the shops. Wednesday and Saturday mornings were market days. The smell of roasting nuts filled the air. Sometimes, since Moe was not there, we got a cookie, or a brightly coloured candy at one of the stalls. Then the bakery, the fish, the flowers, the cheese, the candies. Each stall filled the air around it.

One afternoon, Mrs. Van Surksum opened the door to a loud rap, and Willie and I jumped up from where we had been playing a game on the floor.

To my surprise, Leny, sobbing, told Willie's mom that our aunt had come to take me away to her house in Den Haag. "I want Ria to stay home. I can take care of her," she wailed. "But Tante's going to take her away!"

Without hesitation, Mrs. Van Surksum pulled her apron over her head and placed it on the hook by the door. She ran with Leny to our house. Both crying by now, they begged Tante to let me stay home. Mrs. V. offered: "The girls can play here every day – except Sunday, of course!"

Despite their tears and efforts to keep me home, Tante stood firm in her resolve.

I stood by, confused, petrified. Hot tears coursed down my cheeks. I wanted to hide where she could not find me. My whole body chattered. I hated her.

Den Haag
1948

T ante walked briskly to the train station in Baarn, leaving me running behind, trying to catch up, never beside her but behind her. It was a long way for a person with short legs. I never took her hand. She never reached out to mine.

When the big train station came into view, she turned sharply to the right and moved toward the brick building with its massive entry doors. Smoky train whistles blew and signs and arrows pointed to the stairs, each noting train numbers and destinations. I wanted to know what they said, but dared not ask. I observed the details surrounding me – the sounds, the whistles, the talk and laughter, the ticket booths, the stairs leading down to the tracks.

As Tante headed down the stairs, I got in line behind her and boarded the train to Den Haag. She pointed to the window and placed my bag on the luggage rack; I sat on the plush seat and stared out the window, watching the fields, the cows and sheep, and ditches speed by. My first train ride should have been an adventure. I should have been able to ask about what I saw out the window. I remained silent, sullen and afraid.

The train squealed to a stop. Tante did not give any sign it was time to get off the train. Finally, Tante got up; I followed. We disembarked – again. I struggled to keep up with her, running behind until we reached her house.

Tante stopped, pulled out her key, and opened the house door. She entered, and I followed her, hanging up my coat when she pointed to a rack at the right side of the door. She put my bag by the stairs and continued through the living room to the kitchen at the back of the house. A window looked out to a small plot of the grass backyard with a large clothesline in the middle.

"Pick up the teacup and move it to the table," Tante said loudly, clearly, emphasizing each word as if I was a baby, or deaf. She wanted a fancy cup and saucer for her afternoon tea.

I walked to the counter and picked up the cup.

"Not the rim," she said sternly. "You have to pick up teacups by the ear, not by the rim."

I froze, not knowing how to respond. I did not say sorry. I was fearful, but not sorry.

After dinner, alone in bed, muffling my sobs so no one would hear, I had never had to consider proper behaviour. I missed my boisterous family and longed for familiar surroundings, my street, my friends. I missed the music. "I want to go home," however, never crossed my lips. I was her namesake – she, Rie, me, Ria, ashamed that my name came from such a source.

My uncle, Oom Wim, was at work. Oom Rien (single, Moe's brother) was training to become a car mechanic and lived with Tante, his sister. The dreaded Greetje, my cousin a year older than I, was at school. Soon, they would all be home. Where could I hide?

Days passed with no hints that the end was in sight. In quiet compliance, I waited for bedtime to release the tears that burst forth, my head under a pillow to muffle the sounds. No sobbing out loud.

Ordered to put on a beige wool coat and beret, I stood still with Greetje while Tante took a photo in the backyard on the grass under the clothesline—I pasted a stiff smile on my face. On a later visit to my house, Tante gave the photo to Moe.

Little time to play with Greetje pleased me. Mostly, I sat on the floor and watched as she hoarded her toys and her books. As an only child, she had no idea of sharing, though I had many siblings, but still did not need to share.

The long hours crawled by. I followed Tante wherever she went – to market, to church. She spoke little. I spoke less. I felt her dislike, and I wanted to wither away, to stop the fear, the cowering, but I could not.

The first good news came when I heard: "Let's visit Wim tonight."

Visit Oom and Tante? See my twin girl cousins? Really? I worked to hide my bubbling excitement, but the prospect of being warmly received by my cousins was beyond exciting. My twin cousins had visited us in Baarn before. Maybe I could stay with them, I dreamed.

I could hardly stay still, and eagerly awaited instructions to get my coat while the others found their scarves and umbrellas and shoes – we never wore shoes inside the house.

Suddenly, without warning or a word, Oom Rien grabbed my hand and pulled me down the dark hall into the washroom with a toilet and a tiny sink. He ordered me in.

I heard a lock click. I was trapped inside, shocked, numb, trembling.

Steps on the wood floor led to the front door. It closed with a bang.

Silence. . .

I waited, expecting someone to come, but no one did. I screamed. Still, no one came. I shook uncontrollably.

Beside myself, I sobbed, "Tante! Help!" I pleaded with God. I banged on the door. I screamed my fears. All unheeded.

When I could no longer stand, I groped with my hands and bumped against the toilet lid in the pitch dark, put down the lid and sat.

My teeth chattered. I shook. Sounds of silence.

Hours, it seemed hours – and it must have been. My voice was gone, squeaky and hoarse.

FAINTLY, I HEARD THE CLICK OF THE DOOR, AND FOOTSTEPS ON THE floor, mumbling and laughing, announced they were home. Footsteps, closer.

The bathroom door clicked and opened. Oom motioned for me to leave the bathroom. Not a word – by him or anyone else.

Quietly, I made my way to the stairs and got ready for bed. I had no energy or desire to say my nighttime prayers. If God heard my cries, I did not need to remind him of my troubles.

That entire experience, including the bathroom event, terrifying as it was, brought me a new awareness. *The things we feel as children are extraordinary. Violent passions; terrible grief; rage that burns like paper and evaporates like smoke.* I survived and jump-started my journey toward independence. I carved my way in the world. It began with telling not a soul in my family what happened.

WITH GREAT REJOICING IN THE FAMILY, MOE RETURNED HOME FROM THE hospital. I celebrated, too. I went home. Released!

The living room once again became Moe's kingdom. According to her, she needed to eat fresh grapes to restore her health, so Leny bought bunches of large green grapes daily from the vegetable cart that went down the street, setting them on the small table by Moe's chair in the living room. I looked longingly at the grapes, a large bunch, but dared not ask.

Moe leaned over, plucked a grape, stretched out her arm, and offered me one. In awe, gingerly, I held the pale green grape in my hand and examined it, turning it, taking tiny wee bites to extend my pleasure. Though I looked longingly at the grapes in days that followed, Moe never offered another.

Rehabilitation and restoration were necessary for Moe, but I too needed to be restored from the trauma of my experience. I had not been sick, but I suffered daily – terrified to the depths of my little being when locked and left in the small bathroom.

MUSIC TOOK ON A DIFFERENT FORM DURING MOE'S STAY IN THE hospital. She'd done her job, instilling in us a love of singing. Gré picked up her mouth organ and accompanied our nightly singing. Sometimes, Tinie whistled – she had an exquisite ability to warble like a bird. We continued in our habit of shouting out a favourite song. It was not, as the song goes, *the day the music died*. The music just moved into another sphere.

The welcome home included serenading Moe with hymns and popular Dutch songs. When she was strong enough to play the organ, we resumed gathering around as the sisters cleaned up in the next room. The rest of us circled Moe, already leafing through the hymn book. She started the first hymn. Everyone joined in. The wondrous sounds of the organ and the enthusiastic singing resumed. We sang our grateful hearts out!

Family Life in Holland
1951-1952

After supper, Tinie and Gré cleared the table, taking piles of plates and cutlery to the small, narrow kitchen at the back of the house. The water that boiled during supper was ready and hot for cleaning the dishes. The clanging of the dishes and the sounds of cutlery dropping in the sink accompanied the sounds. Moe headed to the living room at the front of the house and sat on the bench at the pump organ in the far corner of the room. She motioned for me to sit on the bench beside her, cautioning me to listen only, not to sing. Those not doing dishes joined her.

Pa sat in his chair, glued to his book. He didn't join the rest of us. He sang in church, never at home. I wondered why, though I didn't even think to ask him.

Moe picked up and flipped the pages of a small Psalm book, leafed to the section called, *"Gezangen"* (hymns, not Psalms), chose one, and started playing. The others joined in and took their parts, blending voices. Gré and Tinie rushed through the dishes. A robust choir every night. Joyful singing, harmonies blending.

Much later, I learned Pa fell short in some situations. When one of my siblings would ask Pa, "Can I join the choir?" he responded in his standard sentence, without fail: "Go ask your mother." When Moe pulled Tina out of school with only three months left, the school principal and teachers came to the house to plead her case. Pa said nothing. That may cover for little things but not the important ones. Moe made calamitous mistakes, and, in effect, Pa let her.

Chapter Seven

Settling in Canada
1954

Family life continued. Alice worked in housekeeping and childcare. She enjoyed her new family and learned some English. One day, out of the blue, her boss asked, "Does your father have a job?"

"No," Alice said. "He is looking for work."

"I have a job for him. They need workers at the paper mill in Thorold."

"Oh," she said. "I want to tell him."

"If they have a telephone, you can call and see if your father is interested."

"We have a phone," she said. Excitedly, Alice relayed the message on the telephone to our grateful Pa.

A job and regular income from the Thorold Paper Mill! It seemed unimaginable after so many challenges and difficulties. But the drive to the paper mill was too far. Shift work complicated things further. Pa decided the time had come to settle down, to find a house, to live closer. He found a neat, freshly painted white house situated between the first two locks of the Welland Ship Canal in the Niagara region.

"We are buying our own house," Pa announced.

The unthinkable happened – they bought a house, a luxury for most in the Netherlands. The house had a 99-year lease with the Welland Ship Canal corporation. The price? $16,000. They owned an eight-acre property. Pa could develop his own dream, his own plant nursery. And Moe, I know now, finally had her agenda. She was a house owner. Most of my siblings brought in weekly money, and she would find ways to spend it.

The front of the house had a large picture window and a front door leading to a small entry with a coat closet. Against the far wall of the large living room stood Moe's beloved organ. The eat-in kitchen had the popular red Formica table and eight matching chairs. The sink still had a large pump that needed priming by pouring a cup of water into the top. Pump, pump, pump. The water dribbled, then streamed out of the spout into the sink. The well for our drinking water had a circular cement lid with a thick iron handle for lifting when the water truck pulled up.

A very long clothesline, an extra-large garden, an entire field of asparagus, and far off in the back of the property, grapevines filled the window scene from the house. The Canadian classic two-hole toilet, outdoors, had neatly folded old newspaper and the glossy pages of the Simpson Sears catalogues for toilet paper. Beside the outhouse was a chicken coop with chickens Pa raised for eggs and meat.

Siblings Hugh, Gré, and Leny each had a room on the main floor, Pa and Moe had the large bedroom upstairs on the left. Alice, Anne, and I slept in the large bedroom at the top of the stairs with a large window and a sloped roof, each bed with a Dutch blanket on it.

A pot stood under Alice's bed. The early morning ritual was for Alice to take the pots outside to empty before Moe washed them up.

Outside, on the bumpy, untended front lawn, Pa dug out a circle of earth and planted a willow tree about my height on the left corner of the grass, right by the mailbox. That tree thrived. The lawn was another matter. It stayed lumpy and bumpy. Each time we tried to sit out there, our webbed yellow sun chairs wobbled and waved until, after many attempts and repositioning, we balanced the chairs enough to sit relatively safely.

By now, it had become increasingly clear, even to stubborn me, that we were in Canada to stay. The fact did not stop my daily dreams of home. The picture of the ship on the North Atlantic slowly turning away from Canada towards the Netherlands remained my fail-safe sleep cue.

For the first time since arriving in Canada, though, I met and made new friends on Church Road, friends to play with after school right on Church Road. Now almost ten years old, I connected with the Nicholson family next door, Betty across the street, and Barb down the road. To my delight, for the first time since moving to Canada, the neighbourhood had kids my age, close enough that I could walk to their houses.

Church Road, St. Catharines, Miss Elliot
October, 1953

At the corner of Church Road, the bus arrived to take me to Carleton Street Public School. All the others living on Church Road, including my sister, Anne, went in the other direction to McNab school – I don't know why.

The school bus bumped along and stopped in front of a very large yellow brick school, with teachers awaiting us at the bus stop. A huge playground surrounded the building. This certainly looked more like a school!

Nervously, I gathered my lunch, left the bus, and followed the students.

"I am looking for my new class," I said to a teacher in the hallway.

"What grade are you in?" she asked.

"I'm in Grade 5," I answered.

She pointed to the office. Off I went.

Again: "I am a new student. We just moved here. I'm in Grade 5."

"Do you have a report card?"

"No."

"Just a moment," she said, taking out a form. She filled in all the spaces and walked me to the classroom. "This is Miss Elliot," she said. "She will be your teacher."

Yet another school where I bravely attempted to remake myself, to fit into a new environment. My teacher in Grassie had said I would skip Grade 4, given that I had been teaching and learning in Grade 4, all the while sitting in Grade 3 teaching Grade 5 readers.

In Canada, the cut-off date for entering school was the end of December; in Baarn, it was the first of October. My birthday was too late for Baarn schools, but I would see to it that I moved ahead of the Dutch peers I left behind. I wanted to be on the same level as my peers in Canada. I did it and kept it a secret.

My Canadian school history remained unknown to Miss Elliot: an 18-month stint in Grade 1, skipping half of Grade 2, completing all of Grade 3 and completely skipping Grade 4. I tried to tell her, but she took no note. I needed attention. I had been in four different one-room schools in less than two years. This was my fifth school. I was increasingly bewildered, insecure, and vulnerable. My confidence withered.

Miss Elliot put me in the back seat of the first row close to the classroom door.

She seldom smiled, at least not at me. No introductions, no questions. She ignored me, perhaps not knowing what to do, though I was fluent in English at that point. I felt her negative reaction keenly. I felt cut off, an outsider—an unwanted but becoming familiar feeling.

Grade 5 made me increasingly unhappy. Despite my early success, my grades slipped. I did not like Miss Elliot, and Miss Elliot did not like me, so I made little effort to get her attention. It didn't work. In a real school now, with many classrooms and grades, I remained socially awkward, unable to make new friends. My motivation dwindled, and my heart hardened.

In my Grade 5 class, I wanted to be Marilyn Lever, the teacher's pet whose family owned a potato chip company. Everybody recognized the Lever name, and Marilyn never let us forget it. The corner store at Reid Road sold five-cent potato chip bags that read Lever's Potato Chips. Imagine!

Having finished my work quickly and well, I sat bored at my desk, playing with a yellow pencil. Somehow, the lead snapped and ended up in my ear. I sat completely still, debating internally. I poked in my ear but could not get it out. I couldn't very well leave it in my ear till I got home. I had to tell Miss Elliot.

It took all my courage to approach her. Softly, so the students would not hear, I mumbled, "I broke the pencil lead into my ear."

Miss Elliot frowned, scowled and called on Marilyn Lever to take charge of the class, then motioned for me to follow her.

The school nurse took a small instrument and handily removed the lead piece. I felt no relief as I followed Miss Elliot back to our class, where Marilyn confidently sat at the teacher's desk.

Deliberately dismantling my Dutch identity began with the name change from Ria to Mary, thanks to Miss Elliot. "Your name is now 'Mary' and your last name is pronounced Appèl." She was right. "I am *not* Dutch," I reminded myself. "I am now Canadian." Mary was not a Dutch name. With a name like Mary, no one could say "You must be Dutch." I wanted nothing more to do with being called, "Dutchie."

As much as I was able, I abandoned all things Dutch. I refused to speak Dutch at home. Moe did not complain. She learned English from me, learning faster than Pa, who just went with the flow. If he could not find the English word, he substituted a Dutch one – all part of settling into our new life in Canada.

Despite the neglect of my Dutch language, the language lingered in my mind, on pause. Some people claimed they forgot their Dutch – I laughed at such outright fibs. I ignored Dutch, but I did not, could not erase it from my mind.

Pa and Moe were forty-five and forty-eight when they came to Canada. At their age, they needed more time to become even moderately fluent. But by then I was solid in my English. My experiences happened in Canada, in English.

To be true to my Canadian identity, I did not invite friends over to the house for fear my parents' limited, heavily Dutch-accented English would expose my secret. I was building my own identity.

MISS ELLIOTT BRIEFLY REDEEMED HERSELF EACH DAY WHEN, AFTER lunch, she read aloud from the Hardy Boys books. The magic of mystery, boy detectives, new stories! I was the detective; I searched out the clues. Reading aloud, I discovered, was inclusive.

Miss Elliot could not exclude me. I heard every word that everyone in the class heard.

Chapter Eight

Appel Nursery began in earnest. First came planting: small peach trees like a miniature orchard, directly beyond the house and garden in what Pa assumed was bare land. Late in May, much to everyone's surprise, asparagus sprang up. The luxury! Our own asparagus. Moe could not believe it. I picked them daily and Moe added them to our everyday meals, until eventually they became stringy, tall, thin, and inedible.

Proudly in her own house now, Moe set about to furnish and finish the family home. She acquired a wringer washer first. Sloshing water moved the agitator back and forth and then spun most of the water out of each item. An electric wringer – a miracle! – squeezed any remaining water from the clothes and chugged down the drain. Then, wet clothing in her hand, Moe started the wringer and fed a corner of cloth between the white rollers until each piece emerged almost dry on the other side.

But the wringer, I learned, could also be a dangerous weapon. A woman from church got her scarf caught in the rollers and died. Fortunately, I never had to touch that machine. In fact, I rarely touched anything used to wipe or clean or dust. By that time, only Anne and I remained at home, and I conjectured Moe needed to keep busy. She did all the housework, even the dishes. We got fresh lunches in a paper bag, and all our clothes ironed.

Pa hung two long clothes lines outside for Moe's laundry. The clothes flapped in the wind, neatly clipped with clothes pins, every Monday, weather permitting.

Pa made clotheslines in the basement when the snow and outside temperatures made it far too cold to hang clothes in the harsh winter weather. When the wash was dry and taken off the lines, all the rugs, including the dining room rug, were draped over the strong line one by one. Moe stood on the stoop and smacked them with a beater until no speck of dirt or dust remained.

MARGARET ANNOUNCED SHE WAS ENGAGED TO AART.

"We'll have an engagement party," Moe said. "We can set up the basement."

Small tables were taken down the wooden steps to the cement floor. Chairs formed a large circle. Moe bought *gebakjes* (individual Dutch pastries) at the Dutch store and made *Advocaat* (egg drink) with egg yolks and brandy, thicker than eggnog and topped with a swirl of whipping cream. I took one tiny bite. That was enough. I'd wait for a second *gebakje*.

The basement filled with happy new friends and guests. All that was left was the wedding in early December.

EVERY FRIDAY, MOE COLLECTED THE SIBLINGS' PAY ENVELOPES FROM the kitchen table, counted each one and distributed $5 for each to cover bus fares, clothes, wedding, and entertainment. All but Tinie, now with her own household, contributed.

Moe had never been so rich. Something changed in her. She

paid for what she wanted: a freezer with a food plan, new rubber floor tiles, a new bathroom, a green shirred velvet sofa bed for the living room. One door-to-door salesman, very common at that time, convinced her she needed screens on the windows; another one convinced her she needed a set of Seventh Day Adventist Bible stories for children. We never read or touched them.

She filled four glass canning jars with coins and tucked them out of sight against the wall on a shelf in Alice's closet in a neat row, caps tightly screwed on. All the coins were put in neat little piles to pour into the penny, nickel, dime, and quarter jars.

I snuck into Alice's closet and surreptitiously lifted out a nickel. I tucked the treasure in a pocket and dashed to Janet's house across the field, opening my hand to show her. "Want to go to the corner store?" Off we went, running all the way to the corner of Reid Road.

"One Wagon Wheel, please. Here's my nickel. Janet and I want to share, so could you please cut it in half?"

The storekeeper took out a sharp knife and smoothly sliced the Wagon Wheel in half.

We nibbled tiny crunchy bites all the way home down the gravel road, making sure not a crumb of evidence remained. As we reached my house, we looked at each other to say, "Is my face clean?"

Using the jar system, it didn't take long for Moe to save enough to take a trip to Holland – $840 for the flight. As far as I could gather, she neither invited Pa to go nor saved any money for him. In today's dollars, that is not surprising: today's value of $840 is listed at $9,438. A walloping amount of money that did not include spending money once Moe got there. At home, she packed and repacked, took pictures of the house, tucked her cash in the purse. Interestingly, she intended to stay with Pa's family, not her own.

Money collected, tickets bought, and suitcase packed ready, Pa drove Moe to the Toronto airport – quite an undertaking. Fortunately, Pa stayed steady, his sense of direction and fearlessness marking the trip. At the airport, he dropped Moe off, reminding her to ask for help if necessary.

Pa returned to St. Catharines, where our house became a place of "peace that passes all understanding." We lived without Moe for a while.

The day after Moe left, I answered the phone.

"Hello,"

The receiver crackled and buzzed.

Finally, the operator asked: "Appel?"

I agreed, "Yes."

Moe shouted into the telephone repeatedly, "Get Pa. Get Pa on the phone."

Pa strolled, picked up the phone, and calmly said, "Hallo."

Without so much as a how d'you do, Moe shouted: "Somebody on the airplane stole my money. What am I going to do?"

Friends and Neighbours on Church Road
1954

P a solved Moe's money problem. Thanks to him, she arrived
home two weeks after leaving. She said little about the trip
other than that Pa's sister's husband tried to get into her room at
night. She used a chair to lock the door.

Why did she stay with my Pa's family when some of her own
family lived in the Netherlands? I was old enough to suspect
something was awry, but I did not understand the whole story.

We settled uneasily back into the new norms and routines. By
now, as was the norm at that time, we all had proudly adopted
Canadian names.

The Nicholson's lived on Church Road, right beside us, in a
very small rundown cottage with a moss-covered roof. Their house
stood on a large, bald lot of land with only sporadic scruffs of grass.
A driveway ran along each side of the property. The second
driveway had a huge rusted-out truck lying on its side. Thick dark
drapes covered each small window.

Janet became my best Church Road friend. She had three
younger sisters. Her older brother drowned in the stream next to
McNab school a year before we moved there. Millie Nicholson
talked about Dougie and how much she missed him. My brother
Dick never became a topic of discussion. When I thought about it, it
felt like he never lived.

When the weather turned too cold for playing outdoors, Janet
invited me into the house. Together, on the threadbare rug, we sat
in the tiny dark living room in front of their black-and-white TV to
watch *The Lone Ranger, Hopalong Cassidy*, and *Roy Rogers*. I enjoyed
going there. We did not have our own television. Mrs. Nicholson
talked to me, and I listened to her. I talked to her, and she listened
to me. Though desperately poor, she was always the kind optimist.
She never complained. How could that be?

When the weather warmed up, the Church Road girl group went into the small forest at the back of our property and explored the paths through the dense woods. We picked wildflowers and collected loose branches to build a forest house. The forest floor was filled with white trilliums. When we had enough, Janet would say, "Race you home." Off she sped. Janet always won.

IN THE MIDDLE OF ONE COUNTRY-QUIET, STAR-LIT SUMMER NIGHT, MOE awakened to the sounds of music. A deep-toned bass voice resonated through the little window screen, open in the summer heat. Moe recognized the voice: Mr. Nicholson. Quickly, she slipped into her slippers, padded to each bedroom and woke us with: "Mr. Nicholson is singing."

Moe motioned for us to take a kitchen chair to the window. We created a semi-circle and looked out to a vague moonlit image of Mr. Nicholson, slow and heavy, lumbering around his little house. His unmistakable, magnificent booming bass voice rose, and spirituals soared through the night air. Black spirituals – the melodies, the words, completely new to our immigrant family – blessed us.

They did not bless Mr. Nicholson. The following day, an ambulance arrived. Mr. Nicholson came out of the house, half-dressed, socks in hand, made his way to the ambulance's back door and climbed in. The ambulance started up, backed out of the driveway, and headed to Hamilton and St. Peter's Home for Incurables.

IN HER FATHER'S ABSENCE, I WENT WITH JANET TO PICK UP GROCERIES at the little corner store. The owner recorded the amount and date in the register, and Janet signed it. We each took a bag, enough to feed Millie and her family for a while.

Moe proudly nurtured her giant garden with lettuce, beans, peas, sprouts, carrots, potatoes, and cauliflower, which she harvested and canned. Did she send me over to the Nicholson's with baskets of fresh vegetables, asparagus, or grapes? My sister said she did. I don't remember being sent there with an armful of food, but I was eleven and probably paid no attention to such things. If it happened, though, it did not happen regularly.

They continued living – or surviving – until Mr. Nicholson returned after three long months; somehow, the bills got paid. When he was home, they sometimes had Nicholson relatives visit. On one of those visits, the triplets, Faith, Hope, and Charity, came. They brought joy to the family, laughing, singing and praising the Lord in the driveway.

No negative talk about Mr. Nicholson ever aired in our house – a black man in a mixed marriage, an unemployed man, a mentally unstable man. Mrs. Nicholson, despite her husband's mental issues, proudly told of his high jumping career at the University of Toronto. Never a word, though, about why he could not continue or why the truck lay in the yard rusted and unused.

Into the Fruit Fields I go
1954

The summer after Grade 5, when I was ten years old, Moe sent me off to pick strawberries at Ferguson's farm on Lakeshore Road. "Pa will take you to the field. They need pickers."

The Niagara region, known for its abundant fruit orchards and strawberry fields, hired kids to do the picking for what amounted to not much more than spare change. I watched carefully to make sure I did this right. Berry pickers went down the rows on their knees, filling the little empty baskets in the flat until every little basket was crowned with bright red berries. Gentle reminders came to "pick every red berry on the vines or you will have to do the row over again."

I worked as fast as my ten-year-old hands would go. Leaves parted, I pulled out the bright red, ripe berries, making sure I left no ripe ones on the vines. With boxes filled and lined up neatly in the flat, I brought them to the end of the rows. Delivered at the end of the row counted, looked, and punched out nine little holes. The "punches" in the card grew.

Picking happened under a scorching orange sun. No breeze. Unprotected from the intense, early July heat, I roasted. I burned. I sat on my knees in the dirt, from 8 a.m. to 5 p.m., every day, barring rain. By the end of the day, exhausted and dirty, I lined up with the others waiting for the foreman handing out cash pay in the familiar little white envelopes, the same ones my siblings put on the table every Friday. Most days I picked 92 boxes at five cents each ($4.60). I never quite reached 100 boxes a day to get one $5 bill.

I placed my envelope in my paper lunch bag and waited for Pa. My envelope looked like the rest on the kitchen table every Friday. Mine was the only one there till Friday. When I looked again, as expected, my envelope was gone.

For the next five summers, I added a different fruit each season:

strawberries first, then cherries, plums, pears, nectarines, and finally, as September arrived, and peaches, in that order. School started before a full peach harvest. By then, grapes on our vines were ready for picking after school. The blue wine grapes had a solid, slippery green ball in the middle that came out whole and slipped easily down my throat. Not too tasty, though. Only to be eaten when the delicious red grapes became unavailable.

With each new fruit crop, Moe reminded me: "Don't forget to ask the boss if you can pick the last of the fallen fruit when each picking season ends." Each agreed. Bushels, baskets, and boxes mounded with plums, apples, peaches, and pears.

Tina had a large nectarine tree in her front yard, heavy with ripe fruit. She sent full paper grocery bags from her nectarine tree to Moe, who canned enough to last us for the winter. Preparing for canning was a long process, boiling water to sterilize the mason jars and lining up bowls for peeling and pit removal. The work took a long time. We ate from the jars all winter long.

I never complained as I took my brown bag lunch and headed to the fields to find where we'd left off the day before. My best-loved fruit would be peaches, though the fuzzy stuff on the outside made me itch all over. Preferred for picking and eating had to be big, black sweet cherries. With my ladder steady, I climbed the steps and reached into the tree, grabbed a handful of cherries to deposit into a large five-quart basket perched on the ladder's top shelf. I carried each full basket cautiously down the ladder and left it there under the tree for the boss on the tractor to put on the flatbed trailer. He (it was always a he) punched small holes in my card before moving through the trees to pick up more baskets. Throughout the day, I heard, "come and get my basket. It's full." I wanted to be sure all my baskets were quickly retrieved, or they might be stolen, which happened to me several times, much to my dismay.

WHEN THE MENNONITE CHURCH IN VIRGIL, CLOSE TO NIAGARA ON the Lake, opened a summer camp, Moe said, "You can go for a week and stay overnight. It's between the cherries and the plum harvest." It surprised me.

What a wonder to enjoy a week away from the picking season. Moe bought a new matching navy outfit, a top and matching shorts to wear to camp – my first brand new summer outfit. I wore it proudly to the camp, only to be told, "No shorts allowed." No shorts? In the middle of an Ontario summer? Children? I felt crushed. I resented the move to spoil my joy. Memories of the week faded except for one thing: "You are here to get saved."

What *was* allowed, however, was nothing short of harassment: repeated pressure:

"Do you want to be saved? Come upstairs." I blatantly and stubbornly refused. As far as I was concerned, I *was* saved. Every evening before bedtime, I heard counselors coming down the stairs. I hid in my bed. Though the only one remaining in the basement room, I did not cave. I went to church every Sunday. We prayed and read the Bible every day at every meal. Enough, already.

The harassment continued. I explained again and again: "I already am baptized," I said, staying strong. "No altar calls for me," I vowed. By the end of the week, I proudly told myself, "You are the only one left in the room to the last day." I proudly defended my religion. They could believe what they wanted, that I was unsaved. It did not frighten me. I would not bend. No need to be saved again.

Arriving home at the end of the week, I announced: "No more camp for me." Since it cost money, Moe happily obliged. I did not explain, and Moe did not ask.

JANET, MY NEIGHBOUR FRIEND, GOT A NEW PAIR OF LIME GREEN JEANS. They looked perfect. I ran across the field, flung open the door and shouted, "Moe, Janet just got a pair of jeans. I want a pair."

"You mean pants with a fly in the front?"

"Yes."

"Why do you need a zipper in the front of your pants? To have pants with a fly, you need a whistle."

"A whistle? Oh, Moe. Please."

I didn't get the pants with a fly. I had to wait to make my long-awaited jean purchase after I left home, though I still did not have a whistle.

So much happened that summer, including the upcoming birth of my new niece, the first in our family to be born in Canada, and the first grandchild for my parents. Best of all, at age ten, I could call myself an aunt.

I shot outside, ran across the daffodil field, jumped over the ditch, and ran to the Nicholsons' house to announce: "I am an aunt. Tina had a baby girl, Wilma Jane."

"Wonderful," Mrs. Nicholson exclaimed.

"Have you seen the baby yet?" Janet asked.

"Soon," I said. "Maybe I can hold her."

I WAS TEN YEARS OLD. WHAT DID I KNOW ABOUT BEING AN AUNT? MY Tante, I would never be. I loved having a baby in the family. Wilma was adored!

Fortunately, my new niece lived down Church Road, across the street from the corner store. Whenever I was not working in an orchard, I walked to see her. She was a happy, chubby baby, and I loved her.

Swimming and Skating
1954

On warm evenings, we swam in the canal, at first with my sister Alice, and later with my friend Sharon. Moe never checked on us. Great ships moved on the canal, and we swam as they did in an alcove where my sister Alice almost drowned. I rescued her. We did not say a word to Moe.

Once the winter got cold, we skated on the pond in Betty's field, frozen weeds sticking out of the water, a hazard for new skaters. Skating became a daily activity.

Completely unexpectedly, Moe surprised me with a large box. "Here," she said, handing it over to me.

What did I see on the box? A picture of white Canadian skates. I tore the box open. My eyes grew wide: a pair of new Canadian white leather size 8 skates. I treasured those skates. I took good care of them, and when they got smudged, I used white shoe polish to make them shine like new. I skated on the weedy pond, and on Saturdays, I got on the bus at Reid Road that took me to the arena where I skated and skated.

I grew and outgrew my size 8 skates – I now needed a size 10 but didn't dare ask for a bigger pair. Instead, I chose to forgo spending my dime at the arena and go to a small restaurant nearby. Easier on my feet than too-small skates.

My new alternative activity included a visit to a restaurant on the main street where I climbed on a red stool. "One cone of French fries, please," I asked.

"Ten cents," said the man behind the counter.

I had it ready. I doused the hot steaming French fries with vinegar and munched each one slowly and deliberately.

Other times, the skating dime paid for a movie where I made out with whatever new friend I met in the dark seat beside me.

Other times it was the library, where I picked up two or three books to take home. With only my five-cent bus money left, I wandered St. Paul Street looking in the windows at the beautiful clothes and furniture and jewelry. At the appropriate time, I climbed aboard the bus and made my way home. Moe never caught on.

The Uninvited Television
1954

Two men in a large delivery truck turned into our gravel driveway and parked behind Pa's shiny red truck. They exited the cab and simultaneously, like soldiers, marched to the back of the truck. The enormous doors opened wide.

One neatly dressed man bounced up our cement steps and knocked loudly on the front door. My brother Hugh appeared and followed the man to the back of the van. They pulled out a large cardboard box and gently slid it down the truck bed, firmly into their powerful arms, and onto a dolly.

Hearing the commotion, Pa looked out the front window. His gaze met a picture of a television on the front of the box.

For the first time in my life, Pa abandoned his calm, measured self. All hell broke loose. Startling, frightening.

"What is this?" Pa shouted.

"A television," Hugh answered.

"A television?" Pa shouted; his brow furled. "No television in my house!"

Pa wanted nothing to do with monthly payments that he knew he would have to shoulder, given Hugh's non-payment record. Many times, I had answered the phone to hear, "Is Hugh Appèl there? May I speak to him?" The same story every time. Hugh was late on his payments again. Since Pa and Hugh shared the same initials, when Hugh did not pay up, the bill would be directed to Pa. My brother, conveniently, always managed to disappear.

Pa was angry. He stormed out of the house. He stomped, huffing down the road toward the canal. I panicked. I feared he would jump into the canal, though he couldn't swim. Anxiously, furtively, I followed close behind him as he crossed Reid Road and reached the canal.

"Hi, Pa," I whispered.

He lowered himself onto the cement edge of the canal, head down, arms around his knees, looking uncharacteristically despondent. I wanted to hug him. We were a no-hug family, but a peck-on-the-cheek family, so I put my hand on his shoulder and lightly kissed his cheek. I sat beside him, saying nothing. Pa remained silent, too.

When he got up, he dusted himself off and turned back down Church Road. Together, we walked back without saying a word. Pa remained sullen for a day or so. Ever the realist, he picked himself up and got on his way, hoping against hope that Hugh would pay his bills this time.

A week or so later, the grocery truck for Moe's Dutch supplies turned left into the driveway. Mr. L. turned off the truck engine, opened the doors, and put out his step. He climbed the cement steps to the front door, gently knocked, then opened the door a bit, calling out, *"Mrs. Appel, de groenteboer hier"* [grocery man here].

Moe called back, "A minute, please. Step inside."

Mr. L. stepped in and saw the big television in the living room. His face contorted in horror at seeing a television in a Christian home. "I will report you to the church council," he warned. "They will call on you, no doubt!" It proved to be an idle threat. No one ever came.

He ran to his truck, slammed the door, and sped out of the driveway, shooting up gravel and dust balls on the road.

FAMILY FRIENDS MOVED. SADLY, THEY LOOKED FOR A NEW OWNER. They could not keep their Pukkie (small), their miniature collie who always happily swished his tail through the air. "Could you take him?" they asked. Moe agreed.

"I'll take him," I offered. "He's my dog." Pukkie waved his tail madly and followed me everywhere outside and inside when allowed. I loved that dog, and he adored me. We were a matched pair.

SUNDAY NIGHTS AT 7 P.M., WE ALL SAT TOGETHER IN THE LIVING ROOM to watch "Lassie," a larger version of our miniature dog, Pukkie, who filled a gap in my life. I loved Pukkie. Every day he greeted me – no, enthusiastically welcomed me home. Already old, Pukkie got older and became unwell. He could hardly move. One morning before school, I walked outside to use the outhouse and found Pukkie under the clothesline in the back of the house. Stretched out. Stiff. Dead.

"My Pukkie," I wailed. "Moe, my Pukkie is dead."

When he died, I cried myself to sleep for many nights. Pa dug a hole in the backyard and placed my Pukkie reverently into the grave and covered it. I took a piece of scrap wood and made a marker with his name so I could visit him in the field.

Soon after, by some miracle of timing, other Dutch friends offered us a new furry, fuzzy German Shepherd puppy, still fluffy, and I claimed her immediately as my own. I adored her, spoiled her, and took her with me except in the house or to school, showering attention like a new friend or a sister.

Dog was six months old, lighting up my life, when I got to the mailbox expecting her to run, legs askew, to greet and welcome me home.

No Dog. I called out, puzzled, and looked around the yard again.

Dog was nowhere to be seen. I went as far back as the grapes and Pa's new peach trees. I hollered, "Dog, where are you? Come, come!"

I asked each one at home, "Where is Dog? Where is Dog?"

"Haven't seen her," each responded.

Desperation. Heart racing, tears on my cheeks, I walked north to Reid Road, checking along the ditches on both sides of the road, stopping first at the neighbour's farm, calling out and calling out. No response. Not even a weak bark. At Reid Road, I crossed to the other side, looked around intently, and walked farther into the yards. I could hardly see for the tears streaming. Tina had moved. I was on my own.

"Please, please, God," I prayed. I made impossible promises if God would just bring me to the place where I could find Dog.

I stopped. Was that my imagination? Did I hear something? A soft whimpering sound came from a small shed midway in the yard.

"Dog?" I said softly and went toward the whimpers. In the space between two sheds, my beautiful Dog bared her teeth, hissing and growling, white foaming liquid sliding down the sides of her mouth. Gripped by terror, afraid she might attack, I left her there, all alone, not daring to pick her up. I abandoned her.

I ran home for help as fast as I could – what was wrong with Dog?

Pa was at work, not home. No one else listened. I felt abandoned, like Dog. Head down, heart heavy, I cried and cried, alone in my sadness. Later, I learned from Pa that Dog had distemper and would have died shortly after. It explained Dog's death, but didn't make the sadness go away.

Chapter Nine

Church
1955

After church, like other girls my age, I looked for a Sunday church exchange friend who came home with me one Sunday, and I would go to her house the following Sunday. Before long, I found one: Norah became my best church friend. Her family owned the Dutch store right across the street from Montebello Park. We often went there for walks or listened to the band in the classic white bandstand. Sometimes in the summer, we sat on chairs placed in concert style and listened to the brass band or choral or musical band, enjoying every minute. Without a musical performance, we wandered, and as we wandered, we talked of our lives. I don't remember Norah ever going to high school. I think she helped her parents in the store.

Their store was always closed, of course, on Sunday. We'd drive to the store after church and unlocked the door, walking past the large picture window that showed a glass counter including an array of Dutch pastries. Norah's mother let us go downstairs to the store refrigerator to pick a special *gebakje*, served on tiny plates with fancy lace-like edging, with the small Dutch teaspoon alongside. I often chose a flaky pastry with delicious, thick pudding filling, or a puff pastry cone with real whipping cream in it. Norah's mother poured coffee. For lunch, she made Lipton soup with the very fine noodles I loved.

Visits to my house could not compare, though it did start with coffee and cake in the living room. Dessert before dinner. In the dining room, we gathered around the table and ate Moe's delicious *balletjes* soup. Sometimes, when she was in a good mood after cleanup, she slid onto the organ bench, flipped pages in the hymnal and called out: "Come and sing."

Often, for reasons unknown to me, Moe was cranky and grumped around, embarrassing me. My friends disliked Moe; they liked Pa.

On Sunday afternoons at home, Pa and Moe read Dutch books from the church library. Norah didn't like to read, so we dreamed up other ways to have fun. Sometimes, we walked to the canal and sat on the cement ledge and talked, between Locks 1 and 2 at the Welland Ship Canal. A perfect spot for swimming, although Norah was not allowed to swim on Sunday. We watched as the water in Lock 1 rose, moving the massive ship with it. When the lock filled and the water leveled, the ship sailed into the canal and the sounds of cars starting up accumulated on either side of the lifted bridge.

Unlike my church friends, who had very strict Sunday rules, Moe was a Sunday liberal. My friends could not ride bikes and had to wear their Sunday clothes till bedtime. At my house, they borrowed some of mine. No swimming on Sundays or movies any day of the week. No skating on the pond. The only thing left was a walk and talk.

My older siblings set the stage, even going to movies. Once, Tina took me to the movies in Baarn. It would have been difficult to prohibit movies for the younger ones. I really enjoyed that, knowing that my friends were not blessed with a liberal family!

But one thing completely *verboten* (excuse the German word) was shopping on Sundays. Almost worse after arriving in Canada had to be dancing. Card playing was forbidden, but Dutch immigrants did not play cards, so little temptation existed. You could sing, like the Dutch, arms linked, swaying in perfect symmetry. "That's not dancing," they said. Apparently, swaying was not in vogue for 19th century Dutch immigrants.

My sixth school in a little over two years. In Port Weller, every classroom housed only one grade, not all eight, as in the earlier one-room schools. Every day I leaned against the yellow bricks looking enviously at my classmates clustered in small groups. I stood by, hoping even one person would ask me to join them. What was wrong with me? The decline in my confidence played havoc with my motivation. Severely tested in Grade 5, I stopped trying to fit in, stopped trying to be the top student.

Now I started over – again. Fortunately, my Grade 6 teacher, Mrs. Dunn, never raised her voice and spared us having favourites. She made it clear by action and word that we were *all* her favourites. She brought even me into the circle.

Her stories about being an artist, a painter, married to a teacher-painter intrigued me. Sometimes she brought paintings to school and explained each one. I wanted to be a painter! I started collecting paper scraps for drawing, stacking each completed art piece neatly in a dresser drawer. The calm, the comfort of her class made possible a new attempt at reviving my learning life. It started to fall into place: I easily managed the work.

But I could not tell Mrs. Dunn that Buddy, a classmate, poked fun at me every chance he got. When I told my neighbour, Mrs. Nicholson, she said, "Buddy is just acting out. He probably has a crush on you."

"Not likely," I thought. I was probably right, but it was comforting to get Mrs. Nicholson's view; she always saw the bright side. She mentored and supported me.

AT HOME, THE FAMILY CONTINUED THE TRADITION OF CHOIR AT church – there was no such thing as a Sunday church choir, *per se.*

It was a shared activity for all old enough to join; I wasn't old enough, but I learned the music and all the words. Moe sang as she worked, preparing for the next choir concert. I learned every verse of *The Messiah* as Christmas neared. I wanted to join the choir, too.

Feike Asma, a man of great energy and robust gesture, came to Canada from time to time, and dramatically led the choir. When he did not approve of the singing, his arms shot up into the air and as he shouted in his heavily accented English: "More heat! More heat!" the choir raised the temperature.

Mr. Asma wrote a descant to "Silent Night," glorious music that rose above the traditional harmony. I could not hear enough of it. I learned that descant at the organ with Moe. During the Christmas season, the choir finished every practice with "*Ere Zij God*," (Glory to God), the most famous Dutch Christmas song. It stirred hearts and brought tears.

Like all my family, I loved music, all kinds of music, but especially the songs like "Old Black Joe" that Mr. Nicholson sometimes sang in the night. I listened, learned, and sang the songs to myself.

"Teach me the alto part, Moe. I want to sing it with Janet," I asked Moe.

She walked directly to the organ and said, "Sing the melody."

I sang it for her; she joined me on the organ. "Like this?" she said. Moe's voice switched to alto, and I tried to follow. By the third try, I got it. Moe hummed the soprano, and I sang the alto. Then I ran to the door, calling back, "I'm going to Janet's!" Over the field I ran, banged on the door and told her, "We can sing together. I can sing the alto of 'Old Black Joe,' Janet."

We practiced sitting on a huge log in their driveway. We got it. We both got it.

In Grade 7, Moe encouraged me to register for a school choir. We entered a competition in the Kiwanis Music Festival, and I sang alto. Moe helped me rehearse at the organ.

When the day came, the choir stood in the school hallway with a table and three adjudicators. Our teacher director started the choir with a dramatic flourish.

After explaining our marks, the adjudicator remarked, "I heard one lovely voice above the others."

To my horror, I knew: "That's me." I heard nothing else. Head down, red-faced, I waited it out till the dismissal. I am too loud. No more choir for me.

I kept my word.

FOR THE FIRST TIME SINCE COMING TO CANADA, I ENTERED THE NEXT grade in the same school. The teacher, Mrs. B., had a strict unsmiling presence in the class. She took herself far too seriously. I tried to please her, adjusting and accommodating when I could. Her married name, Boikoff, did not suggest that she was Dutch. Like me, she was not particularly proud of it. In teaching, she stuck to her lessons; we read and answered questions.

The entire process bored me. Motivation lagged again; it seemed I couldn't do anything right. I had hoped for an advantage, since she was Dutch like me. On the contrary, she seemed to resent it. The desire to learn slipped ever further away.

Mrs. B. wore a wig. When the wig accidentally shifted, we could see thin spiky hair covering her head. Some kids told us: "She has a disease. All her hair fell out." On the playground, everybody laughed about it. I never told Moe about the wig, but I told her Mrs. B. spoke Dutch, which made it possible for Moe to attend the parent-teacher meetings.

In the first parent-teacher meeting, no doubt Moe expected to hear wonderful things about me and my academic abilities, as she had in the Netherlands. On the contrary, she heard little good news. Mrs. B. complained that I talked too much. I got a C+ in Science (my first, though certainly not my last). Moe learned I was now an average, uninspired student, more interested in chatting up new friends than being a serious student. She came home and pointed her finger, scolding me for not applying myself.

"It's so boring," I said. "All we do is read and answer questions."

This was the year I joined clubs and groups – in Grade 7, it was Girl Guides. That phase lasted long enough to borrow a uniform and hat. But after a few meetings, Pa worked the four-to-twelve p.m. shift at the paper mill, so he could not take me there or pick me up. On to the next thing.

ONE MORNING MOE SURPRISED ME WITH A BEAUTIFUL BLUE SWEATER she'd knitted, sewing on perfect pearl buttons to finish it. Moe proudly showed me the sweater at breakfast: "I worked well into the night, but I finished it. You can wear it to school today."

I took the sweater proudly, stuck my arms into the sleeves, and pulled the front pieces together. I closed several buttons, squeezing and tugging at the knit buttonholes, pushing the buttons through. Satisfied, I walked to the mirror in the front entry and admired my true-blue sweater. So gorgeous! I danced out the door, lunch bag in hand, and skipped to the bus, certain to get compliments and maybe, just maybe, even a complimentary word from Mrs. B.

The classroom was warm from the sun shining right into the two Grade 8 rows. I unbuttoned my new sweater and hung it on the back of my chair, meaning to pick it up and wear it outside for recess. The bell rang. The sun shone before I went outside, so I hung my sweater on my hook in the little cloakroom at the back of the class. At the end of the day, I collected my lunch pail and library book and went to the cloakroom. I looked. I searched down the rows, peeking under coats and sweaters.

Not my sweater, though. No patch of true blue, no knit wool.

Up and down the cloakroom aisle, I lifted each coat and sweater to find mine. No luck. Fear struck. What would I tell Moe? Would I tell Moe? What would she say? I was in trouble.

"Moe," I cried, running up the stairs at home, "My new sweater is gone. Somebody stole it."

No answer. "Moe," I called again.

Through the kitchen window, the laundry flapped in the wind, and I saw Moe's arm hold on to the clothesline.

I ran to the back porch, opened the door, and repeated: "Moe, my sweater is gone. Somebody took it."

Moe frowned and continued her work.

"I looked everywhere, even in the other desks. I looked everywhere in that room. It was not there. I even waited till no one was left in the room." Tears spilled down my cheeks.

Moe said nothing. She did not stop clipping the laundry on the line. She did not get angry or even express frustration.

I'd expected the worst. Her unexpected act of silence made me grateful, ever so grateful.

FOR CHRISTMAS PERFORMANCE, I TOLD MOE, "I WILL NEED A PLAID kilt skirt with a big pin and a ruffle nylon blouse."

On the night of the performance, I arrived, proud of my new clothes that looked becoming but were completely unsuitable for the square dance. I panicked, but a classmate lent me her skirt and blouse for this one dance. I changed before the performance.

I don't think Moe noticed, though she and Pa were in the audience. If she did, she didn't say a word about it.

ACADEMICALLY, I RAN OUT OF STEAM. OTHER KIDS OUTPERFORMED ME. What happened? I had grown tired of trying. But when September arrived, I had tried just enough to pass to Grade 8.

Much to my chagrin, Mrs. Boikoff stood behind the desk in the combined Grades 7 and 8 class. What a letdown. Another year with her? A different school every few months and now the same teacher for two years.

The Grade 8 class sat in two rows along the window wall: fifteen students in all. There I was – in the same school, in the same classroom, with the same teacher. Lessons droned on and the tests kept coming. I knew enough to sit in my seat and do my work and not a stitch more.

When I arrived home, Moe was outside, hanging clothes on the line again, using the classic wooden pinch pins with a spring. She squeezed the end of the pins, tucked the piece of clothing around the line, stretched the item along the line and pinched again on the other edge. Intent on her work, she did not respond when I said, "I'm home. Mrs. B. is my teacher again." I did not smile; Moe just got on with hanging the laundry.

In class, Mrs. B. warned us about a big science test on Thursday.

Tests were a foreign concept to me. I had only ever experienced spelling tests. For me, those required no studying. Not surprisingly, I had little experience or skill for studying. No one explained how to prepare for a test.

When I looked at the test, I saw questions not discussed in class. The number of questions dumbfounded me. I glanced around the room and saw others peeking at their neighbours' tests.

Intuitively, I knew: "You're not supposed to do that." I admonished myself. Across the aisle, on Sharon's sheet, I could read the answers she had neatly written on the paper. I shocked myself. I cheated.

When Mrs. B. looked up from her test marking, she found at least six of us borrowing test answers from our neighbours. She stormed out of the room to report us.

One by one, each cheater was ushered into the principal's office to get the strap. I had never had the strap but had heard many stories. Would it hurt? Why did I look and copy? Maybe Mr. Hutton (uncle to Lauren Hutton, the movie star) would not give *me* the strap. I kept my head down and avoided eye contact.

"Put out your hand," he whispered.

The strap smacked.

My hands burned and went bright red. The outline of the strap remained on the palms of my hands.

I did not cry or say a word to him or anyone in my class. I walked out the door, cheeks aflame in shame, and returned to the classroom. I dared not look at anyone for fear of being called out for cheating again. Papers shuffled, pencils dropped, whispers were heard.

My hand did not shoot up even when I knew the answers. You could be wrong, I told myself. Don't take the chance. I didn't, and neither did many of my classmates.

THE SCHOOL NURSE CALLED EACH GIRL TO AN ANTEROOM OF THE principal's office. When my turn came, the nurse asked a few questions and frowned: "Mmm," she said. I could tell this was serious.

"You are the only girl in your class who does not have her period or wear a bra!"

I put my hand over my mouth, deep down, darkly humiliated. I should have asked: "What am I supposed to do? Could I change that?" I said nothing, of course. My face, a febrile red by now, wore the shame.

I returned to class, slipped into my desk, kept my head down, and went to work.

Next Saturday morning after breakfast, I announced, "I need a bra."

Moe did not say, "Yes. It looks like you need one." She didn't argue or ask questions or give advice. Instead, she took out her well-worn wallet, pulled out a $1 bill and 10 cents for the return bus ticket to downtown and said, "Buy one."

I walked to the bus, aglow in the thought of having a bra, though ill-equipped. I did not have any advice or knowledge about what to look for, ask about, or even how to try it on.

Getting off the bus at one end of St. Paul Street allowed me to walk the entire length of the street, cross over and walk down the other side, browsing every store window for nightgowns and underwear. Near Leon's furniture store, I came upon mannequins wearing bras like my sisters wore, the ones with butterflies on the bottom half of each bra cup. Too embarrassed to get help from a clerk, I just picked one and bought it. I couldn't wait to get home and try it on.

I ran to my room shouting, "I'm home!"

Of course it didn't fit. Too big for my new boobies. To make up for the empty space in the bra cups, I stuffed my too-big bra with hankies taken from Moe's drawer, the ones she used to dab *eau de cologne* on her forehead in church.

I imagined taking that bra and flopping it up and down in the nurse's face who informed me of my physical shortcomings. I chose instead to leave the bra in the drawer till each cup would be mostly filled. I don't know what I wore in the meantime. Probably the undershirts Moe knit for me.

IN CLASS, MRS. B'S SOBER FACE AND STOOPED SHOULDERS REVEALED trouble. More cheating? More poor test marks?

No. She announced that Sharon's father had been tilling the soil in the orchard in front of his house when, somehow, his tractor toppled over and fell on him. He did not survive. Collectively, we inhaled in shock. I wanted to cry. What if I lost my Pa? My Pa had a tractor and an orchard. I was afraid.

Sharon returned to class – oh, so sad. She didn't speak. The accident seemed to have struck her mute. We respected her need for silence.

Not three months later, her seat was empty once again.

Again, a tearful, somber Mrs. B. "Sharon is not here today. Sadly, on the way to Niagara Falls yesterday, her mother was involved in a car accident."

An audible shock rang across the room.

"Sadly," Mrs. B. continued, "she died."

Incredulity sat on all the faces in the room. Paralyzing shock. Losing both parents in accidents in one year? No parents left? Only horror remained. I had no resources to know what to do, say, or help.

Sharon's seat remained empty for what seemed a long time. Her older sister became her parent, but things were hard. When we drove past her house, the last one before the Lock 1 bridge of the Welland Canal, the yard stood neglected and deteriorated. Unruly grass had grown high, reaching up to the lower windows. In high school, Shelly dropped out of school and married at 16. Eventually, the old house, abandoned, lay in ruins, a testament to loss and sadness. That whole story came back to me every time we crossed the canal bridge.

FEW MEMORIES – VERY FEW POSITIVE ONES – REMAIN. I WONDER HOW the experiences of my last two years in elementary school (1955-1957), three to five years after arriving in Canada, shaped my schooling, or education that followed.

Was I learning? Oh, I learned, though probably not what teachers expected. Hugely disappointed in myself, I failed to fire up the motivation needed to succeed. What happened to my school-smart self?

ALICE DIDN'T WORK ON SATURDAYS. SHE KEPT UP HER SHOE POLISHING and ironing for Sunday, shirt by shirt, slip by slip, sheet by sheet, even bra by bra. Moe, very well-endowed, had a bra Alice called "a watermelon holder."

I held up Alice's bra and called out, "Whose is this 'raisin on a breadboard' bra?"

The ironing of a bra was a precise process. Spreading a bra on the ironing board, Alice folded the cup in half horizontally, and struck the hot iron on the white cotton, creating a crisp crease on the bra. She held the two cups and folded them vertically, and again, with the hot iron, created a pointed peak. Big, small, or in between, Alice shaped each bra cup into the popular conical bra – we all wanted to be "sweater girls."

Chapter Ten

The bandana, the Bus, and Weddings
1956

In the front yard, Pa planted a small weeping willow tree in the corner by the mailbox. At the end of the driveway, I sat and watched my brother Hugh and sisters Alice and Leny walk briskly towards Reid Road, a half-kilometer from the house. They boarded a bus that would take Leny to the GM plant and Alice and Hugh on to Thorold to the Scott Abitibi Paper Mill. My sisters wore colorful bandanas wrapped around their heads.

Shielding my face from the sun and gazing down the road, something powerful stirred inside me. I can't explain its source. Looking at the bandanas and the work clothes on my two sisters and brother, I pictured myself walking alongside them, a matching bandana on my head.

I jerked upright and vowed to myself: "You will never, ever wear a bandana on your head. You will never work in a factory." That image, seared in my memory, awakened a deep resistance to my expected life. Would I be forced to walk down the road to the bus, not to school now, but to the factory? Alice stayed in school until she turned 13 years old. I was *now* 13 years old, and I glimpsed a future I did not want.

ON FRIDAYS, THOSE SAME SIBLINGS CAME HOME WITH THE LITTLE WHITE envelopes filled with their weekly wages.

Moe greeted each one, reminding them (as if they needed reminding), "Just put your envelope on the table." She picked them up, counted the cash and change in each one, then took the $2 bills, and distributed them around the table. That $2 was their spending money for the week, which included bus rides to work, saving for their weddings, buying clothes and entertainment. For Alice, it was Saturday night junior hockey games with her friend down the road.

Once, I heard Leny ask for an extra dollar per week to save for her wedding.

"No way!" Moe shouted, obviously annoyed. "You can't get married anyway until next summer. Just to remind you: no money or presents for the wedding from me."

Pa never interfered in Moe's commandeering. His standard response? "Go ask your mother." He neither challenged nor stood up to her – he stayed silent. I felt sorry for Pa. I imagined it was far simpler not to interfere with Moe's agenda. Somehow, all the blame was literally dumped on Moe. But Pa's neglect gave Moe permission to continue.

Every morning as I prepared to leave to take the bus to school, Moe made my lunch: two sandwiches, an orange or an apple, and a cookie. She stood erect by the outside door as I ran to take the lunch out of her hands while she quoted the same maxim: "Too late, too late, an ugly word, does no one any good." ("Te laat, te laat, een lelijk word"). I never learned the rest of that quote – I was already on the road, off and running to catch the bus.

Pa worked diligently to build the nursery, planting new stock, plowing the fields, grafting the new peach orchard in the back of the property. The older ones refused to help. When I turned 13, I began to help Pa. Once, he made lovely bouquets of egg-yolk-yellow daffodils, each neatly arranged and tied with raffia. "I will stay in the truck," he said. "Take a handful of bouquets, knock on every door on one side and then start across the street and say, 'I have lovely flowers. Fresh daffodils only 25 cents a bunch.'"

Without exception came the same reply: "Not today." It deflated me. Each rejection hurt.

I had a hard time telling Pa, who was so proud of the gorgeous butter-yellow daffodils.

Pa worked hard, and along with those still living at home, he brought home his weekly paychecks. Moe spent. As far as the money was concerned, Moe believed, "It is better to receive than to give."

Until that one day when Pa came home, a wide grin on his face; he had traded in his bright green Plymouth for a new candy-apple red truck and neglected to inform Moe. Though she was in the room when Pa made the big reveal, Moe did not let loose.

I waited.

The surprise came when Moe never raised an objection. Did she know she didn't have a leg to stand on? On the other hand, did Pa realize that a truck held only three people? We were seven still at home, which meant that when we had to go to church all together, some had to sit in the back, outside, hair blowing in the wind. Come to think of it, though, we had ourselves a convertible! For whatever it was worth, Pa had his new truck, and proudly cared for it.

My older sisters modelled a life I had no intention of following, though I envied the clothes Alice acquired with her weekly allowance. She hung each blouse, skirt, and dress meticulously in her closet. Sometimes – or maybe a bit more often than sometimes – I surreptitiously took a skirt or sweater or a dress (for picture day or my birthday, for instance), and carefully returned it to her closet before she got home from work.

Work had benefits, to be sure, but for me it also had deficits: Alice, 13 when we immigrated, only completed Grade 4; Leny was taken out of school after Grade 6 to serve as Moe's house helper when she became extremely ill. The promise of return to school for Leny never materialized. Alice, on the other hand, had no intention of ever returning to school.

My world and my expectations for the future remained ambiguous and uncertain. In my young mind, few options existed, though I never dreamed of anything else. A restlessness, source unknown, settled into my mind and heart.

THE SUMMER I FINISHED GRADE 8, TWO OF MY SIBLINGS MARRIED. JACK, who immigrated to the USA, brought Audrey from California to Canada. They married in our church. When I gloomily admitted that I wanted to be a bridesmaid, Audrey found a fancy puffy organza dress, blue as the sky, that fit me perfectly. I was a bridesmaid!

Soon after, Jack returned to California and Audrey stayed to wait for her residency application. A month later, among a family of strangers and her new husband far away in California, she had a miscarriage.

Moe was unkind, dismissive; she treated Audrey badly. I wanted to say something, defend Audrey. I felt so sorry for her. What a relief when she flew home to be with Jack, far out of Moe's range of attack.

LATER THAT SUMMER, LENY MARRIED HARRY. ALICE HAD BEEN Harry's first choice, but "Not interested," said Alice. Harry turned his eye to Leny, who took the attention seriously.

To prepare for the wedding, Leny sewed all the dresses except her wedding dress.

"Moe," Leny pleaded, "come with me to find a wedding dress."

"No," Moe said flatly. That was that.

Harry helped, no doubt. An uninterested Moe, and a no-gift family policy, likely affected Leny, but it did not prevent her from doing all the sewing (including a dress for Moe) and organizing the celebrations.

The wedding came, and Anne and I dressed in matching flocked-nylon yellow dresses as bridesmaid and flower girls. We went to a photography studio before the wedding to have formal black-and-white pictures taken. It all felt very special. It was a lovely wedding.

NOW THAT LENY WAS MARRIED, THE FAMILY INCOME SHRANK AGAIN. Alice, now the oldest daughter at home, continued to deposit her cheque on the table faithfully on Fridays. Alice, however, was not Leny. She did not accept things unquestionably.

She challenged Moe until, exhausted by her defiance, Moe pronounced loudly and clearly, "You bring out the blood under my nails." (*Je brengt de bloed van onder m'n nagels.*)

Desperate for calm, Moe sat down on the organ bench and said, "Alie, come to the organ."

Alice knew the routine. Even before she got to the organ, she started singing a Hank Williams song, or a song by Kitty Wells. Country and western music, new to immigrants, had quickly become Alice's favourite, especially Hank Williams. She memorized the lyrics before she even understood them.

Moe, of course, had no idea of the lyrics' meaning, but she could play the music. Alice joined in and soon Moe contributed her version – some English words collected from Alice but mostly Dutch words that replaced unknown English words.

It worked magic on Alice, and the rest of us who had no choice but to listen to the music. Calmed Alice right down. Her singing continued on her way upstairs. Once in bed, sad tones began anew, drifting downstairs. Sappy, melodic Dutch songs. A song of a mother mourning the loss of her son: *"Oh how the mother weeps . . . her youngest, dearest child will never be with her again."*

Alice sobbed inconsolably before drifting off to sleep.

I can still hear her singing. I heard many of the Dutch words to the songs, and sometimes sang them softly to myself.

High school. Thoughts of Grade 9 filled me with hope and fear. The noisy hall was crammed with students, talking, laughing. I waited nervously, alone.

The 9As lined up for the French and Latin options. At the door, a teacher called out student names. I was the only one left standing.

"Your name?" a teacher asked.

"Mary Appel. I chose Latin and French."

"You're not on this list," he said. "Wait here. I'll find your class."

Not French and Latin, but French and Home Economics, they had decided.

"I am too dumb for Latin," I repeated over and over to myself.

How did the teachers know I could not do Latin? Was Juffrouw Kok wrong? Was Mrs. Boikoff right? Coming to Canada, I had learned English rapidly. But not Latin? Teachers knew more than I did. I must be dumb.

I wore Tina's old brown panel skirt Moe had remade to fit me, topped by a light blue sweater set on the first day of high school. I wore that outfit every school day until the last day at the end of June – the same school outfit every single day of Grade 9. I was teased and taunted mercilessly. "Again?" they would shout. "Again?" Head down in shame.

THE 9C CLASS (FRENCH AND HOME ECONOMICS) HAD ABOUT THIRTY students who, mostly, openly rejected anything academic. At least five were repeating Grade 9.

Shortly into the first semester, some Black girls from my class invited me to smoke in the woods behind the school. I accepted their offers of a puff. When I tried to inhale, the world around me spun. Dizzy, trees swirled around my head. No matter: I could be proud of myself. I was included in this band of girls.

Moe's closet pots were ideal for the coins needed to pay for borrowed cigarettes. Moe would not be able to tell if a few coins went missing, going up in smoke. In the meantime, I hung out with the kids from the classroom. A few of them were repeating Grade 9. One was engaged to be married. One got pregnant.

I thought I belonged, but I didn't. I was caught in the in-between, the nowhere. Maybe I missed something.

Finding my way through the throngs in the hallways to math class agitated me and made me jittery. Algebra went way over my head. The formulas overwhelmed with letters and numbers that failed to register in my head.

The teacher stood in front of the blackboard and shouted every instruction and question, though he could not be heard above the raucous din. Chaos in the room every day. When the teacher turned to the board to write out a problem, paper airplanes soared through the classroom sky, often hitting the teacher. When he turned to face the class, activity instantly stopped.

When the teacher turned to the board again, the scene repeated itself. Intermittently, he tired of the din and shouted, shouted, shouted: "Keep quiet!" "Pay attention!" "There will be more homework and another test!" Nothing changed.

I gave up on math, not doing my homework, handing in nothing – a very low mark on my first and second report cards. Failures in math and English would mean repeating the grade. Grade 9 again next year? The horror.

Tearfully, I admitted to Moe I needed help in math. I described the chaos of the class. A complete surprise: Moe hired a tutor. How did she find one? After a few sessions, I had caught up and fulfilled all incomplete homework assignments and handed them in to the teacher.

THE HOME ECONOMICS TEACHER ASSIGNED THE FINAL PROJECT: "WE are ready to sew a blouse. You will have till the end of term to do it. I will help where needed."

Panic. Was I the only one who had never used a sewing machine? Latin would have been easier. I grabbed the list of the required items and explained to Moe, who gave me the money. I took the bus into the city, browsing in the fabric store, agonizing over colour and style, not understanding difficulty levels.

I found a Simplicity pattern (*Simplicity* was deceiving). Armed with the list and checking it off as I went to the various stores, I brought home light yellow-green fabric, a stitch picker, matching thread, and buttons. I took the bag to school on Monday.

Over and over, the teacher explained and demonstrated. She walked down the aisle with her unfinished blouse to see who needed help. I stitched; I picked out the wandering stitches. I stayed after class and missed the bus. Not surprisingly, I disliked sewing.

Whenever I stayed after school, I missed the bus, so I had to walk across the street to Leny's to wait until Harry came back to drive me home.

I finally finished the blouse. What a complicated mess. At the first opportunity, I crumpled it into a bag and threw it into the outdoor garbage can. It would be many years before I tried sewing again.

ON THE OTHER HAND, I NEEDED NO TEACHER – GOOD, BAD, OR indifferent – to show me the wonders of English literature. Bring it on – novels, poetry, short stories, and plays.

The milquetoast teacher introduced Shakespeare's *Taming of the Shrew*. I was enthralled. I *met* Shakespeare. He called to me from the library. I devoured each encounter in the plays and Greek myths (*Myths and Meaning*); I burned through *David Copperfield*. My hunger for reading led to weekly trips to the library, where I did a "series" reading, beginning with first books by Dickens, Hardy, and Hawthorne.

Shortly after school closed, and before the strawberry fields opened, I snuck out of the house three mornings in a row to wait for the *St. Catharines Standard* to arrive in the mailbox. At the side of the house, hidden from view, I kept an eye out down the road for the newspaper delivery man to arrive, open the mailbox at the end of the driveway, and throw in the newspaper. I raced over, dug out the paper, waved to the driver, and rushed back to the outhouse to sit down to read the results.

The newspaper shook. My heart raced.

Eyes darted across each new page, searching for Grantham High School, then my Grade 9C class. Turn page, scan; turn page, scan. Turn page, turn the page.

My name appeared: *Mary Appel: passed to Grade 10*.

I passed. Passed? I passed?

I wanted to yell, to shout, to punch fists in the air, but of course, I did not.

Still trembling, I walked to the back door with a neatly folded paper and said, "We have to go, Dad."

I dropped the paper on the table where Moe sat finishing her morning tea. "I passed Grade 9," I said, tossing the newspaper on the kitchen table.

Moe did not respond. I walked out to get into the truck and wait for Pa.

F or most of my church friends, school ended by Grade 9 or, at best, Grade 10, with few exceptions. One by one, parents plucked their children out of school and sent them to work to contribute to the family income, like my siblings. Only a few of us remained by the end of Grade 10. It worried me. Would this happen to me? I knew Moe, and I'd heard the stories.

I recalled my 13-year-old self-prophecy: "I will never wear a bandana" when I saw my sisters' heads as they walked down Church Road to the bus for the factory. I never forgot. Why did that stay with me? The uncertainty of my life's journey pushed all deep thoughts of school to the very back edges of my mind.

My friend Sharon and I took the same bus to the high school. She lived in the house closest to the end of Church Road – the unfinished canal lock. Although she was a grade ahead of me, we enjoyed sitting on the bus together and discussing issues of high school and life. She invited me to her house often, a cramped white wooden cottage, much like Nicholsons' house but in much better shape. The outside door opened directly into the kitchen, where a large square country table was often covered in flour. Mrs. S. folded and filled perogies with cottage cheese, mashed potatoes and cheese, and my favourite, cherries. Sour cream sat ready on the table to cover warm perogies. I had never tasted such delights. Perogies boiled to perfection in Sharon's kitchen became my favourite snack. Still warm, smothered in sour cream – I licked my fingers.

Often, when it was warm and light enough, I left the house after supper and hollered: "I'm going swimming, Moe." Already in my bathing suit, with a towel wrapped around me, I crossed Reid Road and called on Sharon. She put on her bathing suit, got her towel, and together, we walked down a short stretch of the road until we arrived at the canal. If there was no ship on the horizon, we dove into the water.

Moe never cautioned me, never seemed to worry about the dangers and undercurrents or warn us to stay in the small bay. I don't think she'd ever been there. I neither worried nor even thought about it. I loved the water, was a daredevil, a risk taker. I taught myself to swim, first by pretending, touching the bottom with one foot, pushing myself up, saying, "I'm swimming!" Bit by bit, the push-offs became redundant, and I floated and swam like a pro – at least I felt like one.

OUT OF THE BLUE, SHARON SAID: "I'M GOING TO THE DANCE LATER. Want to come along? My brother will drive us."

Did I want to? Of course, I wanted to. I ran home, grabbed a change of clothes, stuffed them in the towel bag and headed back to Sharon's, where I changed, tidied up, and stood ready to go to my first dance. Did I just say *dance*? Moe thought I was swimming.

Sharon had no idea that, for me, dancing was evil, a taboo. "Dancing," I heard from church people, "is outrightly wicked. They play Elvis Presley songs there. He shakes his hips. You never know what dancing will do to you."

I needn't have worried. I sat on the school chair all night – the entire gym had chairs backed to the wall. Sharon danced. Others danced. I waited, pathetically, from the sidelines for a prince to dance me to a storybook ending. It never arrived. I did not dance. Not even once.

The house was dark and quiet when I returned. Quietly, shoes in hand, I slipped up the stairs to tell Moe I was home. The clock chimed. *Boing. Boing. Boing.*

Moe heard me enter and hissed, "I called Mrs. Senyk. You were at a dance. Go downstairs and sleep on the sofa bed, but before you do, get on your knees and pray for forgiveness."

Which I did. I didn't mean it. I had no opportunity to tell her, "I didn't even *dance*." Prayer as punishment.

Moving on in High School
1957-1958

R eturning to high school was a relief after a summer of climbing ladders, bending over, lifting, and delivering strawberry baskets to the bosses. High school appealed to me more than hard fieldwork in the relentless sun.

I enrolled in Grade 10—no more Home Economics. To my dismay, my course sheet read the typical academic courses and, in the end, I Elected the course Typing.

Typing? I had absolutely no interest in typing. I did not elect this course. No matter. As it turned out, I fared little better at typing than sewing. My eyes constantly drifted to the keyboard and disrupted the required memorizing of keys and hand positions. Too much effort. Sloppy and incomplete. Detentions to make up for the incomplete assigned exercises.

As the teacher wandered around the class, she often said: "You may not appreciate this now, but you will benefit in the long run!"

Indeed, typing paid off. Years later, when my son, the tech guru, declared he could not fit typing into his Grade 11 schedule, I used my experience. "Sorry, you can't find room in your schedule. Here's what we'll do: I'll register you for an evening class in Typing. That will free you to go on with your schedule as planned." He arrived at the class and thought he had the wrong room – all women. He was the only male, all 6 feet, 5 inches of him.

He grumbled, he attended, and he passed. And, like me, I learned that typing (at least in that era) paid off.

I would not have elected sewing in Grade 9 or typing in Grade 10, but each proved fundamental in my development. Typing became a critical skill later from high school onward, literally throughout my life. Sewing grew into a necessity, allowing me to sew to satisfy my desire for clothes I could not afford. I even completed a couturier sewing course where we produced a complete binder of samples for reference I used for many years. Those courses, least desired, accompanied me through life.

Thankfully, Grade 10 had a different class makeup. Either that or I had changed. I felt more comfortable in classes with more serious academic attitudes. My work, in turn, bore fruit. The great, bellowing male History teacher commented that I, though *only a girl*, had managed to get the second-highest mark in History class. At the end of each class, the teacher said in his loud, low voice: "Boys first." When most of them had exited the door, he barked: "The rest of you can go now."

The girls, including me, snickered and thought it was funny as we walked past the teacher to exit the class. Despite his brusqueness, his constantly furrowed brow, and his dismissal of girls, he taught history passionately and drew me in, inspiring me to love it, too.

Time to Leave School
1957

As I came down to say, "Good night" (mandatory), Moe stood in front of me. With a straight face in her clear voice, she announced: "Go to Mr. Harder down the road. Ask him for a job in the fruit factory."

"Now? You want me to go now? Can't it wait till tomorrow? It's 10 o'clock at night, Moe. It's dark."

"Hurry up!"

Scared, desperately wanting to resist but unable to, I caved. I put on my jacket and walked out the front door into the black, inky night. No lights other than the occasional yellow window light and some distant moonlight.

I walked in the middle of the road, ditches on either side. Slowly, gingerly, I walked past the light of the Nicholsons' side window, the Krauses' barn light, the Penners' light in the large front window. The Harder house was next.

"I'll go to the back door and knock very softly. Hopefully, Mr. Harder is in the front living room and won't hear me."

Into the driveway and up the small hill to the back of the house, I saw the light of the back room, and Mr. Harder bent over, reading the newspaper. I knocked ever so lightly, hoping against hope that he would not look up.

Of course he did. With a quizzical look on his face, he opened the door. "Hello?"

"My mother sent me to ask for a job in your canning factory."

"I'm sorry. I have no jobs. Good night."

Cautiously, shamefacedly, in total dark except for the shining moon and stars, I walked back to my house, again staying in the middle of the road. Deeply humiliated, chilled, I entered the house, went straight to my bedroom, pulled on my pajamas and crawled into bed.

"Did you get a job?" Moe hollered from the upstairs hallway.

"No," I yelled back.

I turned over and lay awake, puzzled about the events of the day.

MOST ATTRACTIVE, SPONTANEOUS, KNOW-IT-ALL ALICE DREW ALL THE attention of boys in our church, particularly when they came to the annual church picnic and youth rallies. Boys called Alice. Sometimes, she'd agree to a date with two or three for the same Saturday night. When the first car arrived, she hollered, "I'm going now," and Moe answered back: "Home by 10 o'clock!"

When the next date arrived, sometimes only minutes later, Moe explained Alice's absence: "She's not home. Went off to a hockey game with her neighbour friend."

"We had a date."

"I'll tell her you stopped by."

Looking out my window, I laughed at the antics of those too-late dates. Each "date" backed his car out of the driveway, spinning gravel. With tires squealing, each turned onto Church Road from our driveway.

No matter who Alice dated, Moe waited for the car to turn into our dark driveway. As soon as the headlights turned in, Moe flashed the outside lights – on/off, on/off. A warning to Alice and her date.

Moe worried. She was obsessed about some guy getting Alice pregnant. Lights flashed again. She wasn't about to settle for a pregnant daughter standing at the front of the church like she'd had to, though I didn't know that at the time.

MUCH LATER, WHEN I LIVED IN BC, I CROSSED THE BORDER TO celebrate my brother Jack's birthday.

"Congratulations, Jack. How old are you now?"

When he told me, I puckered my brow, quizzical, quickly

calculated and said, "Moe lied. She told me you were a year younger!"

We laughed. Poor Moe. Imagine carrying the weight of the shame for the rest of your days. Moe carried it to her dying day, never knowing I knew. Even when she remarried, she reminded my stepfather he'd *had* to get married. She, on the other hand, backdated her wedding date so Mr. V. could not return the favour. Poor Moe.

Schooling Days Are Over
1958 - 1959

Today was anything but ordinary. *Today my life changed.* It started innocently enough in the summer with picking strawberries, cherries, plums, pears, and nectarines, in that order. No lazy, hazy summer days for me, except one day with massive dunes and water and lots of young people: the July 1 church picnic on Lake Erie. I looked forward to that with unbridled enthusiasm.

Moe made enough food to fill a large basket. The substantial church community (1800 members) had many young people. For most, this was our one summer holiday. All day on Lake Erie, running at top speed down the white, sandy dunes. Soon, a group of us ran at top speed to dive into a man-made lake. Oh, it was glorious.

Then back home and back to work.

INCREASINGLY, MOE DROPPED HINTS THAT MY SCHOOLING DAYS WERE coming to an end. Our family was shrinking by marriage and, with it, the weekly income. Moe often quoted the Dutch saying: Each child brings his own bread (*"Elk kind brengt z'n brood mee!"*). Small wonder families had so many children.

But children leave. They are not a permanent source of income. One of those children was me. I avoided any direct thinking about going to work or leaving school. The future remained hazy and mysterious.

Too old for Sunday friend exchanges by now, I spent endless hours reading and working on a detailed portrait of Elvis Presley on a large sheet of brown wrapping paper. Each week, I took it down from my bedroom door and spread it out on the cleared desk to work on a particular section. I was proud of what I'd produced: I accented Elvis' sexy sneer and his thick, glossy black hair. No one mentioned it. I knew enough not to draw attention to it for fear of a smart-ass comment, which could be worse than no comment at all.

ONE WARM, BREEZY SUMMER EVENING, I JOINED PA AND MOE ON THE yellow-webbed folding lawn chairs in the front yard for the traditional not-a-minute-later than 8 p.m. coffee time, as we did most warm evenings. A small, weather-worn round yellow table held three cups and saucers, a speculaas cookie (windmill ginger cookie) leaned against each cup. An ordinary day.

The bumpy front lawn had a graceful swooping willow tree on the corner in front of the mailbox – the one Pa planted. Although we lived at a nursery, the front lawn remained a patch of wild grass filled with dirt bumps. Hardly a showcase.

The little round yellow table that sat on the bumpy grass teetered dangerously, close to toppling the cups and saucers onto the lawn. Chairs wobbled; Pa and I corrected the wobble. Moe talked; Pa and I listened.

Our heads looked up simultaneously at the sound of a car on the gravel road.

Spewing dry dust whirls as it came closer, we saw the bright red left-turn light signal. The wheels turned into the driveway, and tall, well-dressed Mr. Colenbrander emerged from the car and waved.

"Hallo," Pa said as he stood up.

"A cup of coffee, Mr. Colenbrander?" Moe asked.

He smiled and nodded. "Please," he said.

Pa stood and pointed to an empty chair. Mr. Colenbrander found his seat as Moe went into the house and quickly reappeared with a hot cup of coffee and two cookies she placed on the little table before him.

What is Mr. C. doing here? I wondered. He attended our church; I knew his daughters.

After some small talk, Mr. C. began in earnest. "We have a new Christian High School in Hamilton, and we've just purchased a small bus to take students the sixty kilometers from St. Catharines and other points along Highway 8 to the high school. One seat is all we have left, and we reserved it for Mary."

For me? Go to school again?

Moe had her answer ready: "She's done school. It's time to work."

Pa remained silent.

Mr. Colenbrander was not easily dissuaded. An insurance salesman, he knew the art of the sale and the tactics of persuasion. He persisted, smiled, and stayed. Without arguing, he neither raised his voice nor pulled out all the stops; he just gently introduced and reintroduced the possibility.

Through the open front door, I heard the living room clock tick over and chime: 8, 9, 10, 11, 12 times, I counted. Midnight.

Long past her bedtime, Moe was exhausted. Head down, she finally blurted: "Okay! She can go, if she pays for it herself."

Without further ado, Mr. C. stood up, offered thanks, shook Pa's hand, waved good-bye, and drove off.

I waved enthusiastically as the car crunched on the gravel and disappeared into the night. What had just happened here? Did I hear the words right?

Moe had no chance to change her mind. I ran up the cement steps up to the front screen door, called the mandatory "Good night," and nothing more.

But the inciting moment continued as an internal conversation in my bedroom. Why had Mr. C. picked me? My huge church had many young people my age. By now, I hardly considered myself the smartest one. Too excited to sleep, though, I heard the cuckoo clock chime 1, then 2. Time passed. In my mind, I rehearsed the details of Mr. C's proposal. My heart was full.

Did I dream this? Am I going back to school? I am going back to school. "O, frabjous day!" (Thank you, Lewis Carroll.)

MY EDUCATION CONTINUED. MR. C. HAD OPENED A DOOR THAT looked considerably more appealing than putting a bandana on my head to work in a fruit factory. Moe's expectations for Friday pay envelopes were altered.

Here was my hallelujah moment. I knew this was important, critical. I could not, however, have told you why.

Chapter Eleven
～∾∾～

School again?
1959 - 1961

As promised, I filled the last empty seat in the new Mercedes minibus. I picked my best dress (not my Sunday dress) for the first day of school. Pa woke me early; I had to be across the first lock of the Welland Canal in time to meet the little yellow Mercedes bus by 7 a.m.

Pa called, "Ria, time to go. I'll wait in the truck..."

We started each day together in the red truck, driving to the Canal Lock 1. Every day I said, "I hope the bridge is down!" And every day, climbing into his beloved truck, Pa said, "Me too, Ria!" Some mornings Pa, and I groaned simultaneously as the red light on the bridge flashed. Stop! Wait! Pa slowed down; a few cars ahead of us were already stopped. Left and right we looked and calculated the wait time; we grew increasingly accurate, watching the bridge lumber up to make way for the enormous ship to go under it, or the rising water in the lock. The ship sailed smoothly under the bridge. The bridge came down, the green light started, and cars moved, crawling at first. Some days, the process took twenty minutes. Most days, however, the bridge was down, and we were there waiting when the little Mercedes bus arrived.

That first day, the very handsome and soft-spoken driver Tony opened the bus doors to welcome me into the bus. Frazzled, nervous, insecure, and loaded with my school stuff, I climbed into the small bright yellow bus and found my seat. All along the way we stopped for others waiting at the end of their driveways or a corner of Highway 8 until we got to the last two cousins who lived on the same street in Fruitland. Ready to proceed to school! The little bus was full.

Full of new students, full of noise, full of stories. Butterflies swirled in my stomach.

When the bus pulled into the gravel church lot, we poured out of the bus and ran up the steps to the open door, then paused and guardedly moved down the stairs into the basement of a large church.

I don't know what I had expected, but surely, not this. This looked less like a school than the eight-grade one-room schools I attended when first coming to Canada. This did not look like a school. I would call this Basement Basic. A large room with a stage and a piano served as a whole school meeting room for weekly chapel; Sunday school rooms served as classrooms for Grades 9 and 10. Grades 11 and 12 met together in the larger classroom. The kitchen functioned as a science lab. The plainness of it all somehow, oddly, comforted me. It could be the unfamiliar (school in a church basement) with the familiar (church basement).

The Grade 11 and 12 classes had tables in a U shape with chairs backing onto the wall, Grade 11 at the front and Grade 12 at the back, creating narrow aisles along the back of the three walls. Teachers stood at the front of the room, a large blackboard behind them and a tiny table in front to hold their teaching materials. With the name Appel, I always had a front-row seat.

The teachers taught all required courses in the Ontario Curriculum, adding Reformed Doctrine (Grade 11) and Church

History (Grade 12), leaving no room for student electives. Chapel was held in the large room weekly. With Tony Ten Kate (bus driver pianist, teacher) at the piano and Coby on the zither, we sang hymns, prayed, and went off to our classes.

Our teachers – one woman and three men – included Rev. Van Dyk, the principal, who also pastored a church in Hamilton. He had been our pastor in St. Catharines. Not a standout preacher, I'd heard my family say, but for me and the students in my school, he was an outstanding principal/minister. He knew the content of the two religion courses, telling stories of the crusades and John Calvin. He was a beloved principal. As Moe would say, "And my darling, what more could you want?"

Classes at the Christian high school consisted mostly of lectures, long and boring; in that way, it looked like the public high school I attended for two years. The biggest difference? Religion. While my family ritualized prayer, with Bible reading three times daily, hymn singing, and memorized psalms, we never discussed any of it. We knew what we could not do and assumed that was our whole religion. God came up only in formal circumstances, mostly mealtimes with prayers before and after, and discussions related to church people we'd met. God never came up in our conversations. No debates or arguments about religion. God-talk was a new phenomenon for me, and I was curious.

I began exploring my faith and became a hardcore believer in a sovereign, all-controlling God who might or might not love me, depending on how well I did on His earth. Luther's conviction that I was "saved by grace" looked like a victory over the "works" required by the Catholic church, but not so much pertaining to me.

My classmates seemed much better prepared. They argued about the purpose of missionaries and missions. If the Christians approved by God would be eternally rewarded anyway (which was called *election*), what was the point of proselytizing? How would we rationalize the conversion of those who were, at the end of the day, not elected? And how would we know? Or was it that hearts were not moved for conversion unless each was elected "before the world began"? Heavy subjects for adolescents. We scoffed at those who in the Middle Ages debated "how many angels fit on the head of a pin?" but was this any different? The whole thing proved bewildering and fascinating, even exotic at the same time.

School itself was school itself. Teachers talked; students listened and took notes. Teachers asked questions; students answered. Familiar routines.

IN ENGLISH CLASS WE READ *THE SCARLET LETTER* BY NATHANIEL Hawthorne. Miss P. enthusiastically explained the book. I joined her, readily suspending all disbelief to join Hester Prynne on the scaffold, in prison, and later in her cottage, some ways from the town. Forced to wear that disdainful letter A for Adultery, she performed a magical transformation: "On the breast of her gown in fine red cloth, surrounded with an elaborate embroidery and fantastic flourishes of gold thread, appeared the letter A." She wore it like a trophy: I am Hester, strong, brave, and powerful. I wore my own scarlet letter, A for Appel, though not always with pride.

Just before Miss P. arrived one morning, out of the blue, Philip looked around at me and shouted: "The minister did it!"

The minister? "What?" I shouted. "I will *never* forgive you, Philip. You had no business saying that aloud."

Philip stole my anticipation and cut short the detailed work of tracing the clues. I was robbed. But that did not stop me from indulging in every word with care and attention. I played out the movie in my head and saw children on the street eyeing Hester and Pearl walking by, hearing stories. They were prepared to meet Hester Prynne. Fascinated, I memorized their words: "Hark, there is the woman of the scarlet letter and behold, there is the symbol of the scarlet letter running along by her side. Come, therefore, and let us fling mud at them." Imagine young children who no doubt mimicked their parents and repeated it on the street.

To me, Hester was not a sinner but my heroine. I didn't want to care what people thought of me.

Just writing about it inspired me to read the book again. The surprise of the complex and dense language made me wonder how I grew to call that book my top choice. I identified with Hester Prynne, wanting to be as strong and independent as Hester. *The Scarlet Letter* remains my all-time treasured and favourite book.

In the fall, Pa and Moe drove to Hamilton for parent-teacher meetings, and Moe confronted Mr. W. "Why do you skip Mary when she tries to answer your questions in French class?"

"Because she is very good at French; many others are not."

It didn't matter; nothing changed. I stopped listening and stopped doing any French homework.

Speaking of homework – when would I have time? I told myself repeatedly, "I'll do it on the bus tomorrow," but of course, that never happened. Twelve pickup stops collected students from St. Catharines, Vineland, Beamsville, and Fruitland, and the talk and the chatter did not stop.

Sometimes on our way home, Mr. T. gave in to our pleas and stopped at a restaurant along the way where, for ten cents, I would order my favourite French fries in a cone, dribble vinegar on it, and quickly climb back on the bus where all talking stopped while we enjoyed our ten-cent snacks.

For the most part, teachers gave their all to the students, working with scarce support and resources. When math again became a challenge for me, Moe again paid for tutoring, with Mr. T., who taught chemistry in the school (church basement) kitchen on a small counter. The class circled around it while he demonstrated the experiments. We could not do it for ourselves. But then, neither could the teachers do an adequate job. I frankly don't know how they managed sciences. All their materials had to go with them every time they changed subjects and rooms. It must have been so challenging.

At noon, weather permitting, some of us walked to a small, overgrown local cemetery, each claiming "our" stone, like "our" pew in church, and we spent noon hours smoking, talking, and laughing. We bummed cigarettes, paid back when possible, and discussed our life in high school. Teachers rang the old-fashioned school bell on the little stoop to call us in.

Leaving home early and coming home around dinner time each day left little time with my family. This time away became, without intention, a building block in my independence. Most of my classmates, some old enough to leave school and work, had returned to school; for the most part, they were boys. Girls did not warrant, it seemed, the same inspiration and opportunity to continue their schooling. We were part of a small locus of female students.

In the summer of 1960, for the first time since coming to Canada, I felt included and accepted, though not particularly successful academically. My marginal Grade 11 marks might be blamed in some part on the long, long hours on the bus. Excuses, however, did not explain my lack of motivation, my mediocre effort. Others on the bus managed.

It was me, though, who was interested in making my own choices, particularly in reading. But with the state of my marks, I worried. Would Moe send me back to Mr. Harder to ask for a job again? Would I be allowed to continue school?

I now speculated Moe couldn't afford to pull me out of school at that point; that would be a shameful thing. Everyone at church might hear and think she could not afford the costs. I needn't have worried. It was not going to happen, at least for now.

One of my classmates, Bill, found me a summer job in tobacco. He lived in a small Ontario town near many tobacco fields, and his mother agreed I could stay with them and work the tobacco harvest. They arranged for me to be picked up by 7 a.m. each day, six days a week, for six weeks.

The work was back-breaking. The men worked out in the fields picking the tobacco; women worked by the storage and drying sheds, with the hum of the conveyor belt carrying in the sticks with tobacco bundles for drying always in the background.

The table filled with tobacco leaves. Picking up three or four tobacco bunches, I handed them to a woman who tied them onto a stick, flipping over every other one. Full sticks went onto a conveyor belt up into the large storage shed. Repeatedly, the same movements.

At noon, we took turns at the pump, using a thin slat of wood to scrape the tobacco gum off our hands. The tobacco char, jet black, gummed up our hands so badly that it became impossible to fully curl my fingers. It was grimy work and hard, and never a pause allowed without a "Get back to work!" order. The scraper took off some of the tar, but before eating, we soaped and scrubbed our hands, and duplicated the scrub, scrubbing again before leaving at the end of the day.

Each day I earned $10, good money. But Bill's mother took $15 (today's value: $153.00) or 1.5 days of work to pay for my room and board. Looking back and calculating, I wonder how Bill's mother justified that charge, when she knew I was paying for my education.

They spoke Frisian, a different Dutch language, which I could not understand. I felt excluded; I did not fit in.

In the middle of the season, I found a ride to St. Catharines to attend my brother Hugh's wedding, and when the season was over, I put my last remaining money in an envelope and tucked it in my bag for Moe. Ready for Grade 12.

The small grade 12 class moved to a small cement block room in the dark church basement. A small blackboard hung on the wall across from the entrance and exit door. The high mud-splattered window let in only a dimmed light. Our class consisted of eight students, four girls, four boys. Two tables and four chairs faced each other along the walls. A small table stood between the outside rows for teacher notes and books. Teachers squeezed by the table to get to the front. We left class only for lunch break, bathroom, and the kitchen for Chemistry class. Our room was awash in beige – table, chairs, door, floor – everything but the blackboard, and cloudy chalk dust all over everything. Girls sat on the one side facing the outside wall, and the four boys faced us. Some light slipped in from a long, small window, but in the basement dimness, the overhead lights shone perpetually.

For the first time since elementary school, I did not sit at the front! We chose a place to sit at the student tables. With eight students, alphabet arrangements were unnecessary. The boys' table stood on one side under the window, the girls' table on the other. Books, binders, loose papers began neatly organized in front of us in the morning, but by lunchtime, everything was spread out across the tables – things constantly got lost or went undercover.

Mary: "Anybody got an extra pen?"

Bill: "Here you go! Isn't this yours?"

Philip: "Who's seen my lunch?"

Freda: "I forgot my lunch. Anyone got extra you can share?"

Jackie: "We can share my sandwich."

Corrie: "You can have my apple!"

Mostly, we listened and took notes. I expertly used my rote mode for making notes: I did not listen beyond summarizing the lecture. Some classmates worked diligently, completing all assignments in good order. They lived in Hamilton; I did not. They had time; I did not. I was the first on the bus at 7 a.m. and the last one home, at around 5 p.m. or later. If the bridge was not up, I'd walk to the other side to find Pa waiting to pick me up in his red truck.

Small classes, I thought, should result in better marks given the additional teacher's attention. Class size affected me differently. I belonged. Despite that, my marks did not improve. When the marks came home, however, I heard Moe like an echo in my head: "*Hakken over de sloot...*" Heels in the side of the ditch – barely making it, given only my half-hearted effort.

School bus students bonded. We travelled as friends. No worries about being an immigrant – we were all immigrants. No showing off wealth; everybody struggled with poverty and sacrificed to keep their kids in school. The people in this community spoke my language, understood my cultural values and issues, knew about immigration, and came from similarly religious families.

In English we studied Francis Thompson's poem "The Hound of Heaven." It gripped me. I understood the feelings, the draw, and I recalled the opening words many times over the years:

I fled Him, down the nights and down the days;
I fled Him, down the arches of the years;
I fled Him, down the labyrinthine ways
Of my own mind

I imagined myself fleeing from God, my rebellious self in pursuit of ... I don't know what ... a darkness. God would find me, and then what? I felt both lost and found.

LITERATURE STILL ENTHRALLED ME. I LIVED IT. SATURDAYS WERE library days: the 10-cent return trek on the bus into St. Catharines gave me weekly library pleasure. The grand stone stairs with lion heads on each post invited me through the massive oak doors into familiar territory. I moved toward the novel section to locate D for Dickens, H for Hardy and Hawthorn, and occasionally, S for Shakespeare (only the tragedies). I never had enough to read, and I never read enough for class. I managed all the English readings but spent little effort on non-literary school reading. While outside school, my personal reading world grew exponentially.

Jackie and Corrie handed me a small softcover book. "Have you ever read C. S. Lewis?" Corrie asked. I shook my head. She offered me *Mere Christianity*. That evening, lying on my bed, I was smitten by Lewis – philosopher, scholar, novelist – whose brilliant mind examined major world religions before deciding on Christianity. His logical, philosophical framework appealed to me, and I identified with Christianity as defensible, rigorous, and logical. Why had I not known about C. S. Lewis? How did my classmates know this?

I finished the C. S. Lewis and returned it, and Jackie brought me *The Screwtape Letters*. Images of devils startled me: Was that appropriate reading? What if someone found me reading a book of devils exchanging letters with devils-in-training to disrupt any move toward Christianity? This would surely deserve condemnation – "*spotten*" (staining), Moe called it – to ridicule and make fun of religious beliefs! But by now, I was a devoted disciple who looked for logic in my religion. I moved forward and became more open to expanding my world. When I posed the devil issue to Corrie and Jackie, they argued that this new and startling world opened our imagination and had a sound message. I agreed.

The books kept coming. Corrie brought C. S. Lewis's The Great Divorce, a mind-bending imagination-stretching vision of Hell – not as a conventional place of fire and damnation but rather, a place of no needs that led to the curse of wandering in utter loneliness. *Wanting* involved mere *thinking* for desires to appear – no waiting, no paying, all there to enjoy. This astounding view of Hell fired my imagination (pardon the pun) and paved the way for new, alternative interpretations and worldviews I found exhilarating.

I SCORED A PART IN THE PLAY *ARSENIC AND OLD LACE*, NOT THAT THERE was much competition. Rehearsals were held after school, so Jackie and Grace, who lived near the school, took turns inviting me to stay at their houses overnight. Rehearsals happened directly after school.

Performance time arrived. On our first night, the crowd settled onto the seats. A buzz. A hum. Silence. On stage, the play began seamlessly. We remembered our lines and positions. At intermission, actors moved to the back of the set through the stage door. Offstage, we whooped and hollered at our success. Flawless.

After the intermission, the audience clapped to welcome us. I stood close to the back and mistakenly bumped into a fellow actor with his back to the stage door. When the bump became an unexpected push, my fellow actor helplessly slid back. Time moved in slow motion as he bounced against the wall that trembled and shook and teetered forward...but remained standing. Quite a feat.

Spontaneous laughter erupted from the audience. They probably thought this was part of the play. I froze in place, waiting for the catastrophe to unfold. The backdrop wobbled, stuttered, slowed...

And stopped. A communal breath of relief.

I ambled to the front of the stage and blurted out loudly and clearly in Dutch: "More luck than wisdom." ["*Meer geluk dan wijsheid*"]. The audience exploded in uproarious laughter. We actors got back to business.

Chapter Twelve

◦◦◦

Profession of Faith
1961

This year was anything but ordinary. It changed everything.

The principal, a minister, taught Church History to my Grade 12 class. He was always running late. He ran into our class and said, between little puffs of air, "Philip, run up to my office and get my recipe book."

"The attendance record, sir?" Philip corrected, a sardonic, smug smile on his face.

No response. Philip got up.

The religious crusades, the Reformation, the spread of Luther's cataclysmic withdrawal from the Catholic Church entranced me. The principal framed lush historical narratives. As he talked, my mind watched Luther flagellating himself ruthlessly in his monastery's dark, cold cement cell floor until stripes of blood covered his back.

Luther found "saved by faith, not works" in scripture, and it transformed him. The church, dismayed at the declaration of 95 theses he nailed to its doors, put him on trial, charging him at the Diet of Worms (wonderful name). Ultimately, the church split and was forever divided. Was this "the great divorce"? Reformers carried the Reformation to Hungary, France, Scotland, and the Netherlands. I listened in rapt attention to the Reverand's descriptions of the crusades even including children trekking across Europe. First, I was fascinated and then appalled. How could children be sent as messengers to persuade conversion on the masses they encountered? How many died? What percentage survived?

This happens when a church takes charge of its believers, Reverand V. told us. "You must feel it!" he pleaded, elongating the word *feeeel*, stretching the word like a rubber band. "Picture this..." he continued, and picture it I did!

I loved this stuff. History fascinated me. "Believe me, Rev. V.," I wanted to say, "I feeeeel it."

Religion courses broadened my knowledge and opened discussion about worship services, people, events, and the historical experiences that shaped them.

Rev. V.'s upstairs office was located directly above our classroom. A furnace pipe connected them. Sometimes, footsteps paced the floor. We imagined him, head down, pipe smoking, in deep, deep thought. We knew he knew.

Sitting in class waiting for him to arrive, sometimes our chatter grew loud. But as shuffling noises filtered down from the room above, we paused; Jackie uttered a loud "shush," flashed a finger across her lips, and pointed upward. Immediately, we understood. "Be quiet. Tone it down. He can hear every word!"

My voice was significantly louder and more frequent than others. He never held it against me, ever. A passionate theologian, Rev. V. delighted in discussions of faith and beliefs, two areas ironically new to me. In church, theology came as bits and bytes in sermons and songs, and in our family, it did not come at all. Moe voiced her open disdain for anything Catholic, including a warning to avoid all relationships with Catholics, or anyone outside our church. The worst you could do? Marry a Catholic.

Religion, nevertheless, excited me. I faithfully read the scriptures every evening before drifting off to sleep. When some classmates prepared formally to join the church, I told my parents: "I want to do Profession of Faith, too." They agreed, though I was younger by several years than others going forward. Most were engaged and getting married.

I attended Profession of Faith classes at church, culminating in an interview by church elders (all male) who asked questions based on the Catechism. The advantage of my Christian education emerged. My answers never wavered. Within minutes, they approved me going forward with my profession of faith.

MOE TOOK ME SHOPPING IN A GENUINE LADIES' STORE. WE BOTH stopped by a mannequin wearing a suit – a long, pale blue summer wool jacket, matching skirt, and blouse. I looked over at Moe. "Try it on," she said.

A stunning suit. I was already tall, with long, thick dark hair, and the clean tailored jacket perfectly highlighted my build and height. I turned in the mirror to admire a new me.

Moe announced: "I'll buy it."

The tag said $80 (currently valued at $817), but Moe didn't blink. She strode purposefully to the counter and arranged a layaway plan, $20 per week until it was fully paid, just in time for the Profession of Faith church service.

Payments arranged; we left the shop. But Moe was on a tear.

She took me to the millinery shop for a stylish new hat, and to Bata Shoes for new high heels: my 5'10" became 6 feet. Everything matched. The most striking – and costly – outfit I had ever owned. More than the tuition costs I struggled to pay for myself.

THE DAY OF PROFESSION OF FAITH ARRIVED. CANDIDATES TOOK UP THE first two middle pews. The Minister called us to "rise and stand" to confirm our desire to be full (paying) members of the church. Over thirty young people, all older than me, stood in the front two pews. One by one, the minister called out our names.

The minister looked directly at me and said, "Alice Appel." He did not correct himself, obviously not realizing he had made a mistake. I was the family babysitter.

I responded as Alice, however, and said, "I do so help me, God."

I hoped God had a sense of humour and recognized my full commitment to him, even though I was not Alice.

Rev V.'s failed comb-over of thin, reddish wisps fell across his shiny dome and across his face when he ran, which was generally the case. "Mary, I see you have not yet applied to Calvin College with others in your class," he puffed, blowing smoke from his pipe as we passed each other in the little hallway by my classroom.

"No," I said, taken aback.

Who applied to Calvin College? What was college, anyway? Why was I so far out of the loop?

I never considered my schooling could continue. My life had already overreached its foregone destiny: leave school, find a job, put your weekly packet on the table on Fridays, take your $5, get a boyfriend from church and as quickly as possible, get married, get out, stop working, stay home, and produce babies.

I was not imagining things: my six older siblings had followed that exact path. I knew what lay ahead but had no way to identify alternatives or make other informed choices.

Slowly, I shook my head: "I've already bought two extra years of school to finish high school. I'm the seventh child, and the first to graduate from high school in my family. My mother won't ever let me apply to college."

Unswerving in his commitment to his students, in his thick Dutch accent, Rev. Van Dijk said: "Well, den, we won't tell dem. All de paperwork we do here, den I will send it to Calvin College. Two weeks before you leave for college, I will drive to St. Catharines and tell your mother and father: 'Mary is going to Calvin College.' This is our secret. Do *not* say a word about this to anyone, here or at home. I will look after it."

My head spun. Was this another door? Should I go through it?

How did Rev. V. recognize academic potential that I did not see in myself? He convinced me, without saying a word, that I had potential despite my grades, and I trusted him to help me find a way. He stepped in with great kindness and care and took up my cause before I knew I needed help.

There was family history here. My sister Tina was smart, and eagerly looked forward to graduation to take up a promised position with a publishing company headquartered in Baarn. She applied midway through the school year and was accepted by Bosch & Keuning, a well-known Dutch publisher who agreed to hire her after graduation.

Tina describes what happened next:

> "Three months before my graduation, Moe withdrew me from school so I could clean houses and bring home money. I was crushed. I never got over it. I felt robbed. My high school principal and some teachers came directly to the house to plead my case. 'She's smart,' the principal reminded Moe. 'Only three more months,' the teachers said. But Moe, stubborn and contrarian, refused. So, I dropped out of school, to my great sorrow. Moe ruled and Pa did not have the will or the strength to oppose her. It happened."

WHAT IF MOE DECIDED THAT WITH SO MANY CHILDREN MARRIED AND moved out, and only Pa and Alice bringing home a weekly pay envelope, it was my turn to add to the income? What if she cut my schooling short when I was almost finished high school?

Moe, unpredictable and impulsive, made it difficult to trust all would be well. Being part of the immigrant church made things more complex. It had been clear in the Netherlands: we belonged to the poor class and our lives, in many ways, were prescribed and predictable.

It was different with me in Canada. Moe wanted to project a public image that, of course, we could afford Christian school. She would not make herself look bad by pulling me out, though I did not recognize that at the time. The possibilities hung like dark clouds over my head.

On the other hand, I accepted the invitation to enter an unknown educational world. I didn't know why. I felt encouraged, even driven, to move ahead. Where did the conviction that I could trust, believe, so elusive in my thinking, come from?

To my great relief, I finished high school, although my grades remained mostly in the C category; I was average. Why continue in the "almost fail" category, squandering possibilities and not measuring up? Perhaps I planned for failure in case I failed. It's a complex maze that did not appear to have a ready exit.

That summer after high school and before college began with a job offer at Bick's pickle factory in Dunnville. The manager and supervisor, my sister Margaret's husband Art, invited me to work at Bick's and live with them. Margaret stayed home from the time she married, though by the time I arrived some seven years later, they had no children.

I loved being with my sister. We laughed and clearly enjoyed the time together.

Margaret introduced me to Mahalia Jackson, whose soaring voice rang throughout the house whenever Art was out. In his impeccable, neatly pressed green uniform, Art strode the factory aisles hollering and rolling his Dutch r's, stopping ever so briefly to accentuate: "Come on, you crrrrazy women! Get to work!"

Most factory workers were women who stood all day long in rushing water, wearing rubber boots, standing at the production line filling jars with dill pickles (large, small, sliced), gherkins, and relish, moving only for two short breaks and a lunch hour. Thanks to Art, I did not work on the line with the bandana-headed women who, according to him, never worked hard enough.

Assigned to the labelling machine, I faced the humming production line where the bandana women laughed and talked as the jars sped by. I worked alone. Clear glass jars went through the machine that took the label and slapped it on jars. If a label wrinkled or tore, I placed those jars in a large box. With the run completed, I removed the sticky labels and cleaned the jars to be sent for a re-run.

Some called this work a "college motivator," a puppet mechanically bending and picking up, placing, and depositing. A college motivator, however, was for those with life choices. I had vowed at the age of thirteen: "I will never wear a bandana and go to the factory." I went briefly, but I did not wear a bandana. This was my chance to make good on the vow. Even then, I smiled at my naivety.

SUMMER ENDED. TWO WEEKS BEFORE I FINISHED MY FACTORY WORK, I imagined the scene: Rev. Van Dijk driving from Hamilton to St. Catharines, crunching up our driveway, hopping out of the car and skipping up the cement steps to bang on the screen door. He knocked, opened the door, and called out, "Mrs. Appel?" Moe inside, wiping her hands on her starched apron, saying, "Dominee! Come inside. A cup of tea?"

Somehow, the minister convinced Moe to allow me to go to Calvin College.

The Moe I knew endorsed nothing that did not add money to her kitty, but I also knew the Moe whose airs and graces might not admit to rejecting something so prestigious. This was the second time in two years. What if she admitted she had no money, said that I'd had more than enough education? Would he embarrass her into conceding?

Or was it pride for Moe to say, "My daughter Mary is in university"?

The image of a trophy arises.

No matter. Art and Margaret drove me home to St. Catharines and were there when Moe announced: "We are taking you to Grand Rapids to see Pa's cousin."

"Oh," I answered, trying to stay calm.

No story about Rev. Van Dijk demanding I go to college to

become a teacher, but it was he who had arranged for a small scholarship to support me for one year.

In the meantime, I had my brown envelope with the saved money. I counted and recounted every dollar. Was it enough? Would Moe find it and take it?

I sat on my bed to think. I was not being a good daughter; I was letting down the family. Everyone expected to bring in money, but I did not.

Something had changed in me. For a long time, secretly, I had worn the outsider label – not that anyone said it aloud, but I felt bereft. It made me keener to find a way out and move forward, though I had no idea what this meant.

I felt grown up. Independent. I never mentioned money or my savings; Moe did not ask. I pushed all thoughts of relinquishing aside. At the end of the day, I gave her nothing. I kept my treasure inside the pages of a book in the bookcase that ran alongside the length of my bed.

The trip to Michigan
1961

P a placed the suitcases in the back of the truck, carefully covered, ready to drive me to a new, completely different life. Moe had not changed her mind. It was too late; others knew by now. I guessed she could boast that her daughter was a university student.

Off we went. Pa at the wheel, me beside him, and Moe by the window. Much of the time was quiet. Not a word about what I was doing or anything about the upcoming experiences. No advice.

Calm and capable, Pa deftly retraced my high school bus route through the towns and villages along the way until the red truck climbed the Niagara escarpment. A majestic granite wall, a steep rock-face, graced the left side where the road was carved. Wayne, my future husband, would later joke: "Calling it *Mount* Hamilton is a bit of a stretch." On the right, grand vistas: hills and valleys, dense forests, farms and vineyards danced and sparkled in the sun. We zipped by the tobacco fields where Pa had worked one summer. Hitchhiking home one weekend, he walked and walked, lifting his thumb to ask for a ride, but no one picked him up. He walked all the way from Tillsonburg until he got a few short rides to St. Catharines. We were frantic with worry at home, until finally, around four or five in the morning, a noise sounded at the front of the house. I flew to the front door. My Pa was home, safe.

Ten hours later, we arrived at Pa's cousin's house in Grand Rapids.

The door opened and there stood a man who looked like Pa: smiling, red-cheeked, with thick black hair. Easy to talk to, warm and kind, he welcomed us with open arms. Pa felt at home; they talked and talked. Moe, on the other hand, was socially awkward. She needed attention.

TWO DAYS LATER, NEAR A MANICURED KNOLL ON THE CALVIN CAMPUS on Benjamin Street, Pa got out and walked to the back of the truck to set my well-worn suitcase on the sidewalk.

A kiss on the cheek and a smile from Pa, and the truck started up and eased onto the road.

I waved limply as my parents drove off to begin their trip home, waving until they turned the corner and went out of sight.

Still standing on the grassy knoll, I heard myself say, "Free at last. I'm on my own!"

And then, "Free at last? On my own?"

I stepped out into a void – I don't know why or how I did it. Although I had little knowledge of what to expect, this I knew: my heart housed the rock-solid conviction of rightness, even a sense of a calling, to Calvin. I was grateful for my basement basic high school education.

At age 17, with $54 in hand and a receipt for paid tuition, I began a four-year journey that would forever change my life – a miracle fed by unexpected and incredible interventions and experiences.

Against my will, I became an immigrant again. Relocating. New country, so much new here. I had never seen a campus. Here, lawns and grand sweeping trees reminded me of Montebello Park in St. Catharines. Unlike the clichés, apparently professors did not wear flowing black robes or hold on to their mortarboards in the wind as they walked across the campus. Only age distinguished student and professor.

Tucking my suitcase behind a bush and covering it with spindly branches, I walked around the campus. The administrative building with grand Greek pillars and a pure white copula housed most of the classrooms.

Everyone one but me, it seemed, had friends and knew where to go. I had no choice but to stop strangers on the sidewalk with "Please point me to" or even "Can I follow you?" if they were on the way to registering. They pointed or led, and I followed, feeling hopelessly out of place. Too much like the hymn, "I am a stranger here / Within a foreign land / My home is far away . . ."

I paid close attention to markers: a large gingko tree with heart-shaped light green leaves; the back of the administration building where the classroom windows neatly aligned on each of the three stories of the building; the low, modern commons building; the library and music booths; and the science building that ran along Benjamin Street. I silently rehearsed the names of the buildings, the orientation, the Benjamin Street location. Could I do this? What was I thinking? I paid particular attention to Benjamin Street, since that would be my starting point of entrance and exit. I would be living there.

Chapter Thirteen

At Calvin
_1961_

Locating my suitcase (impressive, Mary!), I lugged it along the sidewalk to the house where I would work for my room and board. As the house numbers increased, I crossed the street, found 315 and nervously walked up the short driveway to the front door of the grand red-brick home.

Trembling slightly, I knocked softly on the door and heard footsteps in the hallway.

Mrs. Rosensweig and her little five-year-old son Joel stood in the doorway. She introduced herself and Joel, told me her older son would be off to university soon and her thirteen-year-old daughter had just returned from Interlochen, where Van Cliburn, then the most famous classical pianist in America, taught piano in the summer.

I dragged my heavy suitcase up the carpeted stairs, following the daughter. She pointed to her room. "You'll stay in my room until my brother leaves for university in two weeks."

Kindly, she introduced me to the music of Van Cliburn, playing Tchaikovsky's Concerto #1. Van Cliburn had won the international gold medal for his performance in Russia. I had thought *we* were a musical family, but now I learned about new, unfamiliar music.

Downstairs again, Mrs. R. instructed me on caring for Joel, who hid behind his mother's skirt and peeked around the edges. Precocious, dark-haired and brown-eyed, he was a delightful, charming boy. The following day, my job began. I took him to school and picked him up, fixed him a snack and drink, and asked, "How was kindergarten today, Joel? What did you do?"

Back inside, Mrs. R. had begun cooking dinner, peeling potatoes and tossing them into the pan on the stove. Steam and unfamiliar smells rose.

Dr. R. returned home just in time for dinner.

"You will eat in the kitchen," Mrs. R. nodded her head towards me, rather coolly.

By myself? I had never eaten alone! My big family talked and laughed and read the scriptures with each meal. Deeply humiliated at being excluded, on the one hand, but on the other hand, happy not to have to take part in unfamiliar discourse, I carried on.

The door to the dining room shut, and I was left to sit at the small kitchen table. Lamb, potatoes, and one vegetable were on my plate. The smell of lamb filled their kitchen every day. Mumbled talk emerged from the dining room. I was, once again, an outsider, an immigrant. I didn't want to stay. But I had no choice.

THE EVENING BEFORE REGISTRATION, I SAT AT MY DESK TRYING TO figure out schedules, tinkering, choosing which classes to take, depending on time (so I could fit in the work I needed to do), and cross-referencing scheduled classes to avoid duplication. It was a challenging task in light of conflicts and late afternoon classes.

In the morning, I set out to register for classes at Calvin. People crowded around the doorway of the rectangular, red-brick dormitory.

"Do you know where I go to register?" I asked.

Little groups gathered on the campus lawn waiting to join the line. I did not hesitate to ask questions about direction and processes. Talk and laughter rang out everywhere. I checked my time on Day 1, got into the snaking line around the red-brick building, and waited to enter.

Registration was in the basement of the men's dorm – a very large athletic room used for basketball, commandeered twice a year for registrations.

I followed those ahead of me and entered a stark, cavernous room lined on each wall with long tables, files filled with cards, and scrap paper. A large poster on the wall announced course days, times, building, and instructors. Professors sat at every table ready to help, reorganize, and suggest alternatives if courses were full.

At last, I stood before the table and announced my name: "Maria Appèl."

When a counselor explained "accepted conditionally," I was not surprised, and only dimly aware of its meaning, I ignored it. "On condition" it had said on my Calvin acceptance letter. My barely sufficient high school marks leading to conditional acceptance seemed to prove I did not belong, at least not yet. However, with a large store of resilience and determination earned through events and models in my life, I worked hard to stay. Returning home was not an option.

With a lot of juggling, I registered for English, History, Biology/Lab, Psychology, and Religion, in classes that ended by 2 p.m. so I could be home to pick up Joel by 2:30.

THE FLEDGLING CHRISTIAN DAY SCHOOL SYSTEM IN ONTARIO desperately needed teachers (one year of college sufficed, or even a high school diploma), and on that pretext Rev. Van Dijk had arranged a scholarship for $200 to be added to the Calvin College account when I arrived. With my summer earnings, I had the money needed to pay for the tuition and books, two semesters. No extras. Little spare cash.

But on the way out of registration, proud to have completed this first complex task, I found the bookstore and rewarded myself by buying a pocketbook of poetry, the first book I ever purchased and owned, and a small red binder with the Calvin logo on the front. The outer circle read Calvin College and Seminary and the inner circle read cor meum tibi offero domine, prompte et sincere: *My heart I give you Lord, promptly and sincerely.*

On the bus, immigration kept crossing my mind. Was I still an immigrant? I felt again like the outsider: a Canuck, a Dutchie again. I put "reset" on my identity. I would not think about myself as anything but a wannabe American.

Classes Begin
1961 - 1962

"How many stops to the downtown shopping area?" I asked the bus driver, who promptly answered, "Eight."

I found a seat near the front and counted and pulled on the cord to signal I wanted to exit. Fulton Avenue, the main street, had stores like Steketees and Herpolsheimers, grand department stores with massive front windows. I had never seen the like. Windows filled with stylishly clad mannequins showcased ladies' wear. Farther down Fulton Avenue I found Woolworths, where I purchased a caramel-coloured pleated wool skirt, a dressy white cotton blouse and proudly wore them to the Orientation Days and after.

I toured the campus with small groups of Freshmen, all of them more familiar with the college concept – to me, the campus seemed endlessly, hopelessly huge. They all seemed to know where they were going. I came from another world entirely.

Classes began. The classic cupola of the main building shone a brilliant white in the September sun. I climbed the expansive stairs to the second floor, walked along the corridor to find the room for my English 100 class. Found it. Took a seat, took out my small cranberry-coloured little binder with the paper needed to take notes. Waited. Expecting to see a professor dressed in a black flowing robe, I saw, instead, an ordinary man standing in the front of the room with a suit and tie.

Later in the morning, a woman professor taught a class. *Women teaching? Who knew?*

I familiarized myself with my surroundings and learned to navigate the campus. My courses included two sciences, psychology, English, and History. The Liberal Arts program covered all major disciplines and was intended to broaden our perspectives, opening possibilities for new thinking and practices. I had not been any good at sciences and math in high school, but fortunately, the math credits required in high school prevented the need to take any additional math – or French, for that matter. Not so lucky with sciences. I postponed the two required courses in Biology and Chemistry as long as possible.

MY FIRST BIRTHDAY AWAY FROM HOME FELL ON A SUNDAY, A LONELY day. No classes, just church. I didn't say a word about my birthday to my room-and-board family. On Monday, I ran all the way home from campus and found, to my utter delight, a package with my name written boldly on the front. A package! For me! I sat down on the stair and opened it: inside was a birthday card and a set of flannel pajamas from my sister Alice. She remembered my birthday. New pajamas, a perfect fit. A nice birthday card to put on my little table. Thank you, Alice.

Every day for the next week, I ran home expecting a gift from Moe. No card or gift came. Not Monday, not Tuesday, not Wednesday. By the next week, I gave up. It took me back to my last Sinterklaas in the Netherlands, a painful admission and feeling. Nothing, for my first birthday away from home? Disappointment settled despite my earlier hopefulness. I should have been better prepared, less expectant. I carried the thoughts with me: lower your expectations and do not give up. Keep up, instead.

Despite my new commitment to my studies, things did not go smoothly. As the first semester began, so did quizzes, tests, and final exams. Multiple choice and fill-in-the-blank tests overwhelmed me. Never having written such exams, I was mystified and fearful. What if I failed? What if I was ingloriously expelled? Was I making an "unconditional exit?" Somehow, I was spared – again – to have another chance the next year.

In my bedroom, before leaving for my first year of college classes, I counted pennies and scooped up enough to get a five-cent cup of coffee or the cherry Coke. Coffee and Coke came with new friends gathering around a table describing courses, discussing professors, debating issues, but I worried about how I could earn enough money in the summers for the year to follow. I never thought about returning home. I was going to do this on my own, so I didn't have to worry about Moe insisting I stay home.

Every other week, I fell in love with someone new – by sight only. So much choice, so little time. First it was Jack. Then John, a standout. Unfortunately, others agreed and the battle for John's heart became a fierce competition. It came down to three of us: a high school classmate, my friend Jackie, and another student studying at the Reformed Bible College, down the road from Calvin. I lost. Placed third out of three. I was heartbroken for a while. Years later, when I ran into him at a Christian school teachers' conference, I could not believe I'd adored this short, ordinary guy. What was I thinking? Thankfully spared, I told myself, smiling kindly at him.

On campus, I ran into friends from high school and the St. Catharines church. Coincidentally, I crossed paths with an old friend and called, "Liz!" She shouted back, "Mary!" We chatted excitedly, both at Calvin with no knowledge of the other being there. Liz invited me to the House of Lords, her new boyfriend's home. Liz said when she wrote to her mother, "I go to the House of Lords every day," her mother, she told me, assumed she attended church daily. She did, in fact, attend faithfully, but it wasn't a church; it was a frat house filled with eight male students. Henk lived there and loved – still loves! – Liz.

"Come on over tonight. We're going to celebrate my birthday at the House of Lords."

"Don't ask me twice," I declared. "What time should I be there?"

That evening, I popped my head into the living room to say at the house, "I'm going out."

Mrs. R. reminded me: "Be home by ten."

EARLY IN OCTOBER, LEAVES ON BENJAMIN STREET FORMED A GLORIOUS canopy. On every campus sidewalk, leaves whispered in the trees above and rustled at my feet with every step. I was joyful. I skipped on the sidewalk. Going to a party – so different from my birthday.

The classic Grand Rapids house had a big wraparound porch with wobbly spindles, and well-worn chairs stacked here and there. Yellow light shone through sheer curtains.

Henk answered the door, Liz at his side, and welcomed me to the piano that sat by the front window, invitingly. Henk sat down and belted out a familiar song. I was transported home, gathered around the organ, voices blending in harmony. I belonged. I was at home here.

All sense of time disappeared with delicious freedom. We told stories, discussed issues, courses, professors; dished out recommendations (take that course/professor, or don't!), and being Canadians at Calvin. The evening passed too quickly, and by the time the first "See you later" came and I checked my watch, it was well past my 10 p.m. curfew.

DUTCH IMMIGRANTS TO CANADA WERE THE POOREST STUDENTS ON campus. Like me, almost all girls from Canada worked for room and board. Here I was an immigrant again, trying to survive in another unwelcoming culture. What drove me to carry on? I could not put my finger on it, other than to say that a force outside of me advocated on my behalf. I forged ahead.

As it turned out, I was an incurious student. Well, English interested me. For the rest, I mainly focused on the exact balance in my account at Calvin and the brown envelope always under my pillow. I kept meticulous records of the remaining funds out of terror – that if I failed to drum up the funds, I would have to go home, head down in shame.

Christmas Holiday
1961

I returned to Ontario to find a changed family. Only Alice and Anne still lived there, though Anne stayed in Hamilton from Monday to Friday to attend the same Christian High School I had attended. Things were thin at home with only two salaries coming in. Incredibly, unlike me, Anne did not have to pay. Moe paid her room and board in Hamilton, her tuition, her transportation, and any other related expenses.

I got out, and I was grateful. Period. On my own at Calvin, joyful even if I had to work for room and board and eat in the kitchen. A deep sense of guilt emerged, however, in knowing that I enjoyed a new world, unlike anything I had imagined. My church friends in St. Catharines had already been working in factories for a couple of years – some had married early. But I had been plucked out, rescued from the doldrums of work and little play.

AT HOME, THE ORGAN SINGING AFTER SUPPER GRADUALLY STOPPED AS the family choir shrank. Moe now played the organ throughout the day, a game she called, "clean a room, play a song." Only one, though. I heard the music and sang the words along in my mind. Moe had a lovely voice and, like my older sisters, she faithfully attended choir every week for years. She never sang to herself while playing the organ, although she sang as she dusted and folded and cooked. I knew every word of Handel's *Messiah* because she rehearsed the English lyrics until she knew them by heart.

That first Christmas holiday at home, I invited (with Moe's approval, of course) Henk and Liz and other friends to our house for coffee after church, to talk, sing at the organ, and enjoy a "balletjes" (meatball) soup lunch. Moe sat at the organ, never needing music; she only opened the hymn book to read the words and begin to play. The singing was loud and happy. Sitting in a circle around the living room, someone asked, "What are you studying?" Without a pause, and a big grin on my face, I answered, "I plan to major in psychology." Henk laughed aloud and said: "How do you know that? You've just started college."

IN CHURCH LATER IN THE DAY, DURING A CHRISTMAS SONG, THE ORGAN stopped mid-verse. An awkward silence. Spontaneous hush. The minister climbed to the pulpit and solemnly brought us the news: a horrifying accident occurred. Ria (just graduated from HDCHS and former member of the church) and her boyfriend, John, on their way to meet and join his family for Christmas were hit by a large transport truck. Ria died immediately; John was in serious condition, in a coma.

Gasps and tears all around. A solemn silence filled the air as we noiselessly left the church pews.

A few days later, Liz and I took the slow, sad journey up the wide cement church steps for the funeral. As I entered, my eyes fell on the casket at the front of the church where an open casket stood, with Ria positioned, sitting up in the coffin.

I slumped to the floor. Simone and Els supported me to a pew. Ria's family walked in, each wearing a black armband. I had never seen that. Sobbing. Tears poured down my face. Ria had travelled with me on the bus to the Christian Highschool. I knew her well. This was no way to celebrate Christmas.

Chapter Fourteen

Calvin, Semester 2
1962

Preparation for my upcoming January exams evaporated. By the time Henk picked me up for the return journey to Grand Rapids, books, notes, and paper assignments remained untouched.

Six of us crowded in for the journey to Calvin. Telling stories, taking naps, singing and asking questions "how much longer?", we waited to arrive back at Calvin and breathe again – although I dreaded going back to my eat-in-the-kitchen job.

My unpleasant situation mirrored most Canadian women students assigned to working for room and board. American female students did not work for room and board; they lived in co-operative housing across the street from the Franklin campus, called *coops*, with a coop mother. They had social events, meals together, roommates. One of my high school friends lived there. I asked her questions and dreamed of living there. The cost, $25 per week, far outpaced the funding available to me, but it did not stop the dreaming.

Dr. John Timmerman taught my English class, and his passion for American Literature was contagious. He loved teaching, and his warm and gracious nature soon made him my favourite professor. Regardless of the temperature outside, even in the coldest blustery winter weather, he dressed in a light beige linen suit, with bright flamingos and birds of paradise dancing on his colourful wide tie.

Reading aloud, he often stopped to chuckle or reminisce about the character or the theme. I made detailed notes in my small red binder, especially when we read and studied *The Scarlet Letter*. His sweeping literary knowledge, storytelling, and soft chuckle welcomed all his students. I accepted his invitation to journey through his much-loved literature and through him, made it my own.

Returning late from the House of Lords one night, I found both the Rosensweigs sitting on a small dark blue velvet sofa in the living room.

Dr. Rosensweig pointed to the matching chair, signaling for me to sit. They had waited up to inform me I'd broken the 10 p.m. curfew. They reminded me of their earlier warnings.

"We need to talk," Dr. R. said.

I listened. An hour later, they dismissed me. Now what?

With legs of lead, I trudged to the Dean of Women's office on campus to plead for another placement. She rifled through some papers. Fortunately, the Barnes family in East Grand Rapids needed a nanny for their kids, a boy and two girls, ages 8, 10, and 12. To my delight, they agreed I could start immediately. "Just be home after school to give the kids a snack, play games, and take them to the park until it's time for dinner," Mrs. Barnes said. At the Barnes's home, I was welcomed. I ate with the family at the table. I was happy and felt like I belonged.

It was too far to walk to Calvin, so I caught the bus on the corner of the street. Living so far from campus, I could no longer run over to the House of Lords. I sorely missed the social connections. Back to skipping classes.

Els, a friend from St. Catharines, lived across the street, and we met and chatted on the sidewalk. Our charges played together. We both complained about the distance and the idea of needing to work for room and board. While my place felt safe, hers did not. She told me her boss had called out one evening, "Come into my bedroom, Els, I have a headache." Wisely, she went to her bedroom, shut the door, and jammed her desk chair securely under the knob. Fortunately, I was spared such horror.

Insufficient funds dominated my life. A letter from Calvin College announced: "You have an unpaid library fine that will prevent you from writing the semester exams. All outstanding fines and tuition must be paid by May 1, 1962."

Another letter arrived, this one from my brother Jack, now living in Washington State. What could that be? I stuck my hand into the letter, tore open the top. A cheque fluttered down. $100? Utter shock, joy, overwhelming relief. Saved by the bell. I could make the final payment and write exams. I could not wipe the grin from my face. In a most unusual move, I called Moe to share my great news. "Moe, I cannot believe what happened today." I told her about the cheque and Jack, and the amount I needed to pay before exams. Without a moment's pause she responded: "Jack meant for you to send me $90. I will pay you back."

Completely confused, I obeyed unquestioningly, found an envelope, and counted and wrapped nine $10 bills into a folded paper, tucked it in the envelope. In the dark I walked to the local mailbox. The envelope slipped in easily.

I never heard from Moe about paying me back. Years later, I understood what should have been instantly apparent: of course, Moe had never contacted Jack, never asked him. She made it up. She lied. Ashamed, I told no one. How did I not know, though?

Life in the calm, happy Barnes family was *too* comfortable. After the others went to bed, I quietly made my way down to the kitchen, to the fridge full of snacks including buckets of ice-cream. I gorged.

In a brief span of time, I added the "Freshman 30," resulting in an unprecedented fat me. My clothes no longer fit; I wore my coat as a constant cover.

Mrs. Barnes never said a word, but at the end of the year, the Barnes family decided not to renew my room-and-board job for the next year. I can't say I blamed them.

I had to find a third place for the next semester. I was not cut out for room-and-board work; I was certainly more like my sister Tina than my sister Margaret.

I had imagined majoring in Psychology. What makes people (actually, me) tick fascinated me. At what point did I not fit into my family? What did I do? I hoped course work in psychology would point the way to some understanding.

But studying for True-and-False tests required meticulous attention to detail and memory. Improperly prepared, I took the test and failed. It was the first and last course I failed, though I had come dangerously close far too frequently.

I picked myself up and registered again for Psych 100. This time I passed.

SPRING BREAK IN ST. CATHARINES ALLOWED ME TO RECONNECT WITH friends. I caught the bus to the city and met Norah who had a boyfriend now. We took in a concert at Montebello Park, walking across the rich green lawn to the gazebo where the band gathered and tuned their instruments. Before the concert began, Norah confessed that two of her sisters *had to* get married in the past year. Each one stood up in church and confessed her sin.

Though I was not there to see it, the injustice of it scarred me. Why them? What if they hadn't gotten caught?

AT CALVIN, CANUCKS LIKE ME, PARTICULARLY FROM ONTARIO, WERE the butt of jokes and derision. We had no spare cash to buy cars or new clothes or even books. Men generally worked off campus.

Some joined the choir (free), but took part in few, if any other, extracurricular activities. Most Ontario students were young men with aspirations to go to seminary and become ministers to fill the new start-up Canadian churches. They were respected, revered, and supported by their home congregations. Two men from my home church had already graduated and become ministers.

Other Canadian men took philosophy courses with Evan Runner and joined the Groen Club to study Reformational theology. They read Dutch theologians such as Kuyper and Dooyeweerd. American students poked fun at them.

Ontario women, like me, worked for room and board and had little interest in, or time for, Groen Club. Fewer in number than men, and often at Calvin for only a year or two, women left the college to fill vacancies of elementary teachers and secondary teachers in the new Christian school system. Most hung out together, sheltering against an unwelcoming atmosphere.

I could not shed the image of feeling like an immigrant. The irony. Had it not been for my immigration from the Netherlands, I would not have been in college. Yet, I resented being the butt of jokes. I didn't want to wear hand-me-down type clothes., but I could not afford new. I still remember each piece of clothing I purchased, and picture them as I write.

Despite the challenges, I had not followed my brother and sisters (bandanas on their heads) to the bus and the factory. I didn't leave my paycheck on the kitchen table every Friday. I was lucky: I had glimpsed a future I didn't want and somehow, miraculously, avoided it.

I may not have been the happiest of people I knew, but I would have been far unhappier if I left Calvin and returned home. From that point on, I only went home for visits, holidays, and weddings. The experience of being a university student distanced me from my siblings. We lived in two worlds and little, if any, connection occurred.

My oldest sister Tina though, took an active interest in me and occasionally sent letters of family news, perhaps because of her untimely and undesired withdrawal from high school by Moe just before graduation. She wanted me to succeed.

When I came home after my first year, I went first to Tina's house in the city. She sent her daughter Wilma straight out to the corner store to buy a big bag of mushrooms and whistled while she cut them up and fried them, until a fragrant mushroom aroma flitted around the kitchen. We sat at the table, indulging in fried mushrooms and exchanging stories. Tina's house was my happy place when I came home.

Sophomore Year
1962 - 1963

S ummers meant finding and taking on as much work as
possible, saving for the upcoming year for tuition. I stayed in
Grand Rapids and did my best to earn the required expenses.
Despite the challenges, it never occurred to me to return home and
stay there.

Pa's cousin agreed to take me in while I looked for a summer
job, and my relatives welcomed me in and provided directions and
tips. I set out with enthusiasm. Every door I entered, I asked: "Do
you need an extra employee for the summer?" My shoes were worn
out from walking all day. They all said, "Sorry. No." Sapped of
energy and enthusiasm, I felt a dark foreboding. I was obsessed
with devising ways to earn money and finding ways to stay.

I met my newly discovered cousin Betty from Indiana, who
lived in an apartment with three others: "Unfortunately, we're full
here," she said when I asked her about extra space. In the next
instant, her face lit up. "Just down the street, there's a small house
with four students, some from Ontario, who might have space for
you for the summer."

"Thanks, Betty. Can I leave my suitcase here while I check?"

A block away, Willie answered the door of a classic Grand
Rapids house. "We could use another person here if you contribute
to rent and food."

I nodded – on what basis, I wondered – and told her I was
starting work that day. I hit the pavement in downtown Grand
Rapids, stopping briefly in front of the immense windows of each
department store to admire exquisitely dressed mannequins in the
window. All day, I walked, entered, and asked, but I failed to secure
any work. I could not give up. The only alternative was to return
home.

I heard, "No," "No, no," until I entered Woolworths at the very end of Fulton Avenue. I asked about possible employment. The manager came out and asked, "Are you going back to college? If so, I cannot use you here."

"Oh, no. I can't afford to go back to college. I am happy to work here permanently."

"That's good," he said. "You can start tomorrow. Come and see me when you arrive, and I will get you started. Forty hours a week, $1 per hour."

I learned about retail in different departments. Each week, I took my little white pay envelope and removed $10.00 for room and board and a week's bus tickets—the reverse of what my siblings did at home. The rest was hidden in a suitcase pocket.

Willie, my roommate, planned a trip to Ontario to see her family, and it was timed perfectly for Alice's wedding. She had room in her car. I had one pay cheque hidden in my suitcase and the required $5 to help with gas for the trip. A few others joined. I was the first to be let off. Taking out my little suitcase, I waved goodbye and walked into the house.

My bouffant blue bridesmaid dress hung on Alice's closet door. I pulled it down and eagerly tried it on. The dress, beautiful and flouncy, literally dropped off my body and onto the floor. I had lost weight – the freshman 30 came, and then it went. My dress needed a just-in-time adjustment. Only a day before the ceremony, Alice found a kind seamstress who came to the rescue. A few hours later, a perfect fit.

The wedding ceremony went off without a hitch. Photos taken on the massive cement front steps of the church show Alice indescribably happy as she married "her Bert."

"He's not yours," she reminded me as she belted out Kitty Well's song: "*Jealousy, is there no cure?*" Right.

Honking horns announced my ride back to Grand Rapids. Three women piled out of the car to stretch, stating, "Hurry! We have a long way to go." Suitcase ready, I hollered "Bye!" into the house and left on the welcome journey back.

One benefit of a boring job is that it's a college motivator: "Do you want to do this for the rest of your life?" it asks. "No? Get busy and get back to college, then."

Which is exactly what I did.

The Long Year
1962 - 1963

Returning to Calvin was welcome, but I had not given enough thought or bothered to consider the future. With no place for me to live (again), the Dean of Women (again) made a few calls to secure another place for me, another house in East Grand Rapids. After my interview with Mrs. Young, I put my suitcase and purse on the floor and sat on a chair by the front door to wait.

"Are you assuming you have the job?" Mrs. Young asked, frowning. "I need to think about this."

I pleaded with her to let me stay since I had no other options available, no place else to go. She let me stay. Too bad.

Required to be home to look after lunch for the three kids meant classes from 8 to 11 a.m. It cut socializing during the day, and it cut out regularly attending classes – a bad habit that continued. Again I took a bus to campus and started with 8 a.m. classes. I had to leave campus by 11 a.m. to be at the house by 11:30 a.m. to feed the kids their lunch. I thoroughly enjoyed the kids. Bruce was a classic middle child whose anxiety led him to worry and cry: "I'm going to be tardy!" I assured him we would walk together until we could see the school.

My bedroom had a desk, a chair, a single bed, a small chest of drawers, and a closet for hanging clothes. The cozy room became my escape, a place to smoke and study. I wrote letters to friends. I read good books. I felt sorry for myself, trapped in another work-for-room-and-board situation, but I hung on. Skipping classes became a seductive option – I spent my three-class skipping allowances in the first month of September. Now what?

The harder I worked on an English paper, the more stuck I became, paralyzed by my ignorance and inability to express my thoughts. As I read articles, I admired the language, the turn of the phrase, so I borrowed some for my paper. These bits and pieces propped up my understanding, bestowed it with heft to impress the professor. Fortunately, my professor was *not* impressed.

Dr. Harper, a brilliant English professor, called me in. To my red-faced embarrassment, he revealed he was familiar with the passages and the interpretations I copied. I felt humiliated, humbled. He proposed I rewrite the paper (with some percentage reduction), using only my language to explain, to make it clear. I could not have had a better model of honest scholarship and compassion for the new kid. I was a fortunate learner, indeed.

My second Grand Rapids birthday came in October with no word from my anyone in my family – not even a card from Alice. To celebrate, to my surprise, Mrs. Young invited my high school friend, Freda, who lived in the area to come over. We sat in the basement. I opened a gift from the Youngs: a new leather purse. She brought out some cake, and we celebrated.

Freda looked at her watch and noted, "I'd better get home."

"Unfinished homework?"

She nodded her head, put on her fall jacket, and picked up her purse. I walked with her to the end of the street in the dark and she crossed and walked to her Grand Rapids home.

The work was not difficult or heavy. Time was the problem. I had to be on campus for 8 a.m. classes and home by 11:30 to make lunch for the two boys. I could not return to take other classes because, by then, Mrs. Young would be ready to go to her bridge club. She gave me further directions:

"I finished the laundry. I need you to fold it and do the ironing. Mr. Young's shirts need a crease down the sleeves and leave the cuff buttons undone. Use these hangers." She went out the garage door to her station wagon.

After I put Deborah in bed for her nap, I folded sheets, big and small, then set up the ironing board and swept a hot iron across the top to smooth and flatten the sheets. I delivered clothes and sheets to the boys' room and Deborah's room (stacked outside the door so as not to disturb her), my room and the Youngs' bedroom, just in time to change and dress Deborah and bring her downstairs for a drink and a snack and prepare for the boys' arrival. When they got home from school, we talked about our days. Sometimes, I read stories aloud.

Mrs. Young and I spoke only when necessary. At the dinner table, Mr. Young tried to involve me in some talk. It did not alleviate the darkness, but I continued to be there for the kids, do the ironing, clean up after lunch, and hide in my room.

The year plodded along painfully slowly.

Summer And Year 3
1963 - 1964

"Completely out of the question," I reasoned. "No more room-and-board gigs for me." I took a deep breath and a leap of faith. I wanted space, an apartment of my own, a roommate and a job to pay for tuition, books and five-cent cherry cokes. If I could work for the summer and ten to twelve hours a week during the academic year, I could pay.

A trip to the Dean of Women's office was different this time. No more pleas to find another room-and-board place. I scoured the bulletin board listings of available housing close to the campus. I found an upstairs apartment about a 10-minute walk to Calvin (no more buses) and no more laundry and ironing other than my own. No more frowning Mrs. Young.

After the ten-minute walk to the house, I stopped at #508, a classic Grand Rapids house with a front porch. I rang the doorbell. Quick steps approached, and the door opened to a dark-haired, middle-aged lady.

"Do you still have the apartment for rent?" I asked.

"Yes. Are you interested?"

"Yes, please," I answered enthusiastically.

We climbed the stairs, turned right into a large sitting room with two large windows looking out onto the street. Against the far wall, a double-door closet opened to a miniature kitchen with a stove and fridge and a tiny counter. A drawer held a smattering of utensils and a cabinet for pans and bowls. Two bedrooms – one small and one larger, with a bunk bed – completed the apartment.

"I'll take it," I said. "I will look for a roommate since it has two bedrooms. I will let you know. Can I move in today?"

"You sure can. Two months' rent, please."

Liberation. A load fell from my shoulders. All that's left is a job,

I told myself. Back to Calvin and a careful scan of the Calvin Employment opportunity board. A job at Jersey Junction appeared. Sounded enticing. New. Just opening. Off to inquire and apply.

A bright red schoolhouse had full windows looking out to the street. Mrs. V.'s ice cream shop was decorated perfectly with shelves holding antiques and hooks, with ladles and scoopers hanging down.

The bell rang softly as I opened the door and stood before the glass counter with countless flavours in large, round containers spread along the entire wall. Endless. Labels included dill pickle, black licorice, pumpkin, and peanut butter ice cream, to name a few. Shelves on the walls had small white carton buckets of various sizes for take-home ice cream.

Lively, spirited, creative, Mrs. V. interviewed and hired me on the spot. Full time in the summer (no Sundays), part time during the semesters, 12-15 hours per week at $1 per hour.

I skipped all the way home. Things were coming together. I felt like I bridged a divide.

The ice cream shop proved an instant success. Mrs. Van Allsburg's whimsical flavors and high-quality ice cream drew in the crowds. People lined up to get in. Every imaginable flavour and colour filled the buckets behind the glass.

Lineups were common at the shop. People eagerly awaited their turn to enter and do the hard work of selection. Each day, little Chris V., seven or eight years old, stood in line with the others. He picked a new flavour, took his sugar cone outside and sat down on the bright red bench. Chris, Mrs. V's creative offspring, became a renowned artist and writer of children's books including, *Jumanji* and *The Polar Bear Express,* both award-winning books made into movies.

Money remained scarce, but every penny not needed for room and board went into a brown envelope kept under my pillow. I paid my rent, bought a few groceries, calculated, and recalculated my costs and income. "I can do this," I thought, and remarkably, I did.

I tacked a 'roommate wanted' sign to the Calvin bulletin board. Ginny responded and immediately called to ask for directions. I met her at the front door. We agreed to become independent roommates, always friendly, not friends. She had a boyfriend. I was looking for one. She was diligent and responsible; I hoped I would become more like her.

The arrangement worked. Each bought and cooked her own food. Sometimes my dinner was a paper cup of my current favourite ice cream. We lived separate lives outside the apartment and inside. We each had our own room.

I reveled in my new space and location, basic though it was. No longer required to be home for work (my shifts from 5 to 10 p.m.) improved my life immensely. Mrs. Young asked if I could come two hours a week to iron. Needing additional income, I agreed. She picked me up and brought me home. It was nothing like living there. At one point, I took out the ironing, bedding first, and moved on to the rest, leaving my cigarette in an ashtray on the dining room credenza. I went up the stairs with a basket that had to be taken up the stairs and the linens delivered to each room.

When I came down, I saw my cigarette had fallen from the ashtray and burned a spot on the wood of the credenza. I heard the station wagon pull into the garage. Quickly, I found a book and placed it on the wounded wood. I never heard from Mrs. Young again.

AFTER EACH CLASS, WHEN A NEW CROP OF STUDENTS ENTERED THE Commons, I walked around slowly until I heard my name: "Hey, Mary, join us?"

If that didn't happen, I walked to what looked like a friendly group, preferably mixed, to ask, "May I join you?" If I said, "Can I join you?" some smart ass would say, "Yes, you can, but .... But *may* you?"

We laughed and told stories. I ordered a 5-cent cherry Coke at the counter and set it on the table in front of me. What a difference.

Free to make my own decisions. Free to make my own mistakes. I made plenty of them. Thoughts of classes waned and though it was only October, I had already skipped the allowable three classes for each course. So much for further skip privileges. So much for having learned my lesson.

Chapter Fifteen

The best of times
1964 - 1965

T he landlady excitedly announced on the front steps leaning
to a veranda: "We bought another house a few blocks over,"
and raising her arm, pointed to the rear of the house. "By summer,"
she said, "the whole house will be for rent: three bedrooms on the
second floor and three on the main floor, good-sized bedrooms
with room for two single beds."

Before she could continue, I shouted, "Sold." I did not know
how I would get roommates or pay for the empty rooms. I posted
on the Board at Calvin: Six new roommates needed, large house,
walking distance to Calvin. In no time, the house filled up: two
Canadians, three immigrants. Locals (four of them) often went
home on the weekends to play the church organ, work in a medical
clinic, or work in a restaurant. In January, a new roommate, Lee
joined us. I was unwelcoming. While belonging was critical for me,
I did not extend the same warm welcome to Lee. I didn't want any
change in my life at that moment. I was reminded of Moe, who

often made people feel uncomfortable and unwelcomed. I did not want to be connected to that type of hurtful behavior. I decided to open myself up to Lee, who won me over with stories of Hawaii. I vowed I would travel there one day. It sounded glorious.

A houseful of American Calvin guys lived a few houses down the street. We mingled, met, and played cards during the week. "Bumps," a smart, outspoken rebel known all over campus, became my favourite. He wanted to be a lawyer. I hardly knew what that was, but it sounded big, impressive.

THREE OTHER ROOMMATES MOVED IN FOR THE SUMMER, GOOD FRIENDS from St. Catharines. Kienie and Janna, sisters, and Simone joined us. Laughter rang around the house. Janna and I created grocery cart races, rattling up the street, posing for photos, cooking together. I fully participated and belonged. I could do this. Well, almost.

Kienie suggested: "Let's go to my boyfriend's apartment." As we walked, she described Bob and some of his roommates. Hearing loud music playing through the open windows, we called out even more loudly: "Hello! We're here!"

People crowded into the small living room, and Kienie introduced Peter – a tall, good-looking Canadian guy who quickly sidled over and began talking. We settled down on a single bed together in the living room, cuddling as he described his academic accomplishments. I was hardly able to do the same but was enthralled. I was getting to know an academic star.

Peter claimed he read every footnote at the bottom of each page for all his required reading. He followed up, reading the cited references for each book and article assigned. This was a new academic territory. I had never met a student who read and then also read the entire citation. Did I even *know* about footnotes, let alone follow up and read each one? Absolutely not. I skipped classes and managed only Cs on courses, so needless to say, Peter impressed me. Starry-eyed, I wondered, "Could I do that, too?" As soon as the option appeared in my head, however, I shrugged it off. I should have done the same with Peter, who bragged and bullshit to impress the ladies, including me. Despite that, I fell for him.

Peter called and suggested we go for a long walk. Hopeful, I agreed. In Eastown, crossing the Kroger grocery lot, he confessed he was, in fact, not interested in me – but madly in love with my roommate and friend, Simone. Who wasn't?

He brought a gigantic bouquet of yellow flowers and set them on the veranda, complete with the tag: "For Simone." She came home, looked at the tag with her name, and scoffed. The card said: "From Peter." Offhandedly, she dismissed the gesture, already madly in love with Jim. What a waste, I thought. He should have put my name on the card. I had to admit, though, it would never be me. Time to move on.

Good as his word, though, Peter remembered my birthday and picked me up curbside. I dressed up in a slinky teal blue wool dress, put on a borrowed pair of black patent stiletto heels, and waited by the front door. I felt glamorous. My high heels gave me a new height, though Peter still towered above me. He took me out for a 21st birthday bar hop. I had never been inside a bar. Should I put that on my Calvin sign-in sheet? Peter had chosen four different bars.

His car drove up, I popped in, greeted him, and off we went. At each bar, Peter, the pro, ordered a different drink, a Whiskey Sour first. Never having had a drink, it took only a small amount before I felt loopy. That did not stop Peter from adding a few more bars, plus a Bloody Mary, a Daquiri, and an Old Fashioned. Wobbliness, a spinning head, a wonky stomach and much loud laughter and snickering followed. I stumbled out of the car and began the arduous trek up Mt. Everest (our gently sloped driveway). At 3 a.m., I burst loudly and lustily into song: *Wilhelmus van Nassau.* The Dutch national anthem filled the air. How did I even remember the words? I must have heard them from my singing family.

"Quiet," came shouts from the windows of rudely awakened neighbours and roommates. "Stop!" and "I'm calling the police!" I dragged my wobbly legs into the house, up to my bedroom, and plopped myself into my bed. Instant sleep. The venture, unfortunately, was incomplete. I paid my dues in full during the night and the next few days when the first night's spinach left the toilet bowl green and me groaning.

I GOT A RIDE HOME FROM CALVIN. WITH ALICE MARRIED AND ONLY Anne at home, our Christmas would be small. Pa worked the day shift, so we spent evenings together. Moe greeted me with a severe case of the grumps. My heart sank. Why did I waste my time coming home?

"You're here so long, you'll have to pay room and board," Moe snapped.

I shook my head, looked down to avert her eyes, and walked away, careful not to overreact or say things I might regret. Moe didn't raise the subject again. I could have reminded her, "If you pay me the $90 you owe me," but, of course, I didn't.

I wondered if having a girl in university became such a source of pride, a trophy, that Moe would not force my withdrawal from Calvin. How would it look? How would she explain?

The holidays became an endurance test, but I was not remotely tempted to cave.

"Did you get me a Christmas present, Moe?" I asked, emboldened.

"No." she barked.

No, I decided, was unacceptable. For the first time, I challenged her, then badgered her. "I want a Christmas present."

I wore her down. Finally, she grabbed her well-worn wallet and took out a $10 bill. I grabbed it without so much as a "thank you" and ran to the closet, threw on my coat and tucked the bill into my coat pocket before she could change her mind. I ran down the steps and on to Church Road, relieved, loudly singing songs of Christmas joy. I stopped when the bus put on its brakes to let me board.

Window-shopping the jewelry stores on St. Paul Street, the main street of St. Catharines, I discovered a simple gold ring with a pearl and asked the jeweler if he could tell me about the pearl ring in the window. He walked over, and I pointed to the plain pearl ring. "$10," he said. Bingo.

The jeweler placed the ring on my finger for size (perfect!) and put it back in the small, velvet-lined box. He wrapped it neatly in Christmas paper. The purchase took me a whole day. Totally worth it. Moe neither asked nor looked.

HOLIDAY OVER, I RETURNED TO CALVIN, TAKING PRIMARILY ENGLISH and History courses with my preferred professors. I registered for enough courses to complete both English and History majors.

I liked my classes, my Jersey Junction job, my roommates, and the many new friends I met. I dated mostly American guys, including Butch, one incredibly good-looking vacuum cleaner salesman (not a Calvin student) who had not much else to recommend him. Fortunately, I woke up early enough to know I probably dodged a bullet. He was divorced. A good salesman I did not need.

Early into the semester, Dr. Bud, head of the Education office, called for a meeting. "Student Teaching," he said, slowly shaking his head. "Grades too low." This was news to me, though my report cards should have been evidence enough. This required graduating with a General Bachelor of Arts and adding several courses.

A brisk, rapid knock on the front door. I opened it to a tall, very handsome guy: "Is Simone here?" "I'm Tom. Simone is expecting me."

"She is with her boyfriend," I said, puzzled. "She should be home for dinner. I'll show you around if you like while you wait."

I hopped in his car. We drove around the campus and when he dropped me back at the house, he said, "It's getting too late. I'll head back to Ontario."

Simone, Jim, Butch, and I agreed to go to a movie. We got home around 10 – I went off to sit in the living room, while Simone said goodnight to Jim, who'd parked his car in front of the garage.

Butch left out the front door. Exhausted, I went to bed and immediately fell asleep.

NOISES CLOSE BY. SOMEONE IN MY ROOM? I BOLTED UP IN BED.

"Who is it?" I said softly.

A male voice said, "Oops! I have the wrong room."

Without a second thought, I turned back toward the wall and fell instantly, soundly asleep again. With five women in the house on the weekends, people were coming in and out at all hours: roommates, friends, and boyfriends – in my mind, a mistaken room did not warrant getting up. Of course, I should have.

"MARY. MARY." I WAS JOLTED AWAKE AGAIN AND SHOT STRAIGHT UP.

Simone leaned close, shaking me, sobbing – wet tears were falling on my face.

"Mary, I got raped."

"Raped?" I said hoarsely, wiping her tears from my face, unable to take it in. My heart pounded like it was going to burst.

"He put a pillow over my head. He said if I told anyone, he would kill me."

"We have to call the police. We're going upstairs, Simone!"

"What if he's waiting in the house?"

"He's going to kill me – he's going to kill me if I call the police."

"We have to call."

I jumped out of bed, grabbed an unwilling, fearfully frightened Simone by the hand and tugged her towards the door. I opened the door and peeked around the corner down the hall toward her bedroom.

"He might still be in the house," she warned again, quietly sobbing.

I tugged and pulled Simone to the stairs and then pulled her up each step gingerly, one at a time like a full sack, avoiding making any noise until we reached the top of the stairs and the telephone. I closed the door at the top of the stairs.

Simone trembled. Tears cascaded down her face. She quivered. I could hardly pick up the phone. My hands shook, too. I managed to dial 911 and then to stammer, "My roommate has been raped. We need help. We don't know if he is still in the house."

After taking our address and names, the operator told us, "Stay in the room. Put something in front of the door. The police will arrive in a few minutes."

After what seemed a long minute, two police officers arrived on the front veranda and banged loudly on the door. "It's the police. The police."

Simone stayed behind while I ran down and opened the door to the two officers who showed their badges. They followed me upstairs, where one talked to shell-shocked Simone, who was still hardly able to speak. She looked as though she would throw up any minute. Her voice trembled.

By noon, Simone, after a long, long hot bath, came into the

kitchen and sat on the counter. We all stayed in the dining room as she dialed. Her father answered.

"Dad," Simone hesitantly began, "I was raped last night."

"Raped?"

A long, silent pause. Then the phone clicked. The humming dial tone returned.

Simone looked mystified. "Should I call again?" she asked.

I said, "Wait a few hours. He needs some time to think."

FOR SOME STRANGE REASON, MOE, VIA A FRIEND VISITING GRAND Rapids, had sent a small bottle of vodka for my 21st birthday. I put it on my closet shelf and forgot about it until someone said, "Time to take a sip of that vodka you have in your closet." We met in the kitchen, gathered around that little bottle, and each took a sip.

The police officers who came to the house found it on the shelf in my bedroom while they were getting fingerprints to identify the rapist. They reported us to Calvin's Discipline Committee. We had broken the "No liquor allowed in college-approved housing" rule.

Only those involved in the sips received a notice for a disciplinary meeting. Nancy, who reported us, did not partake of the sips. Fortunately, she moved out of the house that same day. Simone suffered enough. She was spared the inquisition.

Time for the discipline committee. Six of us each took a chair lined up against the wall in the Dean of Women's office. Two discipline committee members sat stiffly in a tiny office with a small wooden table and three matching wooden chairs. The door stayed open, and we heard every word. Each of us responded to their powder keg questions.

Wilma's turn came.

They asked: "What did you do after you had your drink?"

"I hit the bottle," said Wilma calmly.

Those of us still waiting, eyes wide open, awaited the next question.

"You hit the bottle? You drank more?" the astonished professor asked.

We sank down in our chairs, shoulders stooped. We were done for.

"No, no, no," Wilma said. "I *hit* the bottle. I *hit* the bottle!"

"What do you mean?"

"I put the bottle away. I *hit* it."

Phew. A communal sigh of relief for Wilma's Dutch accent, which said "hit" with a "t" instead of hid with a "d."

The two Calvin professors on the committee dutifully confronted us about the "little bottle" and imposed the full arm of Calvin law. They did not express the horrors of the rape, focusing instead on the broken liquor law. So busy protecting campus purity that a student's rape got lost and inexcusably overlooked. We lived in a culture of purity, which meant that instead of offering empathy and counselling to Simone and others present to support and usher in healing, they placed five of us on academic probation. Not a word of warning about the rape or rapist on campus. "Something is rotten in the state of Denmark," I thought.

The year before she moved in, Simone had worked for room and board at a lawyer's house. He heard about the rape and volunteered to represent her. In the process, he interviewed me. He listened as I described the horrors of that night and then picked up an empty Coke bottle and, strangely, started making circles.

"See that?" he said as he looked down.

I looked, confused.

"Watch this," he said as the bottle circled again and again. "Women don't have to be raped. Women only need to move around enough to avoid rape."

Stunned, knowing next to nothing of rape, I knew the lawyer's demonstration had gotten it seriously wrong. It made no sense, but it certainly kick-started my interest in and questioning male dominance and a dim awareness of problems arising when one gender assumes authority.

THE WORST OF IT ALL WAS THAT THERE WAS NEVER ANY MEANINGFUL investigation or follow-up with any of us. No reaching out to Simone, no warnings of a rapist in the area, probably still on campus – no support of any kind for us, her roommates. We were put on academic probation for the last semester of my college career. Fortunately, we behaved ourselves and finished the year with a "clear" sign.

The night of the rape played and replayed in my head, invaded and disrupted my sleep with persistent images of Simone, terrified, sobbing. Night after night, I slept fitfully. I did not, however, sleep it off. I became fearful, suspicious, unable to concentrate or sleep with my face turned to the wall.

I made an appointment with the college chaplain, who listened, let me talk and cry, and assured me he would speak on our behalf. Warm, but not helpful, I decided. Nothing changed.

The impact and reality of the rape did not leave when the semester ended. It stayed long after, messing with my mind, wondering who would do this. Why? I worried and looked around corners. The rape haunted me for many years. Long after having my three children and beyond, someone stayed with me on Saturday nights when Wayne was out of town. The paralyzing event gripped me in its clutches until time finally began to soften the impact and the hold it had on me.

IN THE MEANTIME, LIFE AT HOME IN ST. CATHARINES WAS ABOUT TO undergo a dramatic change. The plant nursery had become a burden too heavy for Pa to carry on his own. Payments lagged and were left unpaid; nursery stock withered. Tina's husband, John, met with Pa and Moe and said, "We think you'd better sell."

Pa's heart broke. His dream shattered. In the end, he swallowed it, as he did most things. Moe, it appears, had not paid the bills regularly or made proper monthly bank payments. They sold Pa's beloved nursery for exactly what they'd paid for it. Zero balance.

From the nursery out in the country to a small apartment in the city. Where were my older siblings living in the area? They moved out of the too-small apartment to a little house in the city.

At Christmas, during my senior year, I visited. Pa brought home a 25-pound turkey from the paper mill, and Moe invited the family over for a proper Christmas dinner. This had not happened in years. Where did that come from? Suddenly, out of nowhere, some surprising, unexpected gesture arose. Was it her way of apologizing?

The family took their old places around a long table in the sunroom for dinner, steam rising, turkey-fragrant aromas dancing around the room. As noisy as ever, we enjoyed a full family meal that ended with clearing the dishes while Moe played the organ and the rest of us sang our favourite Christmas music. It felt like the best parts of home.

Shortly after that, Pa had hernia surgery. Moe tended to him as he lay on a single bed in the small second bedroom, bringing hot black tea (coffee was too acidic for his stomach) and making soups and simple foods to spur his healing. Due to Moe's tender care, looking after him tirelessly for weeks, showing a side of her we rarely saw, Pa healed and returned to work.

Grand Rapids
1965

"A re you a virgin?" Porky asked offhandedly as we sat on the third stair of the staircase in the entry of our Calvin house.

I jumped up and shouted, "How dare you? Get out." I pointed to the outside door, and he jumped up and darted down the stairs, out the front door, slamming it hard as he left. Did I overreact? Perhaps I wanted to lie and say, "No, I am not a virgin." I didn't, though. With all the events we experienced, I knew enough not to admit or reveal any "none of his business" information.

At 21, re-viewing Porky's question, I admit to being taken aback. No one had ever asked me that. Embarrassed. I wanted to be a worldly person who experienced its offerings. That moment had an impact.

Short guy Porky could barely have reached his front door, four houses down the street, when the doorbell rang. Thinking it was the little shit coming back to apologize, I was surprised to see John standing there.

"Anybody interested in a party? It's Tony's birthday!"

"No. I have had enough for one day," I responded, far too harshly.

Others piped up, "I'll go," and "I'll go," and "C'mon, Mary," and, "It's early!"

I groaned. If I didn't go, I'd be alone in that house, and I didn't dare do that. Even thinking about Simone's rape set my nerves on edge. I could not be alone in the house, let alone try to sleep. Grumbling, I grabbed my coat, walked out to John's car and stumbled into the back seat, sitting on someone's lap.

A house full of party goers, beer drinkers, dancers, loud music – and mostly guys – greeted us as we entered. I recognized Tony, the birthday guy, from English classes. As he approached, the kitchen door opened and a smiling, good-looking guy entered.

Tony turned to say, "Wayne, glad you made it!"

"Just finished my shift at the grocery store."

Tony introduced me: "Wayne, this is Mary Appèl. We're in the same English class."

Wayne was like a magnet. We sat close on the long arm of the sofa while others danced around the room. "I'll introduce you to some of my friends," he said, and we got up for introductions to his Alberta friends.

Clint, his lifelong friend and roommate, sat in the corner on a 24-bottle box of beer. Tony, his brother, joked Clint would stay there till the last bottle was empty. Tony was right. Clint finished the last beer and roared off in his hot Corvette.

"In my church and Christian High School, get-togethers never included liquor," I said.

Wayne shook his head in disbelief. "That can't be."

"Truth," I said. "It wasn't because we felt it was sinful, but drinks were reserved only for important celebrations." I persisted. "Nobody had money for those luxuries. You need money to buy beer. Anyway, I am not interested in drinking at all. It doesn't appeal to me."

"Wanna dance?" Wayne said, looking straight at me, and I said, "Sure."

We danced until I could hardly move.

Hand in hand, we stopped to meet and talk to clusters of friends, shouting to be heard amid loud music. After the disastrous date (at least that's how I interpreted it) with Porky earlier that evening, I was having a grand time, complete with dancing butterflies fluttering in my stomach. We talked and told stories about where we lived, came from, our Calvin experiences.

When I could not dance another step, I asked, "Anybody ready to go home?"

No takers. Except Wayne. "I'll drive you," he said.

I gratefully accepted. We pulled up at the door to a completely dark house.

"Nobody is home. It's dark in there. Can you stay until another one of my roommates comes home?" I asked. What would I have done if he'd said no?

Wayne agreed immediately.

The haunting memory of the rape, too raw and fresh, made my handshake in the darkness. I couldn't get the key in the door.

"I'll do it," Wayne said and handily opened it.

"Somebody should be home soon," I assured him. I did not explain my fear and hesitancy to stay home alone. He must have wondered.

We sat on the living room sofa and talked, and Wayne patiently waited for my roommates. Finally, by 6 a.m., my four roommates straggled home. Lights out!

AFTER THE WEEKEND, READY FOR MY THIRD FIVE-CENT CHERRY COKE OF the day, I sauntered towards the Commons. I could see through the glass window people milled about, ordered at the counter, sat down around the tables. Lively laughter. Hushed conversations.

Looking straight ahead through the double glass doors, Wayne saw me. He motioned and pulled out a chair. Delighted, I took my seat with a group of Albertans drinking cokes, heads nodding in animated conversation.

All Wayne's friends, who like him hailed from Alberta, were old-time immigrants, third- and even fourth-generation Dutch Canadians. Their religious ties were with the American Calvinist denomination, not the post-World War II Dutch I was part of. These friends grew up together, went to school together, attended the same church together, and went off to Calvin together. The bond was tight.

I shared the same roots in the Netherlands but from a newer version of immigration by at least fifty years. In those years, the newer immigrants lived through a war, a five-year German occupation, a "Hunger Winter," and cities like Rotterdam left in rubble. It undoubtedly not only affected but shaped the nation. The Dutch admire and continue to celebrate their relationship with

Canada. Culture, religion, church music, philosophy, the economy – all had a distinct look about it. The "new" Dutch immigrants (like me) arrived on Canadian shores far different from their established Dutch immigrants (Wayne). In the literal Dutch translation, we who came later were called "fresh from the boat off."

Wayne's generation did not speak Dutch, though their parents used Dutch at home. Many of them went to school with no English, but English was impossible to ignore once Wayne's generation arrived.

Their families often owned land. They settled mostly in Alberta. Many belonged to the first Christian Reformed Church of Nobleford, Alberta, the first Christian Reformed Church in Canada (1905). They attended Noble Central (Grades 1 to 12). I wanted to identify with this group whose lives differed so markedly from my own and connected more clearly with the Americans at Calvin. Their long residency in Canada let them blend in with their American peers.

We enjoyed being together, and I easily blended into his Alberta friends whose families, along with Wayne's parents' parents, had settled their land at the turn of the 20th century. The tight, restricted community proved ripe for teenage rebellion. Young people acted against their repressive standards. Inviolable rules of life (absolutely no alcohol, for instance) were broken by the young folk, who took every opportunity to find friends old enough to buy them beer. That tradition came with them to Calvin. They told stories of ripping through grain fields in trucks, shooting pheasants, and collecting gopher tails. They drank beer and drove, not on the roads, but in the fields. They smoked shredded newsprint. "Tasted awful," Wayne said.

At Calvin, they had a much easier transition time. They came with lifelong friends. They stuck together and lived together (Wayne's roommate Clint shared rooms with Wayne all four college years). They didn't wear sandals. They wore nicer clothes. Most owned cars. Third-generation Wayne and his friends drank beer, and their parents paid their tuition and other related costs (travel and books, for instance). Wayne was ambitious and worked at various establishments: a grocery store, Oscar's gas station, and night shifts at a factory one or two nights a week to earn extra spending money. Hard-working and incredibly fastidious, his small closet was divided into separate sections for shirts, pants, sports coats, and jackets. Shoes and boots lined up in perfect pairs. (I would never show him my closet.)

This world was new to me. Moe sending me money for tuition? Moe writing me weekly letters like Wayne's mom? My sisters mailing me homemade cookies? In all my time at Calvin, no one letter arrived from Moe.

To my growing delight, Wayne dropped by several times a week. The first time he picked me up, we drove to the Grand Rapids airport. In the dark, walking along the fence, he talked about flying, about jets and his passion to become an airline pilot. We watched Lear jets take off and land until they didn't. Exotic dreams of flying airplanes. Dessert? Big Boy's famous strawberry shortcake. This went well.

Each time he dropped by, Wayne came ready with suggestions. Our first actual date was to see *Goldfinger,* the movie. We spent weekends at parties and time between jobs and classes during the week at the Commons or at my house.

Wayne never skipped a class or church. I never skipped church. Often, we went to the evening service together. Wayne insisted on going to Fuller Avenue church so he could sit in the balcony, right in front of the massive organ capably played by the minister's wife.

I invited Wayne to the Junior/Senior banquet, and he immediately agreed. I purchased a new long slim pale-blue formal dress and had my long, dark hair styled. The picture shows us standing in the living room. I felt elegant, like the suit I wore for my Profession of Faith. Wayne wore a black tuxedo and very shiny black shoes. A banquet with my date dressed in a tuxedo was glamorous, so far from my lived realities. Was I falling in love? Certainly. Wayne and I became friends and lovers.

Wayne couldn't stay for my graduation; his family was ready to immigrate to Washington State to join other Kooy relatives. His father had made an offer: "Go to Calvin one year to see if you like it. When you come back, you can choose: Go back to Calvin or take over the farm." When Wayne returned and his dad asked, "Well? What's the decision?" Wayne responded without a moment's hesitation: "Calvin." No farming; no Nobleford. Wayne had other, far more out-of-the-box ambitious plans. No arguments. His father sold their farm to the Dutch immigrant family renting it. They moved to Lynden, Washington, settled primarily by "old order" Dutch immigrants.

A LETTER ARRIVED FROM ST. CATHARINES. I TORE IT OPEN. "JOHN AND I, with Pa and Moe, are coming to your graduation," Tina wrote. Full-scale panic. Graduation? I was not really graduating. Switching from Education to a General BA required different, additional courses. I fell short by a few courses. Ironically, I had to take Latin – the language my high school had found me incapable of learning. I had no choice but to prove myself. Shy of a C average and short some courses for a General BA, I could not graduate with a B. Ed. or a B.A. I needed two courses in Latin and two other courses of my choice. What now?

I rushed to meet with my advisor. "Please, please can I walk in the graduation? Unexpectedly, my parents, sister and brother-in-law are coming. Our diplomas are blank anyway…" I pleaded. To my surprise, he agreed. Phew! My name went on the list. At least I formally graduated with my class.

Pa and Moe, Tina, and John stayed with Pa's cousin. They arrived at a never-before-seen sight: a gym crammed with family and friends to witness my university graduation. Glorious music started off the processions. Faculty wore the robes representing the university of their own graduations. Students followed, all in black robes and mortarboards, tassels representing their program/faculty. The litany, the music, the invited speaker, the student valedictorian, and the switching of tassels on the mortarboard made for a memorable ceremony.

My family enjoyed the pomp and grandeur. I failed to inform anyone that I did not really graduate. The shame of my non-graduation kept me humble and quiet. I shielded my secret shame for years, even from Wayne.

My family left, as had Wayne. I stayed behind in Grand Rapids, taking two courses. Per usual, I aced everything for the first few weeks. When interest flagged, I faded. The strong start gave me a B+; I had to do better. I shook my head and asked myself, "What will it take?"

I sent out teaching applications to a few Canadian Christian schools as close as possible to Grand Rapids. Not needing a teaching certificate to teach in a Canadian Christian school, I sent a résumé to Sarnia Christian High School, right on the border with Michigan. Unsuccessful. Few Christian schools existed in the southern part of Ontario. I continued the courses, the applications, and almost daily letters to Wayne.

Fall, Summer, Teaching
1965 - 1966

"We need you here," Frank said in a phone call while I was still in Grand Rapids. "Please come."

I thought about the teaching position in an elementary school for a few minutes, wobbled a bit, and agreed, conditionally: "I guess I accept." I could have been more grateful and enthusiastic – the Christian school system allowed me to teach without teacher certification, so I qualified.

Fifteen miles from the border city of Sarnia, Ontario, Wyoming seemed the best I could do. Wayne would be far away, but we would figure it out. I needed a job.

Frank, the principal, attended my church in St. Catharines before leaving for Calvin. He taught my sister Anne to play the accordion. A talented musician, respected by my family, he promised I could live with his family until I found a place of my own. Reluctantly, I agreed.

I'd be teaching Grades 3 and 4, and Frank reminded me (far too often) I was replacing Ria, the teacher catastrophically killed in an accident on a Christmas trip to meet her boyfriend's family the year before. Ironically, my Dutch name is Ria, but I had little in common with Ria, beloved by all.

A week before school opened. Frank invited me into their second-floor apartment, where we sat in the kitchen. He spread out the curriculum, books, and workbooks. He talked about the children, their families, school duties, and staff meetings. I eagerly took the books with me, familiarizing and understanding of the curriculum. The apartment was filled with not only Frank and his wife Celia, but their two boys and two recently adopted Native girls. I got a bed in a small room with two cribs.

Any new teacher will tell you: teaching is complex, overwhelming – and I would add, particularly so for unqualified teachers, of course, who are less able to rely on their own school histories to interpret and apply the curriculum for the students.

The red-bricked school, a square two-story building with incredibly high ceilings, looked every inch of its history, a former standard Ontario public school. A playground surrounded the school. Double front doors, massive and heavy, opened to a grand staircase. Classrooms sat on either side of the stairs for Grades 1-2 and 3-4; up the stairs were two more classrooms for Grades 5-6 and 7-8. A small alcove with a large window served as the teachers' lounge, with a table just large enough for four mugs of coffee. Frank's small office was at the other end of the hallway on the second floor. Shining wood floors and two sets of large arched windows graced every classroom.

"This is your classroom," Frank said as he swung open the door on my tour.

Three neat rows of desks for Grade 3, and two neat rows for Grade 4 faced the front blackboard. Piles of books sat on the large oak teacher's desk: arithmetic, readers, work sheets, fresh notebooks. Reading, writing, and mathematics were important, but Bible teaching surpassed all other subjects. I was grateful for my high school Bible teaching.

My first teaching responsibility included making a schedule of memory verses and psalms to be recited on Monday mornings and handed in to Frank. My first choice: Psalm 42: *"As the hart panteth after the water brooks, so panteth my soul after thee, O God."* My father's favourite, and the first Psalm I memorized at school in the Netherlands. I learned it in English along with my students in this school. At the end of each day, we left the room singing, "Lord, dismiss us with your blessings."

Two grades in one room required imaginative divisions of attention. I often thought of the one-room schools with not only two, but eight grades waiting for attention and support. I scoured the curriculum for common topics and subjects. It made sense to use the Grade 4 Social Studies and Science programs for the Grade 3 students. Language Arts and Arithmetic had textbooks and workbooks. The students followed my explanations in the textbook and then worked through the workbooks. They learned, though not as quickly and less than I hoped, or maybe not at all. I walked along the rows, stopping by any student in need of help. I enjoyed the students and meeting their parents, who went out of their way to connect. Marking notebook after notebook, however, failed to inspire. Report cards overwhelmed.

I knew nothing beyond the "mimic" stage of teaching. I only knew how to "play school." Luckily, the students had been to school for several years and knew the drill.

At some point, I made the wholly irrational decision to teach diagramming grammar to my Grade 3 and 4 students using branches to identify and locate verbs, nouns, adjectives, adverbs. Each morning, undaunted, of course, I had to start again, the same thing over and over. They still did not get it. No epiphanies.

I wanted to showcase my knowledge, the genius of my (untrained) teaching skills. I failed to consider these 8- and 9-year-olds tried hard to please me. It should have been an "aha" moment for me, but I ignored the signals. When Frank observed in my classroom, he gently questioned the wisdom of teaching grammar this early. I took it personally, though. Of course, he was right. I was more concerned about making trophies out of the students than focusing on what they actually learned.

THROUGHOUT THE SUMMER, WAYNE AND I HAD WEEKLY TELEPHONE calls and frequent letters. I missed him. At the end of the summer, he drove across the country back to Calvin, where he settled into a basement apartment with his Nobleford friend, Clint. "Apartment" was an overstatement: all dull grey cement, small clothes closet for each, a sink, stove and refrigerator. Dark, thick drapes hung across one side hiding two beds. A small sofa and a chair finished the furnishings.

Our bi-weekly weekend visits between Grand Rapids and Wyoming began. Every other week, one of us travelled: me on the bus to Windsor and across the border to the Grand Rapids bus station, where Wayne picked me up or Wayne drove to Wyoming. We each arrived biweekly Friday evenings. For a fee, Fred, a colleague, offered Wayne a spare bed at his place. I loved these times.

FRANK'S APARTMENT WAS TOO CRAMPED. "THE TIME HAS COME, THE Walrus said, to speak of many things," I told myself. Time to find my own place. It made sense to convince Ginny, the Grade 1-2 teacher, to share a place. She was well settled, paying room and board to an elderly lady from the church. Initially, she resisted. Finally, she came along to see some places. The first place, some way out of town, had steep stairs outside leading to a small landing and a door above a garage. The inside was one large room with a bit of furniture, two beds, a few cabinets. The landlord kept insisting: "This is snug as a bug in a rug" and "only $25 per month." The second apartment, much closer to school, in the back of a classic Ontario farmhouse on Main Street, had two levels and two bedrooms, furnished, for $40 per month.

The side door of the apartment opened into the living room with a sofa bed, reading chair, coffee table, and a black pot-bellied stove in the corner. Wooden stairs led up to a bathroom and two small bedrooms. The upstairs was unheated, which didn't bother us in early October. The small kitchen, rubber tiles on the floor, held a narrow white cooking stove, and a tall, thin refrigerator. A small dining table was pushed against the wall.

"Sold!" I said to Ginny, but she hesitated, saying, "$40 seems too high." I promised to pay the whole rent for one summer month, even if I did not return. Ashamed to say, I never did.

We moved in. Ginny was an introvert who spoke only when necessary, making it easy to focus on my daily planning and marking. Evenings consisted of quietly sitting at the red Formica kitchen table, one at either end, carefully stacking workbooks and worksheets so as not to mix them up. Ginny, a recent graduate of the one-year teacher education for elementary school teachers, had skills and knowledge I did not. Frequently, I sought her help and suggestions.

Each morning on the way to school we stopped to buy lunch, either at a small deli or at the little butcher shop, where we ordered one good size square of ham to put between the slices of bread tucked into our lunch bags. Ten cents a slice. Off to school.

Chapter Sixteen

Long-Distance Romance
1965 - 1966

On alternate Fridays, immediately after school, I stepped aboard the bus, leaving my little suitcase on the sidewalk for the driver to stow in the underbelly. It was past 7 p.m. when we went through customs at Windsor through the tunnel into Michigan. Passengers stepped out, picked up their suitcases from the sidewalk, and moved into the US customs line.

"Next?"

I walked up.

"Open your suitcase, please."

As I unhooked the clasps on the overstuffed suitcase, the top sprang open, and on either side of the counter and the floor, tampons flew into the air.

The officer's face stiffened in shock. Avoiding my eyes, he bent to pick up the tampons and gingerly slipped them into the top of my suitcase, while I retrieved the rest on the counter and added them to the accumulating little pile in the suitcase.

The customs officer shook his head and mumbled: "Close the suitcase and take it back to the bus." Without a word, I did.

My eagerness to see Wayne kept sleep at bay on the long trip. Always prompt, he waited for me at the Grand Rapids Bus depot. We hugged, piled into his car, and drove to the basement basic apartment, where Granny welcomed me. I paid for a room on her main floor for two nights.

Wayne and I spent magnificent times together. Saturday nights, friends gathered to drink beer, talk and listen to music. I was so homesick for this world every day of teaching, but it ended, of course, as I boarded the bus for the long return trip to Wyoming.

I STOPPED, EYES WIDENING, CATCHING A GLIMPSE OF A GLISTENING NEW navy blue 1966 GTO that pulled up into our gravel driveway. Wayne, with the grin of a Cheshire cat, was in his glory. He'd picked up the new car in Detroit and driven it to Wyoming *post haste.* A brand-new car? Such a show of wealth. Sheer luxury.

I ran out, threw my arms around him, and gave him a big kiss. "Wow! I'm so happy to see you! How was your trip in this beautiful car?" Wayne cherished that car and tenderly cared for it.

The car gave us some private space. We took full advantage, until some busybody came upon us parked in a farmer's field. He embellished the "you know what I saw" story details he related to Frank, who received it just in time to add to my teaching report.

I'd been, Frank wrote, "seen making out in a car" and "on the streets wearing short shorts." *Short* shorts? Short shorts had been out of style for ages! Everyone wore Bermuda shorts, right down to the knee. They were *shorts,* perhaps, because they were not long pants that reached my toes. The evaluative report reviewed my teaching, and bless him, Frank made no reference to comments about the failed grammar diagramming exercises I abandoned.

Over American Thanksgiving, Wayne came to Wyoming – oh, he was so welcome! We drove to Hamilton, pulling up in the gravel parking area of the Hamilton church just a few minutes late for

Anne's high school graduation. In the semi-dark of the auditorium, I found Pa, who wrapped his arm around me. I stood up and whispered: "This is Wayne, Pa."

"Hallo, Wine," Pa said in his thick Dutch accent.

"Hello," Wayne responded shakily, obviously nervous. With my Dad? Really.

The ceremony ended. We spent the weekend in St. Catharines with my parents in their little rented house in the city.

We had our evening coffee and cookies. The first chance I got, I said, "Let's go to my sister Tina's place." Introductions made. The evening progressed and Tina announced, "I am expecting a baby in May."

I said: "I'm surprised."

"You're surprised? *I'm* surprised," she responded.

Back home, Moe gave us a most special treat for dinner, along with potatoes and green beans. After heating the frying pan smoking hot, she added a little butter and threw in the first piece of meat, the largest for Wayne. The meat sizzled only briefly; Moe flipped it just as briefly before putting it on Wayne's plate.

"What kind of meat is this?" Wayne asked.

"Horse meat," I replied.

His eyes widened, but he ate it. Later he told me, "I think that horse was still alive and kicking when it got to my plate."

Later, when Moe took a nap, Wayne continued with a story:

In my freshman year, Clint and I went to visit my grandpa's family in Grand Rapids. We arrived just as the hostess set out the plates with vegetables. The meat was neatly arranged on a plate. She provided each with a generous piece . . . Liver! I had no idea how to eat it, or if I could even keep it down. I mixed whatever I had on the plate and finished it as quickly as I could. Immediately, the hostess got up and came back with more. "You must really like this. It went so fast; I thought you'd enjoy another slice."

He almost gagged describing it.

I laughed, though I probably would not have done as well.

That Sunday after church, Wayne and I took to the highway. Three hours later, he brought my suitcase inside, hugged me, and jumped in his car to drive to Grand Rapids.

Time to think about school again.

Most teachers dread report cards, including me. Marking arithmetic and reading, notebook after notebook – one "x" after another, recording marks and averaging them challenged me. I was determined to read and mark every sum and item. Procrastinating put off completion. I delayed until time to hand in report cards was imminent, and marking madness set in.

I figured the time required for one page and began multiplying (number of notebooks) and dividing (hours required per day). Despite my careful calculations, the evenings got longer and sleep time and planning shorter. This aversion to evaluation dogged me.

The Phone Call
1966

On a bitterly cold January evening, the phone jangled and jangled. In the dim light, I picked it up and softly said, "Hello?"

"Pa is in the hospital," John said.

I felt as though I'd been struck by lightning. "What happened?"

"He is under observation. They think he had a heart attack."

"Should I come home?"

"No. We are here and we'll let you know how it develops over the week."

Overwhelmed by sadness and worry, I climbed into the downstairs sofa bed that Ginny and I were using because the unheated upstairs was in the grip of frigid cold; downstairs had a heater of some kind.

I began shaking, shaking, shaking nonstop.

"Can you stop shaking?" Ginny asked.

"I can't," I mumbled, teeth chattering.

How I survived that week in school is a mystery, although teaching might have been the distraction I needed to get me through those days.

On Friday evening, the phone rang again. I shuddered as I answered.

"Pa died," John says softly.

"Died?" I shouted. "You didn't call. Why did you not tell me to come home? I asked you. You promised you would tell me when it was time." Tears poured down my cheeks. Rushes of hot and cold overcame me.

I hung up the phone without saying goodbye.

"Frank," I said, "I have sad news. My father died."

Frank contacted a kind, gentle school board member to drive me to St. Catharines, a three-hour drive each way. I arrived and found the family gathered around the table in the little house. The prospect of a funeral home visitation terrified me. What if he was sitting up like Ria in the coffin?

But Tante (yes, *that* Tante) convinced me to go. "You'll be sorry if you don't see him," she said.

I climbed back into the car and said nothing on the trip to the Hulse and English funeral home. Slowly, dragging my feet into the foyer, I turned to the left. An archway showed several caskets, lids open. My Pa was directly in my line of sight, his thick steel-grey hair visible from the entryway. Walking closer, I froze. I could not do it.

I turned, walked out, and went down the stairs to the social room below. When it was time to go, I followed Tina, trying to avoid a look into the coffin room. With a swift glance to the left, I saw neatly combed grey hair, a piece of his white shirt, and the knot in the tie. I could not bring myself closer and see more of him. Saying goodbye when he was dead.

Pa's death crushed me.

Little of the funeral service remains in my memory – not the Bible readings, the songs, the sermon. I was numb. The wind knocked out of me. I could scarcely breathe.

The following day, my family filed out of the church and into the cars that took us to the cemetery in Font Hill, where Pa was laid to rest. When the dedication was over, I ran to the car, where I cried and cried.

"Why Pa?" and to myself, I said, "Why not Moe?"

Why did I not say good-bye?

Back at the house, we sat in the little dining room for dinner, squeezed around the table. Before long, stories and laughter rang out. The phone rang. Moe picked it up, raised her finger to her lips and said, "Sh, sh, quiet. What will they think if they hear you laughing?" Moe loved this: all her kids around, phone calls, all that attention. I did not see a tear, even during the funeral. Maybe she was numb, too. It all happened so quickly.

The world was different now. It was not, as my colleague said at another funeral, "as if life would stop, but that it would be like going on with an arm missing."

Pa died when he was 62. My heart shattered. Just when I was ready to be an adult with him, he left.

On Tuesday, a few days after the funeral, Frank called to ask, "When are you coming back? I can't find a substitute."

"I am not ready," I answered. "I'll call you."

He called again a day or two after the funeral: "When are you coming back?"

"Monday," I responded.

Tina's husband, John, called. "We discussed and decided you should come home again and live with Moe and Anne."

"What? Move back to St. Catharines? I don't belong there. Too much distance lapsed. I've been gone for almost five years – so, no, John, I am not doing that."

Being able to stand on my own two feet and make my own decisions served me well.

I did, however, resign from the school at the end of June, planning to return to Grand Rapids to spend the year with Wayne and our friends – and, more importantly, finish my degree.

Go West, Young Ma'am
1966

W ith Wayne in the West for the summer, I returned home briefly to visit Moe, who had used Pa's life insurance to buy a small house in the city. Her kitchen had a large window that framed a verdant backyard with a large garden that needed tending. Niggling guilt surfaced about leaving her on her own, though not enough to change my mind. Moe proudly showed me around her house. She said nary a word about moving in with her. Good thing. I might not have handled that well – or worse yet, agreed to move in.

I saved for the train fare to take a trip to see Wayne in the west, a 4411 km trip over three nights and four days. I had no money for a bed on the train; it was much cheaper to sleep in the seat. Moe packed snacks, fruit, and sandwiches for me to leave first thing in the morning.

That night, temperatures soared and stayed at 100F well into the night. One by one, Moe's neighbours, also unable to sleep, spilled out of their hot houses into the street, and Moe and I joined them. Eventually, after a few hours of sleep, I was on my way to the train station with a small suitcase and a box of snacks and sandwiches, very excited to be with Wayne and meet his family, and to see Canada as the vistas opened on the way.

I checked my ticket, found my seat. Once we were underway, I explored and found the train's glass ceiling car offered spectacular views of the countryside, the expansive cloudless blue sky, the growth of crops, particularly the vast stretches of brilliant yellow canola in Alberta. The vistas sped by.

Lights dimmed. Time to turn in. Not having a berth, I tried bending and twisting to find a position that allowed some sleep. The young woman sitting next to me also struggled. We grumbled and complained and whispered, "Isn't this terrible?"

After breakfast, I peeked into the berths that had their curtains pulled open and envied those able to afford a bed.

"What do you think of sharing a single bunk for the next two nights?" I asked the woman next to me.

Without hesitation, she answered: "Great idea."

We paid for two nights and one bunk. At 9 p.m., we climbed up the ladder. I faced the aisle. She faced the window. My head lay at the other end, on the outside edge of the bed. Worried about falling out and about disturbing my sleep mate, I slept only marginally better than the seat, though at least I could stretch out.

In the morning, the brilliant yellow prairie fields had receded, and I awoke to the *click, click* of the whistling train coming to a stop. Brilliant sunshine poured in the windows. A moment of glory: the shimmering teal blue water of Lake Louise.

I walked outside, completely startled by the glory and grandeur of the sheer rock of the grand high mountains and snowy peaks. It took my breath away. Mesmerized, I felt transported. The moment is frozen in my memory. I wanted to stay, but the husky train whistle blew, and blue-gray smoke poured out of the stacks. Wayne waited for me!

We filed into the train and took our seats for the last day of travel, and at last the train stopped in Chilliwack, BC.

Excited butterflies in my stomach, my legs rubbery, I saw Wayne waving from the platform wearing shorts and a t-shirt in the heat, grinning from ear to ear. Impatiently, I dragged my suitcase bumping down the steps, left it on the platform, and ran to his embrace. It was worth leaving even Jasper. Joy!

We crossed the border to Lynden, Washington, occupied mostly by the Dutch who settled there early into the 19th century. Immaculate lawns and profuse and colourful, perfectly groomed gardens were everywhere. Stopping at a freshly painted old white house with a veranda in the front, Wayne parked the car to a whooping loud welcome from his siblings: two younger sisters, three younger brothers.

Wayne's parents were not home. They knew I was coming. They

were on the way home from Alberta. Wayne's sister Bea took the responsibility for managing the household. She navigated myriad tasks and even took the time to wash my hair for me and put rollers in – just in time for Wayne's parents to arrive.

I had no choice but to say, "Take me as I am. Hair curlers and all."

They welcomed me warmly.

Wayne's five younger siblings ranged in age from four to seventeen. His sister Bea, four years younger, sent Wayne letters, and baked, packaged, and mailed cookies. Sister Brenda sat on the roof of the two-story house with friends watching the 4th of July parade. She waved and smiled from her perch in the air.

Wayne's youngest brother Ted, only four, had been born when Wayne's mother was 43. Wayne, in Grade 11, found the pregnancy deeply embarrassing. His friend, classmate and cousin, Pat, was in the same position. They complained and commiserated.

Unlike my family, Wayne's family came first. They got along. They went places and did things together.

My oldest brother Jack had bought a thriving dairy farm and settled about 10 km away in Ferndale. A yellow two-story wood-frame farmhouse housed the family of seven. The house had a dishwasher, but my sister-in-law, quirky, used it to store pans. She felt it was an over-the-top luxury. Jack was a farmer, proud of his dream. Staunchly conservative, politically, and religiously, they had little time to spare and kept to themselves. I visited them several times during my stay.

In Lynden, Sunday meant going to Bethel Christian Reformed church (one of four CRCs in that small town), sitting in the same pew, in the same order. After church, the whole Kooy clan of four brothers and their families made their way to Grandma and Grandpa's house for coffee and lunch served on lap trays.

They called themselves Dutch, but my understanding of Dutch differed markedly from theirs. I called them Dutch 1 and Dutch 2. When they were young, they'd spoken Dutch at home. Dutch was God's language.

In 1941, our friend Tony's parents took him to be baptized. Three questions were asked about the vows his parents made, and his father answered clearly, shockingly, in English, "Yes," adding: "*In het taal van het land* (In the language of the land)." Instantly, half the church rose from their pews and left the building. English in church was an outrageous, unacceptable sin. Dutch Reformed people expected to go to Heaven, convinced only Dutch was spoken there.

Most church members had come across the border from the US to Canada in the early 1900s, when a family could take possession of a quarter, 160 acres of land. Wayne's family on both sides took advantage of the offer. Later, after World War II, his dad took in immigrants from the Netherlands to live and work on their farm, and improved his Dutch, a valued tool for work and communication. English did eventually find its way into the church, and Dutch waned as the next generation of children attended English school.

Wayne's father delighted in speaking Dutch to me. Impressive, really, since Dutch in Lynden had long ago been replaced with English. Having immigrants on the farm in Alberta made Dutch a critical component of communication. As often as possible, he spoke in a dialect of the Northeast part of the Netherlands. I listened carefully and understood.

His mother rarely spoke Dutch, though I think she could. An introvert, she capably managed the household, cooked, and baked, and served as the office manager for the insurance agency they had purchased when they arrived in Lynden.

During the day, Wayne worked at his summer construction job; I often walked along the main street looking into shop windows. At night, we walked together along Birch Bay Beach, hand in hand, waves shushing in the background. I learned to water ski and attended ball games, cheering loudly for Wayne's team.

Late in August, we drove through the mountains, grand and glorious, to Nobleford (not so grand and glorious) to stay with Clint's family for a day before the trek to Calvin. Wayne told me, "In all the years I lived in Nobleford, Clint was my best friend, but I've never seen the inside of his house till now." Distinctly different from Wayne's family, where the open-door policy meant frequent Alberta visitors.

Early the next morning, Wayne loaded the GTO with suitcases and Clint and Wayne's friend Alvina, whose great sense of humour entertained us along the highways. Stopping only for gas, snacks, and cigarettes, time passed quickly. In Grand Rapids, Clint and Wayne returned to the basement apartment. I planned to return to Grand Rapids to complete my degree and see if I could find a job. To my delight, a group of former roommates rented a townhouse literally across the street from Glenwood, large enough to accommodate six, including me. I felt a wash of gratitude: this was more like home than my home, because of friends, welcoming friends.

Chapter Seventeen

Culture and Codes
1966

E arly immigrants (like the Nobleford Dutch) and more recent ones (post-World War II) came from distinctly different contexts and cultures. The first group arriving in the early 1900s, were supported by the U.S.-based denomination, influenced by the American evangelical movement. The earlier immigrants arrived in the mid-to-late 1800s in a strange phenomenon called the "Third Great Awakening," a movement characterized by new denominations, active missionary work (still active), and a Social Gospel soul-saving approach to social issues. All this was Dutch I.

Dutch II immigrants, on the other hand, arrived in the aftermath of World War II. In Canada, we were called FFBO, "Fresh from the boat off," and "Dutchies," as were all European immigrants. Untouched by the American evangelical movement, these immigrants identified not with Dwight L. Moody, central to the evangelical movement, but with Calvin and Kuyper, who shaped the Reformed churches in the Netherlands. Kuyper became the

Prime Minister who proclaimed, "There is not a square inch in the whole domain of our human existence over which Christ, who is Sovereign overall, does not cry, 'Mine!'" Following Kuyper, these new Dutch in Canada soon created a Christian school network, established a Christian Labour Union, a credit union (DUCA), a bank, and the Citizens for Public Justice organization – all still actively functioning. Yet, the American church dominated the Canadian arm of the Christian Reformed church.

At least fifty years separated the two migrations. Over that time, change happened in language, celebrations, songs, cultural feasts, birthdays, Sinterklaas, and New Year's, for instance.

Recent Dutch immigrants celebrated birthdays (with an open house all day), Sinterklaas, New Year's. Familiar foods included *oliebollen, pannenkoeken* (Dutch pancakes with currants, no yeast), *hutspot* (potatoes, onions, and carrot mash), and *boerenkool met worst* (smoked sausage with kale); lacy curtains hung at every window. Dutch stores popped up. Songs infused every occasion. The singular monoculture of the Netherlands made it possible.

At a Christian conference, a speaker said these holy words: "It's important to celebrate. If we don't celebrate, all we have left to remember is funerals. We must attend funerals. We don't have to celebrate." Done. Sealed. I am celebrating all the markers in my life.

Post-war Dutch assimilated as quickly as possible, and that, too, was critical for change. First-wave immigrants at the turn of the century built tight-knit insular societies. Dutch was the designated language of Heaven, and religion offered a stern and somber reality and identity. Deference was critical: stay humble. Associating with those outside the flock for anything other than business and commerce (grain, for instance) was heresy.

The newer waves of immigrants held starkly different world views, probably developed through the tragic circumstances of the war and its aftermath. They came ready to sing and celebrate and be Canadian. English soon became the language of the church.

Dutch disappeared as the language of choice. Some recent immigrants became wealthy farmers. In the Niagara area, greenhouses sprouted up along the Queen Elizabeth Highway to Niagara on the Lake; many acres of glass greenhouses remain, most imported from the Netherlands.

We left the Netherlands behind. The past froze. Things stood still there, though they moved along in Canada. Another sixty or seventy years passed. As they did, so did the frequency of the post-era trips to the homeland, which they denounced strongly. I heard it repeatedly. The growing nostalgia for the homeland, for the time when they left their Dutch homes, grew. "Holland" (they refuse to call it the Netherlands), they said, has "gone to Hell in a handbasket. Things changed there. Nobody goes to church. They showcase prostitution in windows (Amsterdam), use so many drugs and English words now." Little consideration was given that things changed in Canada as well. I heard it so many times that I believed it. Did not question it.

Preparing for the Wedding
1967

In Grand Rapids, wasting no time, I registered for my final courses, aiming for the good grades I needed to complete my BA. The first course, on Teaching Art, proved rumours about art courses being an easy A. It was wrong to copy, but I traced colouring book pages and used pastels to colour in a squirrel with a bushy tail and handed it in; the next assignment was as banal. I quickly lost interest – please, not another squirrel. My A grade dipped to a B.

Edgar Boevé's art course using his own beautiful textbook proved magical. I saw possibilities and played with imaginative art assignments, and earned an A. He enthusiastically presented the possibilities. I was entranced. My GPA rose slightly above a C, to 2.2. Things were looking up!

Officially, I could say I graduated. Did I just say, "I graduated"? Yes, I did.

I COULDN'T JUST TAKE COURSES. I NEEDED AN INCOME.

"I can get you a job at Sullivan's Furniture, Mary," Alvina assured me, in the middle of a fling with the owner. She called in a favour, and it worked. Bob offered me a job working in the office at $1.10 an hour. The two nasty secretaries there ignored me, speaking to each other in whispers. The word *exclusion* echoed in my mind. Wayne reminded me, "Remember who owns the problem."

My illegal work status made me irritable and anxious. Only full-time students could work part-time, and I did not qualify. Halfway through the year, I took a day off work at Sullivan's, the only time I did so. Early in the afternoon, Wilma shouted: "Mary, two people to see you!" Two uniformed customs agents stood in the entry. An electric jolt went through my body and the colour drained from my face. I said only: "I am Mary Appèl. Can I help you?"

"We have information here that you are a part-time student working full-time."

"I am a full-time student. Otherwise, would I be home mid-day?"

"Thank you, Ma'am. Just checking." They turned on their heels and walked out the door and back to their car.

Another holy moment, I'd say. I whooped and hollered for joy all the way to the kitchen.

"I'D LIKE TO TAKE YOU OUT FOR A BIRTHDAY DINNER. YOU AND ME," Wayne said.

"Great," I responded. "A ring?" I wondered.

In the restaurant at a small table for two, he fidgeted, squirmed, looked around, ordered a drink as we perused the dinner menu. A brash, jolly server, reminding us of Hazel on the TV show, brought the meals. "Here's the extra drink you ordered," she said, placing the glass in front of me.

I looked. An ice cube floated in the drink. I lifted it up to take a sip and puzzled, saw a strange something in the ice cube. A ring? Is that a ring? It's a ring!

Wayne proposed as the ice cube melted, and the server looking after our table called out for all to hear: "Did you guys just get engaged? Hey everyone, this couple just got engaged!"

The whole restaurant burst into applause. Congratulations all around. We were engaged. Wayne loved me and I loved him – such a celebration!

Once I'd found the fabric for my wedding dress, a white silk/wool blend, I put the dress together. Then I made dresses for Moe and Lee, my Maid of Honour, and two flower girl dresses for my nieces. Patterns, fabric, lace, zipper, thread, buttons, all neatly placed and labeled for each dress – the dining room table transformed into an atelier, filled with scraps and patterns and fabric. Many conversations happened with the hum of the sewing machine in the background.

Having no formal experience since the Grade 9 blouse-making disaster, I took on ambitious plans. I'd bought a Singer sewing machine during my teaching time and was ready to learn as I went. Soon a wedding dress and a train emerged on the hanger. Hand stitched lace trim ran all along the train. Next, the dresses for Lee, Moe, Rena, and Elaine – the machine never stopped till we returned to Lynden.

"I AM PREGNANT," HOUSEMATE KITTY SAID SOMBERLY. THE ROOM WENT silent. Arms reached for Kitty. Words of encouragement followed. Just days earlier, her boyfriend, a jet pilot in the air force in Florida, crashed and died in a routine flight. The house went into mourning. We promised Kitty our support.

A few days later, Dick, a friend from Alberta, made an offer Kitty could not refuse. "I'll marry you, Kitty."

She accepted. I sewed her wedding dress, a loden green with trumpet sleeves. Kitty and Dick chose a private ceremony in the town hall and moved to Calgary – and almost sixty years later, they are still married.

The Wedding
1967

Leaving Grand Rapids meant I would miss my sister Anne's wedding in early June in St. Catharines. Our wedding, less than four weeks later, still required much planning for our June 30th ceremony. Wayne's mother sent a list of invited guests, each entry meticulously written by hand. Wayne's family invited at least eighty-five of the hundred guests. I was on my own for the expenses – I did not dare ask for a contribution, but I thought about it.

"Why get married in Washington State?" people asked.

"I'm the last in my family to marry – the eighth. This is old hat for them. For Wayne's family, this is the first wedding on both sides. It makes more sense to get married there."

Wayne's excited family, my excited brother Jack and his family, and our excited Calvin and British Columbia friends attended, as did five of Moe's brothers who lived in Washington State.

Wayne and I agreed to stage a proper celebration. The Dutch know how to celebrate. I wanted more than a typical Lynden ceremony and reception with a cup of tea and a piece of cake; we decided on a sit-down dinner for a hundred guests at $1 per plate, to be held in the church basement. The women's committee prepared a delicious feast on beautifully decorated tables.

Moe came from Ontario; Jack and his family came. Wayne's family and friends came from Lynden and Alberta. Some of Moe's family from the Seattle area came.

The organ played majestically as Jack walked me down the aisle (remember those days?). The tune changed. Everything stopped, people rose and turned to the aisle. *"Here comes the bride"* (*"big, fat, and wide"* – what was I thinking?) rang out, and the service proceeded without a hitch. I gleamed, and Wayne stood happy and nervous, all of twenty-one years old.

A small table in the dining area held the wedding cake, made by my uncle, the royal baker at the palace in Soestdijk, the Netherlands, before moving to Washington state in the US. Topped with white doves and real feathers, the wedding cake was breath-taking, and remarkably tasty. Wayne and I walked around and chatted briefly with each guest, with no formal program. Our celebration left room and time for people to meet and greet; on our walkabout, I met Alida, and we forged a friendship still alive today, some 57 years later. The wedding was the talk of the town for the next week or so: "A sit-down dinner? She must be rich." Rich, indeed.

Since we had nothing but personal goods, all household gifts were welcome. I still have the lap lunch trays, and they still come in handy. Gifts were modest and contributed little to building a house. But my siblings, to my surprise, sent a blender that served us for years. Wayne's family gift was a black-and-white tv set.

The honeymoon, such as it was, began in Bellingham at a Slumber Lodge, the teddy bear motel. My first time in a hotel – my first holiday ever. After breakfast at SeaTac Airport, we headed to the Oregon coast and dove into the pool at the Gitchie Goomie motel in Seaside, Oregon. Within two days, after roasting a few sandy hot dogs on the beach, we dried ourselves off, packed the suitcases, and headed back to Lynden. I was eager to open our wedding gifts.

"My dad found us a furnished row apartment a few blocks from town. My cousin Barb lives next door," Wayne reported when we returned to Lynden. "We can move in. It's ready."

I never grumbled. I'd spent years carefully protecting my earnings so I could pay for living expenses and tuition at Calvin. Now, that summer of 1967, Wayne worked in construction. I picked berries with Wayne's sisters.

For us, our apartment was a haven and a little bit of heaven.

Chapter Eighteen

❧

Transitions
1967 - 1968

I tore open the envelope addressed to Wayne. "Report for duty." The Vietnam War? Horrors! I paced the floor, fearful and anxious, waiting for Wayne to come home. When he read the letter, he shook. After his parents moved to the US, he had tried, while at Calvin, to enlist for the flight division of the Navy, but not being a US citizen, he was ineligible.

Frantic, he set off for the Armed Services building and explained the situation: he had dreamed of flying from the time he was a boy when his father took him to air shows in Lethbridge and Calgary. He explained he was moving to Canada to take his flight training there, and that I had a new teaching position in British Columbia.

The man at the wicket nodded, walked into a back room, returned with a letter stating that Wayne now had F4 status: free to move back to Canada and cross the border freely to see family. He walked out of that office, beaming.

After two months in the cozy little honeymoon apartment in Lynden, we crossed the border and moved to Haney, BC, into an unfurnished one-bedroom apartment for $105 per month. The word *sparse* took on new meaning. We had a small coffee table, and a table lamp Wayne made in a high school shop class. But by our standards, particularly Wayne's basement den in Grand Rapids, this was heaven. It would be better with proper furniture, but we assumed that would come.

THE CHRISTIAN SCHOOL PRINCIPAL TOOK ME ON A TOUR OF THE SCHOOL located on the church property; his house sat at the back of the property, hidden by trees and bushes. We sat down in his tiny office as he described my teaching duties: a Grade 1 class with sixteen pupils. We walked around the four-room school while he explained the books and workbooks available. He had arranged a ride to school for me with Helen, the Grade 4-5 teacher I knew from Calvin days.

The school was a meagre building with four classrooms: two up, two down. I taught in classroom #1 on the first floor, sixteen little desks neatly lined up in rows of four, and a big green board across the front of the room. A table under the windows held readers, workbooks, games, and subject tools such as an abacus for each child, building blocks, counting rods. Janet and John and their shaggy dog, Mr. Mugs, an old English gray-and-white sheepdog, replaced Dick and Jane. It had better pictures, but the plain texts and pictures could not compare to real books like W.G. Van de Hulst in my Grade 1 and 2 classes in the Netherlands.

I was no Juffrouw Kok. I knew my teaching needed more. My new friend Alida (also a Grade 1 teacher) rescued me. Her neighbour, Olive, a school district consultant, generously offered a marvelous assortment of worksheets and "how to teach" materials. Things improved. I learned about alternative methods and that worksheets did not a teacher make. Having access to resources moved me away from predictable "playing school" to focus on learning.

My students seemed settled. They loved to hear me read stories, and I enjoyed that as well. Reading aloud included all students and became a significant tool for teaching.

Losing a tooth prompted celebration. We all gathered the child with the missing tooth and recited:

I had a little tooth
I wiggled it
I jiggled it
Did it come out? Oh, no. Oh, no...

Great laughter ensued. "I want my tooth to come out," some groaned.

Not all was smooth. Three December-born boys and one sad little girl in the class were a challenge. I became frustrated and impatient. I am not proud of my behaviour – I can still see their little faces and still feel guilty.

ONE BY ONE, OUR GROWING CIRCLE OF FRIENDS PURCHASED AND MOVED into their own houses and careers in teaching, educational publishing, nursing, and mothering. A house was out of our reach and would be for a long time. Hiring for airlines was at a standstill.

Wayne registered for flight training in Abbotsford, British Columbia. We saved for each new level of certification, such as night flying. Between each certificate, Wayne worked in construction to earn enough to pay for the next flying level (instrument rating, for instance). He thrived. In this joint flight-training project, we both worked hard and saved as much as possible to expedite and pay for the flight training. We were a team.

On one particularly challenging training day, Wayne demonstrated flying straight, wearing a mask covering his face for his instructor.

"Put the plane level, on course, right side up," the instructor instructed.

"Got it," Wayne said. Convinced he had flown perfectly level, he removed the mask. Aghast, he realized he was flying literally upside down, looking down at the earth below. He learned a graphic lesson: you cannot depend on your senses. Trust the instruments.

AT MY SCHOOL, MEN EARNED 10% MORE THAN WOMEN. I ASKED THE principal: "Why is that? Why am I getting less?"

"Men are categorized as breadwinners," he responded.

"In actual fact," I responded, "*I* am the breadwinner. Wayne is a flight student. It's very costly, and we could use the extra income."

No success.

We managed. Wayne was a committed, hard worker, capable and astoundingly skilled. He found construction work that opened times between licenses to earn the money required. We were incredibly, over-the-moon happy.

ONE QUIET EVENING, THE PHONE RANG: "HI, MARY. IT'S DICK. I WANT to come over and introduce my new girlfriend."

With the pot of coffee ready and four cookies on a plate, I welcomed Winnie, a teacher and children's librarian in a Christian School. Winnie was smart and savvy about books and being a school librarian. We connected immediately. Dick, unfortunately, remained the same Dick I knew from Calvin – as we said in those days, he was "stuck on himself."

In the spring of 1969, after only a year in elementary school, I came across a posting for a position at a nearby Christian high school. I applied. I got an interview. Wayne dropped me at the door and went off to see Winnie and Dick, who lived nearby. An hour later, he returned to find me sitting happily on a very large rock outside the front door.

I couldn't wait to tell him. "I got the high school job with a real raise," I said, jumping into the front seat. With the extra pay, we could speed up the flying courses for Wayne.

I formally resigned from the Haney school. Relief at the thought of moving to secondary teaching motivated us to find a new place to live. We found an apartment in New Westminster with a view of the Orange Bridge and the Fraser River out of the large living room glass doors. Scenic.

With our first tax return, we bought camping gear: a tent, two sleeping bags, a propane stove, a lantern, and a cooler. Camping was new to me, but Wayne's family were great campers. From the outset, I loved camping. Wayne's experiences, know-how, and work ethic suited camping. He got it done. We camped every summer weekend, always with friends.

JUST BEFORE SCHOOL STARTED, MOE VISITED. I WAS A FOREIGNER WITH Moe, unfamiliar with her world as she was with mine. Some things stayed the same, of course. At precisely 10 a.m., Moe said, "It's 10 a.m. Coffee ready?"

I deeply resented the reminders. To get out of the small apartment and into the air, I suggested shopping at Army and Navy. We grabbed a shopping bag and walked down the steep sidewalk leading to the main street in New Westminster. The Army and Navy store had bargains.

The way down on the sidewalk? No problem. The way up was another situation altogether. Moe's face turned very red; she puffed with each step. Her hair dripped water droplets onto her face.

"Are you OK, Moe?" I asked.

"I can't go any farther. I will never make it up the hill."

I took the Army and Navy bag from her hand, although that did not make the steep incline any easier. Every ten steps, Moe plopped down in the grass on the roadside, puffing and huffing. When she caught her breath, she reached out her hands so I could pull her up —no mean feat. Luckily, the street running by our apartment complex was relatively flat.

For the rest of her time at our house, Moe repeatedly complained, "You were killing me." I took a deep breath each time.

Time to go to my brother Jack's house. We headed to the farm. Taking her back to Jack would bring much-needed relief. We sat down with a cup of coffee, said our good-byes and jumped back in the car, rejoicing.

Wayne continued flight training in Abbotsford. The licenses added up. The end was in sight. He would soon be ready to search for a flying position. I trusted Wayne to accomplish what he set out to do. Certainly, if determination and persistence were factors, I needed not to worry about Wayne.

I Am a High School Teacher Now
1968 - 1969

Two weeks before school began, new Principal Henk from Ontario took up his position. For our first meeting, he invited the staff to his house. He replaced a principal fired the year before, although a few staff were still devout followers who resented the dismissal. From the start, the staff was divided.

In a circle of chairs, we talked, told stories, and asked questions. The circle was divided into two parts. I chose a side and sat down among the pro Syd (former principal) teachers. I was the new kid on the block. I should have sat and listened. Instead, I was loud. I did not hold back.

Henk was soft spoken. He distributed a pile of paper, our schedules for the first semester.

An unbelievable course load arrived: English 9 (two sections), Business English, 11, Art 9, Physical Education, 9. Forty-five-minute classes. I felt tossed from one course to the next.

Ed, the Art teacher, responded to my desperate plea for help to inspire the Grade 9 students. He took me into his classroom and demonstrated: he took some black paint, put little blobs all over the paper, stuck a straw in his mouth and blew wet black paint across the page until it looked like a tree with bare branches. With little sponges dipped in red, orange, yellow paint, he sponged lightly on the branches to transform them. Fall colours popped on the black branches of the trees. A magnificent jungle of colours.

"Now what?" I ask Ed after Fall Trees had run its course. "Any other ideas?"

I needed to be a student. I couldn't follow in the steps of Mrs. B. from the Calvin Education Department and copy colouring book characters.

First class, English 9: I stood in the front of the room with about 20 students in the traditional row format. A big Grade 9 student in the back row uttered an insult loud enough for me to hear. I sauntered down the window row, reading aloud. I got to the last seat in the row. I reached for him, grabbed his shirt, and pulled him up a few inches from the seat. Without saying a word, I let him go. His bum hit the desk seat with a little thump! I made a friend who never tested me again, though I cannot imagine repeating this trick.

The English classes – I loved the English classes. I had a repertoire to draw from. We read Ogden Nash and Robert Frost, the poets. I cut poems to pieces I stored in envelopes with the name of the poem and poet in the front. In English classes, I read poems and short stories aloud that captured them and learned the art of the pregnant pause.

"More, Miss," they would shout. "Read more."

At home, I went through every one of my English texts to build a set of read-aloud stories appropriate to their grade and age. Reading aloud captured them. Hushed in anticipation, the readings proceeded.

I connected with teenagers, and thankfully, they connected with me. Teaching now felt like a more comfortable fit, though I still felt the "fake," because I was. I knew enough not to try to *be* one of the students. They had a life with their friends, surrounded by people their age. They expected me to lead them in their classroom learning, and I gave it my all. Somehow, it all came together.

Some Grade 11 students in the Business English class had a boring curriculum that even I found stultifying. I read stories here as well. We met at the end of the day. Small wonder they had a reputation for being a tough group. I enjoyed them as students. A small group of girls lingered after class. "What do you think of organizing a banquet for the Grade 12 graduating class?" I asked. Pause. "We could copy the one from Lynden, with its Mexican theme."

Four agreed to work with me on Saturdays. Diligent, reliable, the girls found a hotel for the festivities. We borrowed the Mexican theme from an earlier Lynden celebration, hired a band, and started with menus, name tags, and theme colours. The time together bonded us into a committed cohort. A new experience for students and me. The banquet succeeded, celebrating the seniors as the Mexican band walked up and down the aisles; I proudly served as "Mistress of Ceremonies."

DIVISIONS IN THE STAFF GREW. PRINCIPAL HENK WAS A SMALL MAN from Ontario with three girls and a wife who resented leaving her Ontario home and tending to her girls with no local family help. Sometimes she erupted with threats into the phone: "Come home, Henk, or I'll throw the TV through the window." Henk grabbed his coat and jumped in his car, fearing disaster. To his relief, the TV in the large wooden cabinet still stood on the floor, while Rowena sobbed in the corner. Henk soothed her, then washed up. Deflated, he drove back to the school. I underestimated the difficulties she faced and the stresses and strains for Henk. I could have been kinder to both.

At the weekly after-school staff meeting when "Any other business?" was called, Fred, a teacher I had known from Calvin College, stood stern-faced behind a chair.

"Is there any reason," he began, "that there's a girdle hanging on the three-legged stool in the little room at the back?"

I sucked in my breath.

"Whose is it?" he demanded.

Sheepishly, though with a wicked grin, I raised my finger, not the middle one I probably should have raised, and pointed at Fred. I explained, "Have you ever tried getting out of a girdle and changed into a PE uniform in a one-minute turnaround, and still have time to neatly fold your teaching clothes? Any suggestions? How about a private change room?"

Fred sat down, silent and sullen. On to a more important topic.

Once, when I didn't have time to change my clothes for gym at all, I wore a yellow dress I'd sewed. One day a wasp, tempted by the open bell of the sleeve, buzzing loudly, found its way up and couldn't find its way out. The wicked thing stung and stung until my arm swelled and the sleeve tore open.

Obvious allergic reaction. To the ER. Proof, to me at least, that I had no business teaching Physical Education. Maybe Fred could take over.

EACH DAY WITH GOOD WEATHER, I LEFT MY ROOM AT LUNCHTIME TO scan the skies and see if Wayne would buzz the school. "Make sure you're outside during the noon hour and watch," he said.

"What are you looking at, Miss?" students asked.

"My husband is in flight training. He said he'd fly over the school at lunchtime today."

The rumbling airplane sound approached. I shaded my eyes to watch Wayne make great circles. Students stopped and stared, disbelieving. We waved enthusiastically until the small single-engine airplane disappeared.

Flying, teaching, and camping with a growing circle of friends became our new reality. Most weekends, we trekked to Birch Bay, just across the border, into the lush forest and huge camping spots in nearby Washington state. Often Wayne hooked up the family boat to our car. In the warm bay salt waters, he taught me to water ski. He was an expert; I became satisfactory.

One Sunday, packing up our camping gear, Wayne said with great animation, so all could hear: "It's here. It's going to happen. Anyone interested in watching can come to our apartment."

Excited beyond description, we crowded around our little black-and-white TV to watch the first landing on the moon. Mesmerized, Wayne snapped picture after picture for posterity while the rest of us watched with bated breath. Neil Armstrong took the first steps on to the moon and spoke the famous line: "One small step for man; one giant leap for mankind."

I DISCOVERED TEACHING, AT LEAST WITH SECONDARY STUDENTS, LIVED in my DNA. Many women teachers my age started by teaching dolls, teddy bears, and younger siblings. I had no teddy bears or dolls, so my only available sibling suffered through my attempts. As young women fortunate enough to get an education, I had two choices: teaching or nursing. Teaching appealed to girls who quaked at the sight of blood. That was me. I became a teacher – well, a fake teacher. I stumbled along, mimicking and assuming a false confidence. I'd heard the little voice inside say, "you want to be a teacher."

Ironically, the little voice stilled when I began teaching long before I was properly prepared to do so.

Chapter Nineteen

Another Wedding in the Family
1969

M oe's written address on the front of the envelope? I tore open the envelope, read and jumped up, shouting to Wayne in the bathroom, shaving, "Moe is getting married!"

Someone actually marrying Moe?

I called Tina. "I just got an announcement from Moe that she's getting married."

"Yup! Apparently, a friend a few houses down the street introduced her to Mr. Verkerk, whose wife died less than a year ago. He arrived in Canada only recently, a seaman with only a few words of English. On his left arm," Tina continued, shocked by this in 1969. "He has a giant tattoo that takes up most of his upper arm: a large portrait of his first wife's face with hearts and a banner that says *Maartje* – his first wife's name. Mostly, thank goodness, it's covered by shirt sleeves."

Moe getting married. Who expected that? Some siblings openly resented it, but they were not keen to look after her themselves. Tina, like many adult daughters, had taken on the responsibilities. "The others rarely come to see her. I'm relieved Moe is no longer alone. It'll sure be easier. I've been her main support, always at her beck and call." This will be good, I thought, or maybe, hoped.

WHEN WE WEREN'T OFF CAMPING, WE ATE SUNDAY DINNER WITH Wayne's family and joined them for evening church. On the church balcony one Sunday night, I realized and whispered to Wayne, "I'm out of birth control pills."

Quietly, he slid out of the row to purchase my prescription. To my great relief, he quickly returned and tucked the pills in my purse.

When I asked for a refill, Dr. Dunn said, "You are now twenty-five. I cannot give you birth control pills any longer. Time for babies. You need to have your children by age thirty."

Babies? We have to have babies? We had neither considered nor discussed that. We busied ourselves getting Wayne through the money, requirements, licenses, and the accumulating flying hours. I needed to keep teaching. A baby? What would I do with a baby? Food for thought. Our friends had babies. They managed.

Dr. Dunn was not alone. Grandma Kooy, on our Sunday lunch visits, repeatedly asked, "When are you going to make me a Great-Grandma?"

"You already are a great grandma," I assured her, but she persisted, every Sunday we were in Lynden with the same plea. I moved to another chair. That did not deter Grandma, who, head down, then complained: "Flying is too dangerous. Why can't Wayne get a job on the ground?"

"Oh Grandma," I said, "When Wayne's flying, he's closer to heaven than you and I. Just be grateful."

I ignored her when she asked: "Do you smoke?" Dutch II women like me who came to Canada after World War II smoked. I was a Dutch woman.

"YOU ARE PREGNANT," DR. DUNN CONFIRMED.

Proudly, I announced the good news to Wayne, who joined me in a baby dance. We agreed to say nothing to anyone, to keep our little secret until at least three months had passed. Exhausted, utterly exhausted every day of the first few months, I could hardly lift my body. I spent my days on the sofa.

"What's the matter with you?" Ed, the Art teacher colleague, asked one day when he stopped by. "Why are you staying home? We miss you."

I told him. "I am pregnant."

"Hurrah!" he said. "Congratulations."

When I tabulated the exhaustion of early pregnancy, tension among staff in the school, and teaching only until the new year, with a due date of April, I resigned from the high school. What was I thinking? I had six months to go. We needed the money.

Wayne paid the rent for the next month and told the supervisor, with a huge smile on his face: "we are expecting our first baby."

"Congratulations," the manager said, but her face fell. "You can't have babies in this building. You'll have to move, I'm afraid. I am so sorry."

Not as sorry as I was. I liked that apartment with the windows facing the Fraser River and orange bridge arced over it.

PULLING UP INTO A DRIVEWAY TO A HOME ON A HILL OVERLOOKING THE Fraser River, we climbed out of the car. A woman looked down from the big picture window on the second floor. She thumped down the stairs and met us at the door to take us through the basement apartment: small, old, clean, and two bedrooms. An uneven vinyl floor, a tiny living room, a bathroom, a small square kitchen with a small square wooden table and four matching chairs.

Too hastily, Wayne agreed to the dark basement apartment. I had no car, no job, and I was pregnant. On my own, away from friends. Money was tight. As the days passed, I felt isolated.

Friends, teacher friends or students from high school did not come. They worked.

WAYNE COMPLETED THE FLIGHT PROGRAM AND READIED HIMSELF FOR the airline search. With the scarcity of flight positions, he said: "I'll have a better chance to get work if I get an instructor's license and teach flying." I agreed.

He worked to pay for further training. With his instructor's license in hand, Wayne landed a job at a small airport in Langley, cleaning the planes for $1 an hour; he earned $5 an hour stepping in when an established instructor was unavailable. He was also sent to the mall with a small plane inside to sell private pilot license programs.

THE BABY GREW. DR. DUNN WAS PLEASED. IN MY FOURTH MONTH check-up, Dr. Dunn announced: "The baby is growing towards your back rather than the front. I need to do a minor procedure that will almost certainly correct the situation," Dr. Dunn announced.

I was about four months pregnant. He arranged a hospital bed for the following day (those were the days).

"It's not 100%, but we should be able to move the baby so it can grow naturally," he said.

Wayne took me to the hospital, where an attendant wheeled me into surgery. The next thing I knew, I awoke, fearful, skeptical, praying for a good outcome. A nurse came to do a check: "The baby is fine," she assured me.

I didn't believe her. "She's just saying that," I thought. Tears wet the pillow.

Dr. Dunn came. Before he spoke, I demanded, "Is my baby still there?"

He smiled. "All is fine. Baby will be fine. You can go home today." I felt fine. Baby grew. "A little boy," I convinced myself. By the time I returned home, my spirits were up.

At the Army and Navy Surplus store in New Westminster, I purchased yards of baby-patterned flannel. Out came the sewing machine. The needle zig-zagged its way, making baby sheets, diapers, bibs, and receiving blankets. I washed, dried, ironed and folded fabric, measuring carefully before cutting. I made piles of receiving blankets and diapers and then more challenging pieces for the little crib and window. I made soft receiving blankets to keep the baby warm.

Alida and Winnie hosted a festive baby shower at Alida's new house. It was overwhelming to be surrounded by so many friends with so many gifts I could not possibly purchase myself.

GERRY, A CHRISTIAN SCHOOL PRINCIPAL FROM RICHMOND, CALLED: "Mary, would you, by any chance, be available to teach Language Arts part-time in my school?"

"Gerry, thank you. That would be fantastic. My baby is due in April, but I will stay as long as I can. Thanks for thinking of me." He was a gentle, kind, good-looking man with a shock of grey hair. This chance to teach, with Jerry as principal, was transformational.

I pulled up in the parking lot of a newly built Christian School. As I got out, a car drove up the gravel parking lot of the school, and a foot wearing a pink fur-lined slipper emerged. Out came a boy.

Puzzled, I greeted him and walked to the side door of the building. In the staff room, I asked, "I saw two small feet reach out of the car door in pink fuzzy slippers. I expected a girl and, to my amazement, saw a boy. A boy in pink slippers?" This was 1970, remember. Teachers described how, after the drowning death of their little girl, his parents tried to make their boy into a girl to replace the girl they lost.

On the first day in a Grade 7 class, I asked: "Would you like me to read a story?"

Smirks on faces. Rolling eyes.

I sat on the front of the solid wood teacher's desk, book in hand, and began. Before long, silence fell, heads raised, ears perked up, looks of concern on their faces. I know how to read aloud. When I got to the climax of the story, I looked down at the shock on their faces – I closed the book, and their protests arose: "Miss, keep reading, you can't stop now."

"Tell you what," I responded. "If you finish a little writing assignment, I promise to continue reading to the end. Can you do that?"

"Yes," they shouted in unison.

Reading aloud continued, much to the delight of the students and the principal, who sometimes found a chair in the back of the room and listened. We developed a warm, working relationship. In his gentle way, he witnessed learning in each class. He made me feel like part of the staff, even though it was temporary.

Baby
1969 - 1970

Two weeks before the baby was due, Wayne and I visited Winnie and Dick. As I turned to wave and move down the hall, my heel caught onto the carpet, and I fell down three or four steps and landed on the floor. All three, hands over their mouths, jumped down to help. I felt very foolish, but for some reason, I could not stop laughing. Finally, Wayne and Dick slipped their arms under my shoulders and lifted me up. What a chore! None the worse for wear, though, it seemed.

"Wayne," I said two or three times till he stirred in the bed. "I'm dripping liquid. The mattress is getting wet. I have no idea what to do."

The slow drip continued as I walked up and down the little apartment. I called Dr. Dunn in the middle of the night, and he said, "Get dressed and go to the hospital. I will see you in the morning."

A large towel placed on the seat of the car prevented the liquid from seeping onto the seat and kept my bum dry. Wayne delivered me to the hospital and left, mumbling that he had to be at work, selling flight lessons in a mall. Obviously, having a baby was a woman's work. I had no expectations and simply went with the flow.

So much for sleep, though. Too excited, too afraid. I'd taken birthing classes but drew a blank on what I learned. Not much, I decided.

Unexpectedly, a student nurse entered. "Hi, Mary. My name is Gloria. I'm a student nurse and will stay with you right through the birth."

I was tired and grateful and had not slept since my rude awakening Thursday night. A student nurse would know so much more than I did.

Friday came and passed. Two interviews with the student nurse conducting a case study on labour. Still no contractions.

Noises erupted. Hollering and shouting down the hall. An emergency? A game of cat and mouse?

Family members sneaked in to encourage a woman in labour. They instructed, "Go ahead, lots of noise, shout, yell," and "You want a healthy baby, then holler with all your might." A small group of encouraging relatives slipped in and out of her room.

The scene, though out of my line of vision, left me utterly dreading the prospect of delivery. Would that happen to me?

Gloria explained the chaos next door: "Italian mothers-to-be are told that the louder they yell, the healthier the baby will be."

I laughed. "If that's true, that baby will be strong and healthy!"

That cultural story was maintained for generations. The ward nurses repeatedly asked the moms-to-be to calm down and stop frightening the others on the ward. Finally, the bed wheeled past. Silence. Peace. The stress wound down a bit. My turn.

No contractions. Grateful for my nursing companion, I lay on the bed as the clock ticked, tocked, ticked, and tocked. Sleep remained elusive. Gloria stayed awake.

Although Dr. Dunn approved of Wayne coming to the delivery – an unusual thing in those days – Wayne unequivocally dismissed the opportunity.

"I'm not doing that."

"Why not?" I asked.

Thanks to him, I was on my back in considerable pain and needed his comforting presence. He was too afraid – though I was afraid myself, I had no choice.

On the way home that evening, Wayne stopped briefly at Alida's house and proclaimed, "She never has to go through this again."

Right.

Another sleepless night – on Saturday morning, the ward nurse announced: "Enough waiting. Let's get this baby moving." She placed a pit drip in my arm, moving liquid dynamite into my veins with the promise of speedy delivery. Labour began – relatively painful contractions that, even after a full day, failed to jumpstart the process.

At six o'clock, the ward nurse declared, "Nowhere near ready," and pulled the plug, so to speak, on the pit drip. "We'll try again tomorrow," she said.

My mouth dropped open. "Tomorrow? Are you kidding? I haven't slept a full night since Wednesday. It's Saturday."

She frowned, moved the dial on the machine, and walked out the door.

"Ready! Help! I need to push," I bellowed before thirty more minutes had passed.

"Here we go," Gloria said, wheeling me into the delivery room.

I did not shout out. When the pushing began, I groaned: "I can't. I can't push again."

"You're doing fine. Baby will be here shortly."

Easy for her to say – though, of course, she was right.

With one final push, my legs shaking uncontrollably and not an ounce of reserve energy, and the baby slipped out.

The nurse held her aloft. I look at our naked baby girl. A baby girl? It's a girl? We hadn't even picked out a girl's name.

The baby turned her little face to me, and in an instant, I told myself: "I can do this. This is our baby. I am a proud new mother."

Wayne entered, puffing, red-faced, in awkward awe of his perfect baby girl.

Since bottle-feeding was the norm, a woman nursing a baby made people uncomfortable. As soon as a nurse brought Tracey in and placed her, wrapped in a blanket, on my bed, she drew the curtain all around to keep us in a private space. I enjoyed the calm space to meet my new daughter and to get to know her. How can love grow so quickly?

Wayne visited daily. On day two, his parents arrived with a large, colourful bouquet. Friends came, and I gleefully showed off baby Tracey.

The required one-week stay in the hospital felt like I was in a resort, having a grand learning experience. Someone cooked, and watched my baby at night, and comforted her when she was not with me. Life was good.

And about to change.

On the seventh day, elated, I prepared to leave. Everyone in our ward received pamphlets, formula, sample diapers, butt salve, and soap. We exchanged addresses and telephone numbers with promises to stay in touch, which we did. Wayne purchased the required Ford baby seat and installed it in the car. Everything at home was ready. At least that's what I thought.

After we arrived home, I realized Tracey needed changing. I picked up a white flannel cloth and spread it on the kitchen table while Wayne read Dr. Spock's book on how to fold a diaper. I took step one: transform the square into a kite shape. I diapered, following step by step, until Tracey's bottom was washed and warm, with a fluffy dry diaper. Phew!

A most contented baby, Tracey slept through the night at six weeks and soon outgrew the little basket.

Moe and her new husband came to celebrate baby Tracey. Moe had knitted a gorgeous blanket for her little bed – yellow and white. With no car to take us anywhere and no money to spend, we were restricted to camping chairs on the upper lawn. The coffee was ready at 10 a.m., and the tea at 3 p.m. Moe and Mr. V. slept on the fold-out sofa in the living room. The first night, a loud thump. Mr. V. fell out of the bed. A yelp! Wayne and I both jumped up and helped him back into the bed, and pushed the sofa tight to the wall.

I preferred to be alone with Tracey.

"Wayne, there's a flying job here in Lethbridge. I checked it out. They want you," Ken said in a welcome phone call.

A lifelong Nobleford friend, also a pilot, Ken flew for a small airline in Lethbridge, and as he prepared to leave on a trip, he heard a Time Air pilot say: "We're looking for a first officer."

Without a pause, Ken said, "I know a recently trained pilot. A good guy. Can I call him?"

A real flying job? This so soon after a cross-country trip that resulted in not so much as a nibble or a thanks. No pilot hires anywhere. And here Wayne was – employed.

Mad times ensued: organizing, packing baby stuff, securing a U-Haul. Wayne packed our belongings in the little rented trailer, and we headed to Lethbridge, his birthplace. The twelve-hour trip took us through steep mountain ranges, valleys, hairpin turns, blocked views, and tunnels. On a particularly steep hill, the trailer wove dangerously behind the car, swinging one way and then the other – but in true character, Wayne said nary a worry word until all was well again.

The road wound around the steep, granite, glorious snow-capped mountains. My fear of heights led to imagining myself hurtling over the scant fencing and rolling down the mountains, through trees and brush. My jaw locked. I edged closer and closer to Wayne, almost sitting on his lap. Tracey slept in the back seat in her collapsible carry bed – three months old, she should have been secured in her new car seat.

There, at the top of a grass hill, stood the famous Banff Springs Hotel, in the distance, mountains. Wayne reached for the camera; I reached to the back seat for Tracey, who was red-faced, burning. I panicked. "Wayne, Tracey is red hot. She needs water! Get some from the hotel!"

He ran up the hill to ask for water while Tracey screamed uncontrollably. Her face grew redder, bold red spots on her cheeks from the heat coming in through the window. The summer heat had overwhelmed her. She was dehydrated. I walked back and forth, cradling her, humming a song, soothing her as I went. When Wayne reappeared with the water, I quickly put some in a bottle and gave it to her. Why had I not noticed? Why had Tracey not cried? Frightened and ashamed, I vowed never again to let that happen to my baby.

In Lethbridge, we pulled into a parking area where Wayne's single aunt Gert lived on the main floor of the bungalow where Grandma and Grandpa Withage had lived before they passed. Grandpa, a finishing carpenter, had created a lovely suite for Gert in the basement.

"Come on in," she said warmly, and made a great fuss over Tracey, who looked exactly like a real Withage. "You can stay downstairs in the apartment until you find a rental place for yourselves." Good news.

In his teens, Wayne had sometimes accompanied Gert on her travels, going to world fairs and exploring new cities. She was ecstatic to have us visit – at least initially. She loved Wayne, and she loved Tracey, hugging her and taking pictures at every opportunity. She guided us down the carpeted stairs into the charming, attractively furnished apartment. I was happy to unpack and find places and spaces for our family. Wayne was happy; I was homesick for Vancouver and my friends.

As the days went by, Gert didn't warm up. I felt guilty throwing a wrench into her life.

Wayne reported to Time Air at the Lethbridge airport. A jammed schedule would be ample opportunity to build flying hours. Day after day, he left to soar around the province. The pay, $300.00 per month.

The following day, Wayne began first officer training on a twin-engine plane that travelled among Alberta cities. Soon fully trained, he picked up passengers in the Time Air van, dusted off the airplane, welcomed passengers on board, and flew the airplane. After each landing, he reversed the process. Sometimes, passengers left a tip in a tin. Whenever Wayne accumulated $10, we celebrated with a dinner out and a babysitter.

While Wayne began to fly, I scoured the *Lethbridge Herald* for rentals. Apartments were scarce. Any that were suitable, we could not afford. The intensive search ended with one possibility: another dark basement apartment. When nothing else was available, I reluctantly conceded.

At the airport, out of the blue, someone told Wayne about a low-cost townhouse that had become available in Rideau Court. The cost? $87 per month. We didn't walk; we ran. Anything would be better than another basement.

Rideau Court townhouses were set up around a grassy square. A rental agent opened the door to the entry with a coat closet and an open doorway into a small kitchen (rubber floor tiles in three different colours). A large picture window overlooked a manicured lawn. Steep stairs led to the upper floor, two bedrooms and a bathroom with a tub; laundry and storage in the basement. It seemed just right for us.

"Please God."

The agent stood at the top of the stairs. "What's your income, Wayne?"

"$300 a month."

"Let me calculate. That's $3600 a year. Lucky!" he said. "Our cut-off is a minimum of $3500 annually. $100 a year to spare."

A huge smile covered both our faces.

"We'll take it," Wayne said. "We can move in immediately."

Even with a subsidized townhouse, Wayne's income fell short of covering even the basic expenses. I needed at least a part-time job. Gert, retired from Sears, recommended checking out positions in the catalogue department. Indeed, openings were available, and they hired me on the spot. I worked every Friday evening and all day Saturday for $1 per hour, and a percentage of catalogue sales.

AT CHURCH, A SENIOR LADY INTRODUCED HERSELF, SAYING SHE LIVED close by.

"We need a babysitter for Friday evenings and Saturdays while I work at the Sears order office," I said. "Would you know anyone from church?"

"I am looking for something to do," she said. "Would you hire me?"

"Of course."

The babysitter cared for Tracey. A delightful chatterbox, Tracey loved stories and songs and dancing. At Sears, I learned quickly and skillfully to sell and, particularly, to up-sell ("Did you notice the same colour mat for the bathroom?"). It was boring, so I kept looking for something more than filling order files on the phone or locating packages on the shelves for customers doing a pick-up. I dreaded the weekends.

Wayne, on the other hand, was deliriously happy – he loved flying. He never complained about the hours or the pay, though I admit I did at times. Nevertheless, his dream had materialized, and his hopes for a regular airline position stayed strong. He sent updates to CP Air. Positions were scarce.

The long-shot dream stayed firm. He saved every postcard. We persevered.

AN AD IN THE *LETHBRIDGE HERALD* CAUGHT MY ATTENTION. "WANTED: assignment marker at Lethbridge Community College." A made-for-me, perfect opportunity! I could stay home with Tracey, mark papers and get paid. Shortly after, a letter arrived advising me that, unfortunately, I was not on the shortlist. Upset, I had no choice but to head back to Sears.

About to leave for a New Year's Eve party in Nobleford, Wayne put Tracey in her car seat. On my way out the door, as I was turning off the hall lights, the phone rang.

In the dark, I lifted the receiver.

"Mary Kooy?"

"Yes."

"We have you on record from an earlier application. Can you come in for an interview for a teaching position?"

Teaching at a college? Our New Year celebrations were filled with new promise and hope.

The Call to Teach (LCC)
1971

A few days later, I drove to the south end of Lethbridge to a simple, single-story building with a small sign that read: Lethbridge Community College.

I parked. Cold hands. Nervous, nervous, nervous.

In the Education office, I told the secretary: "I am here to interview for a teaching position."

She smiled and walked me to a door where a man stood waiting. He introduced himself; I introduced myself. He welcomed me into the room, to a chair facing two men seated at a long table. It was good to sit down and keep my trembling and ice-cold hands out of sight beneath the table.

The committee chair described the position – teaching young men who came to Canada from Japan for farming experience unavailable there. Harsh, cold, wind whipping Alberta winters made outdoor farming prohibitive. The college offered to teach English to the men in winter gap times. The class would be divided into three levels of English competence. Instructors would teach full-time for six weeks.

"I am an immigrant who came to Canada with no English. I struggled to master the English language. Since I was only eight, I learned rather quickly." I did not divulge, and they did not ask about teaching credentials. I was still unlicensed, though I had teaching experience in both elementary and secondary schools, which might have been just the ticket. "I don't need a teaching qualification for college," I thought.

My hands warmed up.

As the interview ended, the committee chair said, "Thank you. Before you go, a few final comments. The position pays $10 per hour for a six-week contract that could possibly be renewed."

What did he say? I could not believe what I heard. My insides quivered and my breath quickened. I tried valiantly to maintain a calm presence, trying my "no surprise here" look.

Enthusiastically and gratefully, I shook their hands. "Thank you," I said, waved and moved out of the door.

Ready to explode, to run down the hallway and shout: "Are you kidding?" That went well, I thought, optimistically. My step had a bounce – a gift had fallen into my hands. I reveled in the prospect of teaching adults. New learning, new possibilities.

Naively, I allowed myself not to consider that others would be interviewed. They had not yet offered me a position.

All the way home in the car, over and over, I pumped my fist and shouted: "Ten dollars an hour! Did I just hear ten dollars an hour?"

At home, Wayne and I sat at the red Arborite kitchen table. I described the interview and the questions, leaving any talk of salary to the end. "What do you think it pays?" I asked.

"No idea. How much?"

"The salary is [a pause] $10 an hour!" I laughed.

Wayne looked at me, perplexed, as though he could not have heard me right. I understood. He waited for me to correct the figure.

I didn't. "I may not get it, but wouldn't it be amazing if I did?"

A phone call, and a breathless "thank you" and then much dancing around our living room, arms pumping, rejoicing after I hung up, hand over my mouth. An unbelievable opportunity. How could this be? Hope restored. I could not have dreamed this up. Dancing days for me.

THE CONTRACT ARRIVED IN THE MAIL. A FOLLOW-UP TELEPHONE CALL: "You have a meeting with the two other teachers for curriculum planning, questions, rooms, and resources. They have taught here before and will be glad to fill you in on the details."

The instructors met. We clicked immediately. We worked well

together. We divided the young men into three levels. I got the middle group.

Morning classes focused on improving English. Afternoons sessions were reserved for different assignments drawn from our personal expertise and choice. I elected to teach public speaking with the least experienced English language group.

Studiously, I read and reread each course description and expectations, scribbling questions in the margins as I went. My two experienced colleagues discussed details, content, and resources while I made copious notes. They taught me how to assign competency levels to make three groups – the calm and confident colleagues were remarkably knowledgeable.

I learned and connected with my colleagues and with the students. Something clicked, particularly with the collaborative efforts of my colleagues, allowing me to learn and grow and not feel alone, as I had in much of my previous teaching.

Need a student handout? Submit a copy and the next morning it arrived on a cart, neatly parked at the front corner of my teacher's desk. Have a question? All stood ready. Confidence-building and inclusive.

All three instructors had young children spawning many stories on the rides to and from the classes. We laughed, talked, worried, and openly discussed our failures. We told stories about students, threw out questions, and created helpful resources. Thankfully, we functioned like an idea bank.

Afternoons were reserved for projects that focused on the instructor's interest. I had chosen public speaking. In class, I began: "Your first speech will be about Japan, so I can learn new things from you. You can tell me about whatever you choose." We practiced and read to each other with a Japanese-English dictionary on each desk. I helped where I could. Their basic English skills became a little less basic.

The day of public speaking arrived. Students talked about growing rice, Japanese homes, temples, schools, and cooking. Some brought pictures. I was amazed at the variety and the interest they displayed describing life in Japan and fascinated by the efforts made to help me picture their worlds.

Halfway through the reports, one student stood up in front of the class. Unable to find all the words he needed in English, he gestured to begin his report on Japanese girls. "Japanese girls have . . ." he tapped his face twice before placing both hands over his left chest.

Completely taken aback and puzzled, it was obvious I didn't understand. He tried again, placing one hand to tap his face and then both hands over his chest. The entire class, recognizing my confusion, stood up and applied the same gestures first on the face, then on his chest. My breath speeding, I froze in distress.

At last, one enterprising young man picked up his dictionary, smiled and repeated the gestures as he spoke: "Ah, teacher, Japanese girls have beautiful face and *big* heart!"

"Class dismissed!" I said.

Sometimes my morning homeroom students called on us in the early evening, knocking on the picture window at the back of the house. I opened the door, gripping it (very windy in Lethbridge). Regardless of temperature and snow or my insistence, the students took off their shoes outside before entering. They brought Japanese tea, and I put the kettle on the stove. The kettle hummed, then whistled. Time for tea. Seated on the floor around our Wayne-made coffee table, they stirred, drank, and enjoyed talking English and laughing together: a joy.

Despite the challenges, particularly of oral communication, we managed to communicate. I genuinely appreciated teaching adults.

The first six-week appointment ended when we received the message that the program would continue. As it turned out, I taught with my two colleagues for two more years. Mrs. V., a caring, peppy senior, cheerfully continued babysitting Tracey, who joined her on errands, picking up groceries, going for walks, visiting her friends. She read stories from a pile of her favourite books, sang songs, played with her. Tracey loved her.

Tracey's charismatic and contented personality was recorded in her baby book, including two pages of words she could say perfectly by the time she was 11 months old. Talking, singing, happy Tracey had an incredible language facility. For her second birthday, she filled a cassette tape of songs she sang with my encouragement, but without my help.

Tracey became my pal. In the car, she read signs all along the way beginning, of course, with McDonalds.

FROM THE OUTSET AT MY TIME AT LCC, I OPENED A SAVINGS ACCOUNT for a house down payment. Pay cheques went directly into the new account that accumulated, not surprisingly, faster than our regular chequing account.

When I became pregnant in the fall, the need for a real house ratcheted up a notch. Wayne and I, with Tracey in tow, began walking through open houses in Lethbridge.

Wayne continued flying long days and ridiculously long hours. Once a month, I transcribed his scribbles of scheduled flights and recorded them neatly in the required logbook. With his intense schedule, flying hours soared, and he was promoted to Captain, doubling his wages to $600.

FOR CLINT'S WEDDING, WAYNE PROUDLY WORE A BURGUNDY-PURPLE polyester suit. We both admired it – it was so fashionable! The wedding offered an excellent opportunity to meet Wayne's friends. I went around the circle: some I knew, some I just met.

One man said he had a thing for immigrant girls. Taken aback, I said: "I'm married."

"So am I," he responded. I moved to another chair.

ON A SUNDAY AFTERNOON, A NOBLEFORD FRIEND INVITED US TO GO water skiing. We packed a lunch and sat on the shore, taking Tracey for water splashes and walks. She gleefully enjoyed the experience.

As we packed up, a crowd gathered in the dock area across the lake. The sound of happy water play dimmed.

We stopped at the spot, and I went out to ask: "What is happening there?"

"A young boy drowned."

"Drowned?" I repeated, disbelievingly. "With all these people here?"

"He was at the end of the dock, got pushed in and did not come up."

I felt myself blanch and become lightheaded. So sorry. I was so sorry.

"That will never happen to our children," I told Wayne. "I am registering Tracey for swimming lessons tomorrow at the Y."

"Agreed," Wayne said.

On Monday morning, I got the information, schedule, and costs for the program. I called our friend Pat and explained what had happened at the lake. "I am registering Tracey for swimming. Do you want to join me with Carmen?"

"Sure. When? How much does it cost? That will be fun," she said.

Pat and I met at the pool twice a week. Tracey loved the water from the moment the lessons began. I might have guessed, given she always resisted leaving the tub at home. She loved the splashing. Orange blow-up arm bands kept her afloat in the lessons, and she needed me only to walk or swim alongside.

"Great work, Tracey," I repeated.

Her progress amazed me and most bystanders. After three months and two sets of lessons, Tracey no longer needed the armbands and swam, unassisted, the length of the pool. She was eighteen months old. Proud mother!

Chapter Twenty

Wayne Begins His New Career
January, 1973

Wayne continued flying for Time Air, though every month, he forwarded letters to CPAir noting the changes in his flying hours (critical) and command time as Captain. As always, polite rejections came back. In time, just postcards, with an orange CPAir plane on the front, arrived. The back of the card read: "Thanks for your application" and "We have your resume on file."

Two months earlier, Chuck, Wayne's First Officer at Time Air, had received the CPAir call two months before. He called to say, "Get out here, Wayne. CP Air just bought two 747s, with two more on order. They are hiring."

Gloomy, Wayne shook his head. "Just this week, I got another postcard rejection, with thanks *but no thanks* written on the back!"

As quickly as I realized what had happened, I bolted up the stairs and threw two small suitcases on our bed. I hollered down: "I'm up here packing, Wayne. No time to waste."

"What? I'm not going!"

"Why not come with Tracey and me?"

After some heated discussion, Wayne relented, packed, and drove to the Lethbridge Airport. Inside, we passed the sign on the wall behind the counter that I promised myself not to read or even look at: Time flies. Why don't you? I couldn't resist giving it a brief glance and a smile. We won't be looking at this again.

WAYNE DROPPED US AT ALIDA'S HOUSE. I EXPLAINED: "WAYNE IS going to the CP Air office to see about a possible interview."

"Of course. Come on over. I want to hear all about it."

The following day, Wayne drove to the CP Air building at the Vancouver International Airport, returning hours later, bubbling over with excitement, fear, and hope.

"I introduced myself at the desk, advised them I'd just flown in from Lethbridge – I handed over my logbook with the flying hours and airplane types, and requested an interview." Wayne quoted the secretary: She said, "Hold on a minute, let me check," and came back nodding to say, "Wait for your name to be called." Wayne choked back tears.

"The interview lasted a long time," Wayne continued. Several around the table in the room commented on his university degree, the only one in hundreds of applications. Who knew a degree in political science would make a strong pilot candidate?

"Please return to this office tomorrow at 2 p.m.," the secretary informed him.

As instructed, Wayne returned the following day.

All went smoothly until one heart test detected a murmur. "Your records," the doctor said, "will be sent to Ottawa to confirm that the potential heart valve issue would not be an issue for flying."

Deflation.

Waiting challenged both of us. We had to return to Lethbridge to await results. The heart murmur report delayed the course start at CP Air. In the meantime, we talked and talked, waited, and hoped. Wayne, as always, kept things close to the chest. He knew the implications of this report. At twenty-seven, he was in the final year of his eligibility. No one twenty-eight or older (changed now) could qualify. This was it—his only chance.

To our surprise, within a week, notification arrived from the Canadian Ministry of Transport in Canada (MOT) in Ottawa. Hands shaking, Wayne deftly slit open the envelope and pulled out the letter. The paper shook.

He read aloud: "Your medical report for the airline has been approved going forward."

His hands shot up in the air, shouting, "I can fly! I can fly!"

This was the stuff of dreams. Well, almost. Lengthy, rigorous course flight training awaited. Not all in his class of fifteen would become CP Air pilots.

Wayne packed up and left Lethbridge early in January. We bade a tearful goodbye.

He reported to the CP Air Office in Vancouver on January 11, 1973, a memorable day. Pilot position openings were rare. Though under incredible pressure, Wayne was also capable, determined, accomplished, and fiercely committed.

Success.

A Lethbridge Good-Bye.
1973 - 1978

Tracey and I stayed behind in Lethbridge to complete my LCC course and pack the boxes for the move. While I packed, Tracey, almost three, danced around the little living room like an ethereal fairy. I prepared mentally to build a new life in British Columbia.

We had much to celebrate. College teaching, a new baby coming, moving back to BC and being with our longstanding friends – all in one year.

In the car with my LCC colleagues toward the close of the semester, I announced, "Wayne secured a pilot's position at CP Air. We are moving back to Vancouver. I will miss you, my teacher friends, and I will miss our students. You've taught me so much, and I am grateful."

The teaching had turned a significant bend, a professional growth spurt. Confidence had grown, as had my skill. I belonged here. The college took a risk. I accepted and filled a new role, grateful for a call to teach in a new environment, for colleagues, for students. I had hope. I could be a teacher. I would be an actual teacher.

At the end of January, my courses for the semester ended at the LCC. I prepared for the move. I thought as I worked. I knew I would miss my students, who regularly walked the hall to the cafeteria saying, "Ah, teacher, you too big." They meant tall, and they were right. The Dutch are the tallest people in the world.

Wayne's flight training on the DC 8 shifted from being a captain on an 18-seat airplane to a very large, ocean-crossing jet. It both intimidated and exhilarated him. He was stressed, but stoic. I was stressed. Not stoic. He got hives. I did not. Everything depended on Wayne's training success. Wayne succeeded. Three of his fourteen classmates were excused.

Somehow during the training terrors, Wayne located a house, set up bank accounts, changed our address and telephone number. The new duplex was in Tsawwassen, with an unfinished basement and a two-bedroom finished second floor, very common in the area. Close to the water.

"CP Air will move us and any items too big for the car trunks," Wayne told me. "I called Chad in Nobleford. He offered to drive your car from Lethbridge to Tsawwassen. He and I will convoy across the mountains; you and Tracey can fly."

Tracey and I flew to Vancouver on a clear, bright, sunny day. In her window seat, as we approached Vancouver, Tracey looked out at the Coastal Range Mountains, puckered her brow, and exclaimed: "Mom, look at those big Coulees!"

I laughed. "When they're that big, Tracey, we call them mountains," I said.

We reunited at the airport with tears of happiness. Being without us during critical and high-pressure training must have been challenging for Wayne. Or maybe it was better Tracey and I were not there; we might have made things more complicated.

Wayne set out the furniture in our new home in Tsawwassen: kitchen table and chairs, the little sofa, coffee table and lamp and table, and of course, beds.

Even though it was winter and cold, though not compared to Lethbridge, Tracey and I walked every day, meeting old and new friends. With Tracey in the buggy, we bumped along on the sidewalk that needed repair. "Stop, Mum," Tracey shouted, swinging her arms. Pointing to a bed of purple, early crocuses, she continued excitedly: "Look, Mother. These flowers are as small and delicate as I."

Where did that come from? I can only conclude it came straight from a story I read to her. Nevertheless, her mother was very impressed. Like me, Tracey loved words.

On a visit once, Moe told stories about me as a baby: "When you were about ten months old, in the middle of the war, I took you to the doctor. While we waited in the office, I pointed, and you spoke. You identified each item clearly, without baby talk. People looked and asked, 'How old is she?' Ten months, I replied." Simultaneously, they spoke some version of "Unbelievable." A whiff of trophy there.

CP AIR DID NOT PAY DURING INITIAL TRAINING. MY LITTLE NEST EGG of $3,500 – our house down payment – shrank as we dipped into the savings account to cover our basic living costs for at least four months. Each withdrawal hurt, though the cost of the admission to the airline was far beyond any sacrifice. I was grateful, at least, to have the funds available. What would we have done otherwise?

The good news arrived. The stamp, as it were, of "passed," thrilled us. How can that be? I had little familiarity with dreams come true. This was a dream come true.

Soon I connected again with Winnie, who announced that she was also pregnant.

"Wow, Winnie, great news!"

Our babies were due around the same time in June. Another gift to enjoy.

Tony and Sue and their boys joined us at Tsawwassen beach. Tony had introduced me to Wayne at his birthday party. Busy exchanging news, sitting on towels on the sand, Wayne looked up to see Tracey and Brett far away on the beach, running without a care into an incoming tide. Wayne and Tony leapt up and raced toward the kids, shouting as they went, "Stop! Stop!"

The kids, of course, didn't stop. The crashing sounds of waves muffled the sound. Mercifully, Wayne and Tony caught up, exhausted. Each firmly held Tracey and Brett's hand until they got back to our blanket. Shades of the Lethbridge drowning at the lake clouded my thoughts. Relief. Safe.

A biannual medical in December, the day before Christmas, Wayne's x-ray showed a shadow on his lungs. I pleaded for him to stay home; he went. Weekly, he reported, and weekly, the shadow grew. Terror gripped me. Wayne grew increasingly sullen and terrified. What was this? "Don't tell anyone," Wayne said. Being the traditional stay-at-home wife at this point, I told no one.

On a sunny, cold day, I stood at the sink, immobile, weeping and heard a voice, "Wayne will be fine." Where did that voice come from? I don't know, of course, but it comforted. Finally, in April, he went to the hospital for tests on his liver. At home, I cried and hugged the kids all day long.

Once home again, we awaited news. Day after day, nothing. Finally, I said, "Why have we not heard? Please make an appointment with Dr. K. I pleaded; he agreed. When he came home, he described what Dr. K. said, "Do you feel sick?" Wayne shook his head and said, "No." Dr. K. called the lab; results were in. "No sign of any shadow. In the clear!" Hallelujah!

Sue called, "Tony broke his leg playing baseball. Wayne just brought him to the hospital."

"Oh, no. Is he OK?"

"They set his leg. Wait, I see Wayne bringing Tony to the front door; he's home."

At home, Wayne called Sue: "Tell Tony I'll come to mow your lawn."

"Sure. Thank you. When can you come?"

"This afternoon."

We parked on a steep unpaved driveway, road noise just beyond their yard making a constant "whoosh" of zooming cars. Tracey danced into the house to play with the boys and Wayne got the mower from the shed and started it up with a roar. In record time, the lawn was sheared, and the lawnmower delivered back to its home in the shed. With a rake, Wayne gathered the cut grass and threw it into giant paper bags while the kids played outside, running barefoot on the freshly cut lawn. Squeals of delight as their feet turned green.

"Why not stay for dinner?" Sue said.

"I can't say no to that," I answered.

It was too much effort to cook now. Delivery time was at hand. Three days from due date. Being so close, I packed a small suitcase and placed it in the car's trunk, just in case.

A few phone calls later, a group of mutual friends dropped by. With the kids in bed, the fun began with a game of charades. Puzzled looks around the circle. Vern, Alida's husband, got quite tipsy by the end of the evening and stood up to play – or try to play – his charades role. Accidentally, he stood on Sue's foot and remained there, unaware. She winced stoically but stopped short of asking Vern to remove his foot. Vern sat down and, as he did, released Sue's foot. Mercy.

On another note entirely, I spontaneously declared: "Whoa, I think I'm having contractions." Others chimed in, laughed, carried on and thought I was joking. Sensible Sue brought a pen and paper to record contraction times and length. Since contractions came relatively close together now, I called Dr. Dunn: "Better go in. Second one."

"Well," I thought, remembering Tracey's long birthing process, "I sure hope so!"

By midnight, I announced: "The time has come/The walrus said."

Lots of "ha ha ha," around, but Sue looked out at the others and said: "She's not spoofing," adding: "Tracey can stay here with us – Tony and his broken leg, and the little boys can keep her company."

I thanked her profusely and went out to the car in the cool summer air.

Once in the car, my legs shook uncontrollably. I was afraid. Images of the lengthy process with Tracey came back in technicolour three-dimensional clarity. My legs shook uncontrollably. I had no desire to have another baby now.

Too late, I told myself.

"Can you please take me to Surrey Hospital? That's where Winnie is," I said to Wayne. We arrived about 12:30 a.m., and by 5 a.m., with Dr. Dunn nowhere in sight, baby number two arrived.

"This one will be a girl," I told the intern delivering the baby.

"It's a big boy, a big boy!" the intern shouted.

Unbelievable. Unexpected. So much for my certain knowledge. I did not seem to get it right. Now for a name.

In the meantime, Winnie's baby, Sherry, had been born the day before. Settled in my bed, ready to sleep after a hard night's work (though much slicker than my first delivery), Wayne stole down the hallway, found Winnie's name on the door, knocked lightly and peered in.

Winnie whispered: "A baby, too?"

"This morning at 5. A baby boy. All well."

"Congratulations, you two," Winnie responded.

Our new peaceful baby boy looked exactly like my brother Jack and me. A few sprays of black hair. Now for a boy's name – not a girl, but a boy. What would Tracey think of her new brother? Not much, as it turned out. She diverted my attention whenever possible. "I am here," she reminded me. "Pay attention."

The next morning, Winnie and I met and immediately set off down the hall to admire our new children.

"Have you got a smoke, Winnie?"

Handing one over, she asked, "Got an extra peppermint, Mary?"

I handed her one large round King peppermint.

After a day or so, a concerned nurse arrived to say, "Your babies both have very upset stomachs. Stop the peppermints," she said.

For Dutch people, peppermints are holy morsels used only during church, not maternity wards, apparently. The nurse made it clear. We obeyed. No more peppermints after a cigarette. We should have said no more cigarettes, too, but that did not occur to us.

Winnie, ever the adventurer, took me to survey several sights in the ward. In one room, she showed me the umbilical cords that were examined and stored there. She explained, in detail, the reason for the umbilical cord. I was intrigued. After five days together on the ward, Winnie prepared to go home.

Two days later, it was my turn to pack. Wayne, of course, was flying. Feeling lonely, I waited in the entryway for a friend to pick me up; Kent gurgled and cuddled in my arms. Shortly after we got home, Wayne's mother arrived.

"Oh, let me hold that baby. Let me rock that baby," she said.

No one better with babies existed. She cuddled, she talked, she rocked, she sang. When she cuddled him, Kent cooed contentedly. In between, Grandma made meals and tea and snacks. During the night, she heard Kent mewling before I did. By the time I walked to the bedroom, she had already picked him up, hugged, cleaned, and changed him. Imagine! Baby up and diapered before I could even get to him myself. A wondrous but short-lived reality.

Each evening, I placed Kent in his little white crib with the embroidered linens and a little blue tucked-in blanket on the bed. Within an hour or two, intense, high-pitched crying would begin.

Wayne's mother left, and so did my milk. During the nights, Kent awoke hourly. Neither he nor I got a break. I felt pressed, against my better judgment, to supplement using the Similac powder included in the hospital package.

By eight months, Kent was biting the edge of the crib, gnawing, rubbing his sore gums till they became infected and filled with thick, yellow pus. He must have suffered terrible pain.

The doctor said, "Bring him in immediately. We need to look after that." The doctor took one look, grabbed a small instrument and, in a flash, lanced Kent's upper gums. Kent protested loudly, thrashing about. The pus stormed out and disappeared.

Calm washed over Kent. It held, at least, during the day.

Chapter Twenty-One

The Family Grows
September, 1973

At three, a precocious Tracey walked to nursery school at the end of our little cul-de-sac. She adored her teacher and friends up and down the street and in her class. They played in our house or backyard and on the street. Tracey read endless books at home and knew every word.

"I want to be a ballerina," she announced.

"I think you're right. Let's see if we can find you a ballet school."

A studio in Tsawwassen had an opening. Lessons began. She danced with joy until she was thirteen and had entered high school.

Tracey's first school year was in an out-of-district public school kindergarten, on friend Tony's recommendation. His work with an educational publisher took him to schools regularly. He praised the school, which thankfully admitted Tracey. Tony had hit the nail on the head. Teacher Bunny was herself a delight; she also delighted in

Tracey. She learned Tracey could read books on her own, and like my beloved Juffrouw Kok, selected books for her.

Every day, Tracey was excited to go to school. To keep her occupied and interested after kindergarten, she often played with her friends in the cul-de-sac. Sometimes I packed up to see friends or invited them to our house, which was challenging.

By now Wayne had successfully completed another set of his training, and his flight schedule took him away on three- and four-day flights at a time. Kent still woke up throughout the night; neither of us could get enough sleep. I knew it wasn't his fault, but I could not understand what was happening to him or why.

I went *au naturale,* breastfeeding Kent, supplementing only when necessary. I sat in the rocking chair and lit up a cigarette. Curly clouds formed in the air with every puff. I left the cigarette in the ashtray on the coffee table. I got up to get a drink of water in the kitchen. Smoke curled up from the ashtray on the counter.

A thunderbolt: Nursing Kent with two cigarettes going simultaneously? Why did I still smoke while embracing healthy breastfeeding? Seriously? I vowed to quit.

One day at a time. Home with Tracey and Kent, Wayne, on a new six-week training course in Seattle. I fidgeted, I fussed, I fumed, but I did not smoke. On Wayne's first weekend home, I greeted him with: "There's only one thing worse than what I just went through this week, and that's starting to smoke and doing this all over again."

My smoking days ended.

My getting up every hour or two with Kent proceeded uninterrupted.

THE LANDLORD KNOCKED ON THE DOOR AND ASKED IF I COULD TAKE A tour of the neighbours empty house. I grabbed the kids and followed him up the stairs next door. The neighbors, now gone, had bred and raised small dogs. Often, six or seven pups could be seen in their backyard. We followed the landlord up the stairs. The door opened to animal poop on the floors, rotten food on the counters, the carpet filled with black round cigarette burns. Cigarette burns in a semi-circle around the toilet base. Frightened to the core, I asked: "How did the house not go up in flames with me and my two children right next door?" I now understood why my landlord wanted me to be a witness to the damage the renters had done. We lived innocently, unknowingly, in the other half of the duplex. What a relief to see the backs of them.

"I HAVE A GREAT LOT IN LADNER I COULD SELL YOU TO BUILD A HOUSE. Would you be interested?" Nick, the builder, said to Wayne after church.

"Yes," Wayne replied. "Give me directions so I can look at the lot."

"I'll take you," Nick said.

Nick was right. A cul-de-sac would be perfect for a family home.

After scouring house plans, meetings with the Construction company and the bank, the first, checking in with Wayne's father, a new house was on its way. On days off, Wayne worked with the construction crew. They built a beautiful new house with a carport, back yard and a spigot on the deck for gas, so I never ran out of fuel for the BBQ. I decorated the house boldly: orange shag carpet, red cabinets in the kitchen. We chose teak furniture, orange drapes and an orange shag rug (it's the '70s, remember).

"IF WE WANT ANOTHER BABY," I SAID TO WAYNE, "IT MIGHT BE GOOD to get started. I am already past thirty. The two others took a year each."

Miraculously – I am Mary, after all – I was pregnant in literally no time. Exhausted by the lack of sleep and Wayne's absences at critical dinner and night times, I'm pretty sure thinking had nothing to do with this. Kurt was my "No sooner said than done" baby.

Kent failed to sleep through the night and by association, neither had I. He worried me. His speaking, by 18 months, composed of a mumble-jumble that no one, including me, understood. He needed attention. Without words, he gestured in desperation and frustration. He perfectly mimicked and gestured his best *Sesame Street* characters and events. He stood, arms spread like a blessing, and recited: "Welcome, welcome to the Association of 'W' lovers."

Shortly before Kurt was born (too late to change my mind), I took Kent, now eighteen months old, to the doctor to inquire about his hearing and lack of speech.

The doctor pulled out a tuning fork; Kent responded.

"He can hear," he said confidently.

"Why can't he talk?" I asked.

"You just want him to be as smart as your daughter, Mary. He is not going to be."

"I would remind you," I said with conviction, "I am the only one of nine children in my family who did not need some kind of ear surgery. Hearing issues should not be unexpected. I am not making this up."

"He'll be fine," he said. Dejectedly, I left the office, but turned to Dr. K.: "If I was phobic, would I not obsess over all three kids?"

No answer.

Recently, I read an article that sparked an *aha*: "Medical gaslighting includes dismissive attitudes by healthcare providers that depict patients as non-credible and may lead them to doubt their own perceptions and symptoms." Of course, I doubted my own perceptions. I knew in my heart, Kent needed attention and care.

KENT SAT ON THE CARPETED FLOOR IN THE FAMILY ROOM. FROM THE kitchen, I watched him saunter to the bench, throw the long bench pillow to the floor, and open the toy box/bench lid. "E, E, E," he shouted.

I ran downstairs and dove into the toy box and threw things on to the floor. "What do you want, Kent? Do you want this? Do you want that?" I picked up a large wooden letter E.

Kent smiled and took it out of my hands.

Does he know the letter E? I wondered.

The wooden letters were still on the floor. I spread them out again and walked back to the kitchen. Kent played quietly.

"Time for lunch, Kent."

He ignored me. I looked at the floor and saw a neat line of numbers from 1 to 20. Right under it, a perfect alphabet ordered from A to Z. What is this?

"Wow, Kent! You know all the numbers and letters? Did you learn that from Sesame Street?"

He looked me straight in the face and nodded.

I stocked up on books and strategies from the library and the Teacher's Store to encourage his speaking. Every day, Kent and I sat at the kitchen table spreading pictures to match or describe, retelling a short story. He identified animals and objects, but only after I told him, "Duck."

He recognized it, but could not formulate the word.

"How are you?" I asked.

"How are you?" he mumbled back.

Perhaps Kent had echolalia, not knowing the difference between *him* and *me*. He needed to learn to use "I" – as in, "I am fine" – at least that's what I assumed.

The quest continued for Kent and me. Every day. One hour.

Kurt's birth was imminent, with only weeks to go, when Kent slept through the night for the first time. The entire night. As did I.

I jumped out of bed and half ran to his room to see if he was breathing and asleep. He was. I slipped out of his room and accidentally hit the knob with my ring. Kent awoke.

LITERALLY ON MY DUE DATE, I GOT UP AND A WASH OF WATER SPILLED onto the kitchen floor. I cleaned it, changed. More water, more cleaning, more changing.

Wayne, surprisingly, was out of town (just a joke), so I called a friend who kindly took me to the hospital while our neighbour stayed with Tracey and Kent.

I put a call through to CP Air to contact Wayne, now flying over Lethbridge. "Tell him I will deliver soon and please, ask him to come to the hospital straightaway."

Though in the middle of a flight, he agreed. The CP Air scheduler found a replacement, Wayne disembarked and drove to the hospital. He entered in full uniform as his wife (me) lay moaning in the bed, swearing that this was enough.

"Three strikes and you're out," I reminded Wayne.

With no Dr. Dunn, and interns on strike, the nurses took over.

"This is my last one. Can I have a mirror?" I asked.

"Of course," they said.

One push, and a 9-pound, 8-ounce baby arrived. "It's a girl," I gushed.

Simultaneously, three nurses piped up in chorus: "No, it's not! It's a boy."

Another boy? I can't even call it when there's a mirror?

"Do *not* tell Wayne! I want to tell him this time," I pleaded.

"Congratulations! Congratulations!" Wayne said, hugging me till it hurt, which did not take much.

At Kurt's first official baby doctor appointment, Dr. Dunn suggested: "You really should have another. You were made for this."

"Will you guarantee a girl?" I quipped.

"No. No guarantee," he said with a smile.

"Well then, I can give you this guarantee: I'm done."

We often camped at Birch Bay or Lake Whatcom in Washington State, less than an hour from home. We walked the trails and sat with the kids on the water's edge as they explored and threw stones. Some friends often joined us.

Women fed and put kids in bed while the men built a big crackling fire. It was idyllic. Grown out of the tent, we'd moved on to Wayne's family tent trailer. I loved camping, particularly when the tent became a luxurious tent trailer that even had a little toilet.

By 8 p.m., with the kids in bed, adults sat around the fire to shoot the breeze, as they used to say. In the middle of a story, I looked up and saw Leon, three years old, literally shoot out of the tent trailer, hit the ground, and nonchalantly keep sleeping, not stirring.

Dick jumped up and gingerly picked Leon up, took him into the trailer, put him in his bed. Leon kept sleeping, none the wiser. The snap, snap, snap of the trailer curtain pieced together, Dick took his camp stool and sat down again by the fire.

Sometimes other friends stopped by to visit and brought a bottle of sweet rosé and talked me into a glass. I often gave in. A few hours later, in bed, regret kicked in. I felt it coming. I jumped over Wayne and whipped down the steps of the trailer to the nearest bush, where I dispensed the wine in short order. "Why did I agree to a drink?" I asked myself during the trip back to the trailer and, hopefully, a quiet night's sleep.

Back at home, Winnie, a school librarian, brought books along to read aloud and for the kids to enjoy on their own. With a library a short walk from our house, we became regulars. I saved boxes for weeks to prepare for the annual book sale, five cents a book. Winnie awoke a passion for stories captured in children's books. The bright orange fireplace in our family room became our read-aloud corner.

Stories engaged the kids. They never got bored, though Kurt was not as attentive as the other two. With each book, I introduced the title *and* the author. When they requested certain books in school or in the library, they asked by title and the author's name. Kurt's all-time favourite book was *Sylvester and the Magic Pebbles* by William Steig. It was the first book he asked for in Grade 2.

"It amazes me how Kurt asked for books by title and author," his teacher said.

TRACEY CONTINUED SWIMMING AND, BY AGE NINE, COMPLETED THE entire program. Waiting until she was eligible for the Red Cross certification at age 16, she joined a local swim club and swam competitively for the in-between years, hopping on her bike at 6 a.m. and again 6 p.m. for practice every day from May to September.

For a fundraiser, without much ado, Tracey slipped into the water and swam 200 lengths without a pause, using smooth, ballet-like open turns at each end. When shouts went up, "You did it, Tracey!" she sailed on, completing three more lengths before realizing she was done. She loved the water.

The boys shared Tracey's love of swimming. At the large pool, they dove from great heights before kindergarten. Lessons, however, were a different matter entirely. Kent performed up to standard, failing and re-doing a few courses along the way; Kurt loudly and adamantly shouted his distaste for swimming lessons. At one point he rode home on his bicycle to report: "I failed again," he yelled. "I have to repeat the course for the fourth time."

Unsympathetically, I responded: "Too bad, Kurt."

Swimming lessons shaped our summer days. The pool, only a few blocks from our house, was a handy distraction, and ultimately, gave the boys a lifetime skill.

LIVING IN THE MOUNTAINS MEANT SKIING, WHICH BECAME A FAMILY thing. Wayne took each of the kids, starting with Tracey, to the local mountains after school. She flourished. Kent's turn: he was a natural skier. Kurt, in true form, objected loudly, completely in line with his character; he refused to try. Wayne exhausted himself encouraging Kurt – though once he took to the slopes, he didn't quit. All except me learned to ski with skill and grace.

Frequently, I packed up the three kids and headed out from Ladner to Surrey in the summer to visit Winnie and pick berries with the kids. They ran through the fields and filled up with the fresh, ripe berries. The love of berries showed on their faces – strawberry/raspberry red, blueberry purple. They were a sight to see. Often, Winnie drove to Ladner to visit us. Eventually, she moved there.

Since we shared a passion for spontaneity, this proved very convenient.

"Want to go strawberry picking? Want to hit kids' clothes sales in Lynden?"

"Want to go to the library sale?"

"Want to buy a pressure canner to can cherries, peaches, and beans?" We took turns driving to the BC interior to purchase bushels of apples, peaches, and black cherries. We packed and froze peas, corn, strawberries, raspberries, and blueberries that we picked in Richmond. We did it all.

Winnie and I agreed to buy an applesauce maker. It worked. The kids argued, "It's my turn to turn the crank on the applesauce maker." They delightedly watched the clean, smooth applesauce leave one end and the cores, stems, and pits slid into the other. A magic machine.

I baked every week, though most importantly for birthdays. Out came the birthday cake book with pictures and instructions for about twenty-five cakes. Every cake began as a sheet cake. Instructions and diagrams showed how to cut the pieces to create a masterpiece.

Kent often chose a rocket, and Kurt an airplane with round

chocolate disks for windows. My favourite: Tracey's ballerina, a perfect bun in her hair, arms arced over her head, leg raised against her knee. It duplicated the pale blue satin ballet outfit Tracey wore for the Christmas ballet recital with pink leotards and ballet slippers. For Christmas, I made a doll to match. Birthday parties were exciting, like their Christmas wish lists. They decided how to celebrate. The wave pool proved the best excursion. A hit.

EAGER AND AMBITIOUS AND IN THE FLYING GROOVE NOW, WAYNE SET up his own construction company and bought a lot two doors from our house, where he built a beautiful house. In the hot market, the house sold in a few days. He called it "keeping himself occupied between flights." I could not have disagreed more.

I often wished he was more present, though I might have misjudged that. Tracey later wrote that she "had the only dad who came along on school trips, especially skating." Of course, it was "normal" to them. Well past the 18-month trial period at the airline, he earned a good salary, meaning that finally, the house got furnished.

Visits by Moe
1978

M oe and Mr. V. came every September – poor timing,
though, since I was organizing, buying last-minute school
items in preparing for school.

Moe did not say, "I will stay with Jack."

She didn't enjoy staying with my brother. My sister-in-law
Audrey casually tossed hot baked potatoes around for everyone to
catch. "How uncivilized," Moe said. The indignity was too much
for her. I should have asked, "Why do you like staying with us
more than anyone else?" But I didn't. I was always afraid and
stressed for the entire visit.

As always, Moe announced a reminder: "It's 10 a.m. Where is
the coffee?" or "It's already five minutes after 3, where is the tea?"
or "Shake up the potatoes after cooking them. I like them better
that way."

Privately, Wayne said, "Don't shake the potatoes. I don't like
them that way."

Anxiety. I stood between them, feeling like a pushmi-pullyu.

WAYNE'S FLIGHT SCHEDULE KEPT HIM EITHER AT HOME OR FAR AWAY ON
a 24-hour clock. Every week a different schedule, though they
scheduled his flying for three months at a time.

Step by step, painfully, I learned to accommodate. I began
carefully. From the time we moved into the new house, everything
closed at 5 p.m.: drawing the drapes, locking doors, turning on
lights when dusk settled, or even when it didn't. On Saturdays, a
babysitter stayed overnight. Being the only adult in the house
terrified me, though I never let the children know. Every week, the
Saturday shivers brought back my friend's rape and with it, dark
dread surrounded me.

I had to register kids, bring them to birthday parties, watch them play baseball, dance, ice skating . . .As a matter of course, scheduled flights fell on birthdays, anniversaries, at the birth of children, holidays, Christmas, and long weekends. Eventually I had no choice but to forego inflexibility ("Christmas is on December 25th!") and rigidity ("We cannot change that!") to adjust and accommodate. Make the best of things.

One Christmas, the telephone jangled loudly at 4 in the morning. "I have to go to Japan and fly every day there until the 2nd of January," Wayne called out, in a rare fit of frustration. "How can you cancel a seven-day trip on Christmas Day? I would never do that." He was right. He would never do that.

"Wake up! Time to open Christmas gifts," I shouted, running up the stairs.

Bedraggled, rubbing their eyes, the kids asked, "Why? What happened?"

Wayne was already in full uniform. Piles of unopened gifts were spread out under the tree. Making up (and then some) for the Christmases I did not get presents, I over-purchased for my kids to outrageous levels (although the pile included new underwear, pajamas and socks). "Hurry, hurry. Dad has to go."

They tore through the packages. Wayne left. We continued our own small Christmas. I became Santa. Together we crumpled all the wrapping and ribbons and put them in large paper bags. Opening Christmas gifts never waited until the 25th of December again. We opened gifts about five days before the actual holiday when Wayne was home.

On alternate years, everyone came to the Kooys in Lynden. Wayne was excused. The kids loved their cousins. Gift opening met with joy and laughter. Games indoors with Grandma.

Alternate summers, Wayne's family hosted a Kooy Kamparee. The adults had a golf competition while the cousins played, ate, and sat around nighttime campfires together. The importance of family was a living thing. Cousins knew each other, their grandparents, their aunts and uncles, and even great grandparents.

It took time for me to adapt and adjust; my family had no such loyalties, other than the occasional Christmas dinner. With Ontario so far away and Wayne's schedule so fluid, we never visited my relatives in Ontario for Christmas. I probably would not have gone, even given the chance. I treasured the idea of my kids having a relationship with their Kooy cousins.

EVERY WEEKEND I FULFILLED MY PERCEIVED OBLIGATION AND CALLED Moe. It got more difficult to find something, anything, to talk about. Frustrated, I could feel my body tighten and my face get frustration red. Mostly, I listened. Moe never asked about me or Wayne or the children. It's true, though, that she never forgot about Wayne's church attendance: "How many Sundays does Wayne work this month?"

I grimaced. By her standards, one Sunday of flying was not perfect (B grade) because he still worked (flying) and ate in restaurants (making others work). Missing four out of four Sundays was an F, no redeeming it.

I rejected outright this Pharisaic, self-righteous approach, but I did not say so aloud. I just brooded.

No congratulations. No curiosity about my life. No concern for Kent and his hearing difficulties. It made me angry, yet I did not challenge or ask for explanations.

Chapter Twenty-Two

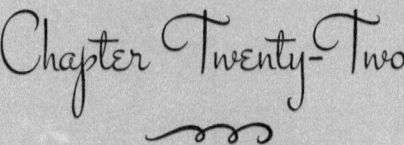

The Accident
1978

Tonight *was an ordinary peaceful night until in the middle of the silence, the phone rang. It changed everything.* Loud ringing, jangling sounds. The phone? Too early. I stumbled out of bed, lumbered down the stairs and gingerly picked it the receiver. The big clock in the kitchen read 2:30 am.

The speaker on the phone, slowly and somberly, said: "Mrs. Kooy?"

"Yes," I whispered.

"I am so sorry to report an accident that has resulted in one death, though the individual has not yet been identified."

"I have four names here: Winnie, Sherry, Jake, and Dick." Passengers in the accident included my best friend (Winnie) and another teacher friend (Sherry), along with their husbands, Dick and Jake.

"We will let you know as soon as the identification is completed," she said.

A blow. My body stiffened. I wanted to block this out. Start over. Why was I the first to hear this? How would they know to contact me? Why was this happening? Thanking her, I gently I hung up the phone, headed to the bathroom, two stairs at a time, yanked up the toilet seat and vomited. I stood paralyzed. What do I do now?

My three kids slept soundly in their beds, unaware of the storm in the kitchen. I was on my own, weeping, waiting, praying. I trembled and shivered uncontrollably. What do I do now? I grabbed a sofa blanket, spread it on the cold kitchen floor, lay down and waited.

A SECOND PHONE CALL. HANDS SHAKING, LEGS QUIVERING, I SOBBED; the receiver shook as I raised it to my ear. My teacher friend Sherry, deceased; my best friend in a deep coma. The two men survived, both with broken bones.

Wayne arrived the following morning, opening the front door with his usual jovial greeting: "I'm home!" I ran into his arms, face swollen and red from the crying. He held me tightly. "What happened?" In my calmest, blubbering voice, I relayed the events, Sherry's death, Winnie's coma and the men's broken bones. Tears rolled down our cheeks.

This started the cycle of hospital visits. Winnie remained in a coma. She did not move, though occasionally, she seemed vaguely aware – an eyelid flutter or a spontaneous jerky arm movement.

The nurses caring for Winnie warned me, "Don't discuss anything you don't want her to hear. She can hear you even when she doesn't respond." I took that seriously. I told Winnie stories of our kids, reminisced about our six-day stays in the hospital with the births of our children, Kent and Sherry, our hopes for making applesauce again.

On one visit, I heard a husky, completely unexpected voice say: "Where are my legs?"

I was dumbfounded. It was week seven since the accident, and I'd only once barely seen Winnie move, let alone talk. "Under the blanket," I said, gently. Groaning, gently shaking her head, Winnie muttered, "No." She turned away from me with no more words or even gestures.

Two days later, in church teaching a church girls' group class, a friend approached. No need to say anything. I knew. The feeling of numbness took over my body.

"WINNIE PASSED AWAY," SHE SAID SOLEMNLY AND TEARFULLY, AND turned away. I grabbed my purse and coat and opened the door to a drizzling rain. Climbed in the car, tears flowing.

I had failed to realize that Winnie would die. This was seven weeks after the accident. My world became so small, so focused on my pain, that I could not be the mother I wanted to be or that the kids deserved. There is reason, you might say: I was inconsolable, bitter, angry. All of those things. I slogged my way through caring for the kids, making meals, household chores, and birthday cakes. For seven weeks, I visited the hospital to spend time with my silent friend.

MY DAYS WERE FULL; THREE YOUNG CHILDREN TOOK CENTRE PLACE. I struggled to keep the pieces together. Every night before bath-time, I gathered my brood nightly to sit around the family room fireplace and read stories aloud. Dr. Seuss's books, astounding picture books, funny, sad, rhyming, and heartwarming were added to the repertoire. They were a powerful buffer.

Winnie was my best friend. The loss proved heart-rending. She was the companion who often filled spaces left by Wayne's away times, camped with us every weekend, and shared books for children. I was utterly bereft.

There was a reason to be inconsolable, bitter, angry. I was. I slogged my way through the care for the kids, household chores, birthdays and other celebrations, dance recitals, baseball, soccer, and, in summer, swimming. In short, I could not be the mother I wanted to be or that the kids deserved.

REV. G. CONDUCTED WINNIE'S FUNERAL IN WHAT I HAVE COME TO call a "no name" service. Winnie's name was not mentioned. I felt sick for the ignoring and a deep anger. I needed more. I wanted comfort. I sought out a James Wendell Johnson poem, "A Funeral Sermon," which included, in particular, these deeply moving, comforting (for me) words:

And God said: Go down, Death, go down,
. . . And find Sister Caroline.
She's borne the burden and heat of the day,
She's labored long in my vineyard,
And she's tired --
She's weary -
Go down, Death, and bring her to me. . .

And Death began to ride again—
Up beyond the evening star. . .
On to the Great White Throne.
And there he laid Sister Caroline
On the loving breast of Jesus.

And Jesus took his own hand and wiped away her
tears,
And he smoothed the furrows from her face,
And Jesus rocked her in his arms,
And kept a-saying: Take your rest,
Take your rest, take your rest.

I memorized sections of the poem to recite, sometimes orally, sometimes silently, "She's resting," I repeated to myself.

My functioning was reduced to feeding and cleaning. I was depressed, morose, lonely. The kids walked on eggshells, knowing something was askew in the world; they were eight, four, and two years old at the time. I felt unhinged, connected to nothing. Without Winnie, the days stretched out in slow motion. Wayne's flights seemed longer. The entire world felt askew.

AMERICAN RADIO BROADCASTER PAUL HARVEY HAD A POPULAR SHOW on ABC called *Paul Harvey News and Comment*. Each show introduced a moving, powerful story. Midway, he stopped and went on with the program, leaving his frustrated listeners eager for more. Relief came towards the program's end when he famously ended with: "*And now for the rest of the story.*" And now, I say, for the rest of my story . . .

About a year after the funerals, my husband Wayne (home between flights) said: "Let's talk. Seems you can't pick yourself up. How can I help?" I nodded in agreement. It was true; sorrow had moved into my body and settled there. Wayne continued: "I know you planned to return to school when all the kids were in school full time, but that is a few years off. What if you started now? Started small? Stay till you are satisfied you have reached your goals."

"In the meantime, I promise you that on the days I am home, I will take care of everything with the kids and the house and the class trips, so you have time to study." He made an offer I could not refuse. Wayne was (and remains) my saving grace.

Kent
1979

K ent's speech problems increased. Four years old now, he still was difficult to understand. He often just watched on the sidelines at the kids on the street. Neighbours warned their kids, "don't play with that crazy kid," and most did not.

Overwhelming sadness overcame Kent and me. A pivotal, critical moment. How could they judge Kent for something completely out of his control? I watched my little boy, lost and sad. He mourned for Winnie: she had loved Kent, and he loved her. He understood sadness. He missed her.

"Kent! Kent!" I called when I couldn't find him in the house.

Frantic, I flew out the front door, worrying that he had found his way into the deep ditch behind the house across the street. I called neighbours to help. "I can't find Kent," I hollered. When we didn't find him, I ran back into the house, taking the steps two at a time, opened the bedroom door – and to my incredible delight, Kent sat quietly on the end of my bed, watching television.

I ran to him, tears running down my face, hugging him again and again.

After more than a year of teaching him with little progress, I knew I needed help. I registered him in a new, most-interesting local nursery school that accepted typical and atypical children. They had a bevy of services to meet the varying needs. A godsend. He went happily as we walked down the cul-de-sac to the school located in a little old white church at the end of our street. I approached the staff at the pre-school for strategies and practices to advance his learning, and asked a teacher: "Could I make an appointment to discuss my son Kent's speech difficulties?"

"Of course. The audiologist is here every Thursday." "He can't hear," the audiologist said. "He needs to be tested at Children's Hospital in Vancouver.

After Kent went through the hearing test, the audiologist called me over. "His hearing is very limited. We need to test it further." Surprised, I said, "But my doctor tested him with a tuning fork and said he could hear."

"The problem was the tuning fork used by your doctor. It rings out only a singular pure sound, but the world consists of multiple sounds that mix and mingle. He needs to be fully and thoroughly tested."

For that, I needed Dr. K's signature. Wasting no time, I went to see Dr. K. and explained. "You don't need to do that," he said, when I handed him the documents. "I have a friend who's an audiologist. I'll contact him."

I didn't know what to call it then, but it amounted (again) to gaslighting.

Calmly, I responded: "I don't think so. See this chair I am sitting in? I'm staying here as long as it takes for you to sign this paper. I have been working with Kent daily on his speech for about two years, and he still cannot be understood. You told me he could hear, based only on holding a tuning fork to his ear."

I waited. I repeated: "I am not moving."

Grumbling under his breath, he signed.

This time I did not say "thank you" when I left the office.

The need to help Kent overrode any need to follow a family doctor's advice. I felt strong. I was Kent's mother. I loved him and wanted the best for him. Whatever it took. Finally, I felt strong enough to hold up my son and take deliberate action. He needed help I could not provide, so I worked until it became possible.

Wayne and I took Kent to the Children's Hospital for three days filled with a multitude of tests. On Day one, we entered a room with a large glass window. An audiologist explained and demonstrated to Kent. Looking him straight in the eye, using gestures, he said slowly enough and loudly enough: "When you hear a *beep*, throw a block into this little bucket."

Intently, the way he watched television, Kent focused on the audiologist. I figured he was watching to see when he moved ever so slightly. Each time, he turned to me: "Wasthatabeep?" Then he tossed the block in the little bucket.

After the first day, a doctor met with us and confirmed Kent could hear in the first test.

Day two, a blow. The doctor suggested Kent probably only had an IQ of 80, because in the tests, he drew only heads. Bodies were missing. I sensed the doctor simply wasn't aware yet that Kent's minimal hearing had skewed the hearing test results negatively.

On day three, tests measured pressure on his eardrums. They stayed completely flat. No movement. It looked as though nothing penetrated. Discussing the final report, the doctor said, "Good thing you have such a loud voice, Mary. Some of that voice obviously came through."

Kent needed surgery for repairs in his ears. I stayed with him overnight. The following day, after successful surgery, we headed home and sang songs all the way and carried on little Sesame Street conversations. He knew every word.

At home, sitting at the table, Kent dramatically put his hands over his ears: *"Too roud. Too roud,"* he said. Within a month, he spoke clearly enough to be understood.

Oh, the gift of that little nursery school, there the moment Kent needed it. It changed Kent's life and ultimately, also my life and my teaching.

Ladner, BC
1979

My days were full; three young children took centre place. I struggled to keep the pieces together. I gathered my brood nightly to sit around the family room fireplace and read stories aloud.

Wayne often had scheduled flights three or four days a week. It seemed he either arrived at the end or left in the middle of things. To meet the challenge, I overcompensated. Gifts at Christmas almost buried the tree. My children acknowledged they pretty well got everything on their Sears catalogue list for Christmas, and I made birthday cakes of ballerinas, airplanes, and rockets. I spent entire evenings wrapping and writing names on sticky tags. Piles of gifts included their entire wish list. Every year, I told the kids: "This is it. I must tone it down." It never happened.

"It's been almost a year since Winnie died, Wayne said. "You're still so sad, Mary." I could hardly disagree, but neither could I offer a solution. Wayne continued: "I have a proposal: how do you feel about returning to school? We decided long ago that you'd go back when the kids were in school full-time. It's a little ahead of plan, but this seems like a good time."

Shocked, surprised, and even happy to have something else to think about, the offer astounded me. Wayne was strong, dependable, and knowledgeable. He just knew how to do things.

"If you agree, we'll use my three-month schedule. When I'm home, I'll take complete responsibility for the kids and chores like laundry, shopping, extra cleaning, driving to lessons or games and school trips. Your extra time will be for reading and studying. What do you think? You could start with one course a semester and see if that works."

Astounded, my eyes lit up. Could this be a tipping point? A way through? Paul Harvey famously ended his popular radio show with: "And now here is the rest of the story:" You could imagine the audience leaning in. Good stories do that.

"WHERE CAN I FIND THE BUILDING FOR REGISTRATION AND VISITOR parking?" I asked the attendant at the UBC wicket. "Would you have a campus map?"

He reached out with a map and explained and pointed. From the nearest visitor lot, I made the journey on foot to the Administration building. In the main hallway, a sign overhead read: Registration.

I stood at the end of a short line, waiting my turn at an available wicket. My hands were sweating, but I was not tempted to leave. I waited.

A large square woman with a brush cut (completely new to me) called out in a loud, clear voice, "Next?" With essential papers in hand, I moved forward, greeted the woman politely, and explained: "I'm here to have my transcripts evaluated." I slid the papers under the raised glass, my mind a whirlwind: why did I think I should come here? I will never be admitted.

Brush cut quickly secured the papers and skimmed them – her hands stopping when she saw *Calvin College* across the top. "I hope you didn't attend some little sectarian school," she sneered. "We don't give credit for religion courses."

"I'm not looking for a bargain," I assured her. "I want to know where I stand and what I do to get registered for one course." Was that my voice? Did I just say that?

Brush cut frowned. "It will take time to evaluate this. Count on a minimum of six weeks."

"Thank you."

Feet heavy, I walked and plopped, exhausted, into the car and took a big breath before driving out of the visitor parking lot and into the scenic Point Grey waterside.

A LARGE BROWN ENVELOPE ARRIVED WITH THE UBC SYMBOL ON IT. MY hands trembled a little as I gingerly tore open the top. "Your Bachelor of Arts," it read, "fully satisfies the academic requirements."

I read it and read it again – Wayne was not home to enjoy the moment, so I indulged myself with a piece of cake and read the rest of the letter until I'd almost memorized it. Within ten days after the wicket woman, who, for some unknown reason, failed to intimidate me, the whole thing was settled. I was able to take any two courses to give evidence of my academic ability before removing the condition and continuing into a specific program. I'd been there before, all the way back in my one-day kindergarten career. "I can do this," I thought.

The wait for the transcript review led to many conversations about how the frighteningly challenging options would materialize. Wayne and I agreed that, if accepted, I would take one course per semester and complete the course readings (available before the course began) during the summer. The kids still needed a lot of my time and attention, but they developed independence. Tracey was going into Grade 3, Kent would start kindergarten in the Fall, and Kurt was in morning preschool. This would be possible.

I headed back to UBC to register for two courses: *Victorian Novels* and *Assessment in Education*. When I completed registration, I flapped my schedule in the air and confidently shouted (to the car): "Victorian Novels, here I come!"

THE *VICTORIAN NOVELS* CLASS MET ONCE A WEEK FROM 5 TO 8 P.M. IN the UBC English building. One empty seat along the back wall remained. I sat there rigid, freezing cold, hands folded on my lap. I nodded to students filling the seats around me—I was by far the oldest person in the class.

Right on the minute, the professor, nattily dressed, each silver-grey hair in place, entered the classroom and introduced the course.

The voice thundered again: "The paper is due the last week of the semester. I want a 5,000-word paper on *one word* from one of the assigned novels.

One word? I must not have heard that right. Five thousand words on one word? Anxious, unable to imagine myself even remotely capable of managing this assignment, I climbed into my car, tears rolling down my cheeks, shoulders hunched. Slowly, I made my way behind a row of cars to the campus exit and home to Ladner.

Ultimately, I chose the one word, "love" for the paper.

The process drained me. The one course became a full-time endeavour. I used every minute when the kids were in school. I had time.

Exam time. It had been fifteen years since I last wrote a three-hour university exam. Panic. My hands cramped, cold and trembling. "Get a grip, Mary," I reprimanded myself. No choice but to put all books under the desk and begin. My arms tensed as I picked up the exam and scanned it. Three questions.

I started with the first. My hand flew over the paper—so much to say! I began on the second question, again racing non-stop to include everything I had learned and understood. I checked my watch. To my horror, only fifteen minutes of the three hours remained. I stoked the fire inside and scrambled to scribble until the professor said, "Fifteen minutes."

Exam submitted. I walked out into the darkness to the car. Why had I not kept track of the time? Would I even pass? Much hung on this course. Grades arrived: First course? B.

Second semester: *Assessment in Education* offered lessons in learning and teaching. Just what I need, I thought.

The instructor, a professorial caricature, read straight from his yellowed pages of chapter notes through the entire class while a Teaching Assistant stood awkwardly by. I read and reread the required chapters on evaluation to prepare for class. Weekly quizzes. The first two quizzes left me disappointed. True/False still confused me, as it came in small, unrelated bits and pieces. Sometimes, each option fit. No explanations required. I did better with the bigger picture.

My mark for the first quiz fell in the 60s; the second in the 70s.

The TA stopped me on my way out the door. "Mary, can we talk for a minute? You wrote the right answers for the hard questions and the wrong answers for the hard ones."

A small two-pronged epiphany: first, focus on the questions I knew first. Second, I switched from pleasing the professor and started taking the course for my own benefit. I needed to drive myself *for* myself.

The TA gave me the confidence to change. Each weekly quiz from that point on reaped an A. I received an A in the course. When was the last time I'd had an A in a course? Too long ago to remember.

My fears of inadequacy softened. How was my motivation spiked? Thanks to Wayne, room for new vistas and goals became possible. No more hunching and averting eyes. Motivation blazed. I was on fire with a passion for learning and teaching. The letter came soon after the two completed courses. The letter noted that two successfully completed courses were removed from the conditional status. I was free to apply to the Faculty of Education's one-year program. Could this be an end to my years of "fake teacher" status?

A UBC EDUCATION DEPARTMENT LETTER NOTED THAT IN THEIR FINAL review, they found a missing course: "Outstanding requirement: *Philosophy of Education.*"

In going through the process of admission, I thought I had taken all the necessary steps. I found an advisor who read my transcript and initialed "full credit" for the course. What happened?

Concerned, I asked for a meeting.

Dr. B. said, "Good thing you didn't approach me on this—I

would not have accepted it, but as you say, the credit has been awarded. So, on you go."

When the Dutch face a challenge, people wish them strength. I needed strength to store all information carefully and to question, even challenge, where warranted. Taking responsibility and ownership made me grow. As the popular posters of the day noted: "Bloom where you are planted. I was blooming. I applied and was accepted into the Teacher Education program.

ADMISSION TO THE FACULTY OF EDUCATION TO DO A B.ED. WOULD remove the "fake" status from my evolving teacher self. I eagerly looked forward to student teaching and seeing how the public school compared to the Christian schools I'd known. I dug in. My teaching experience reduced my required practice teaching to just one six-week session at Richmond High School.

In the relatively small high school with 600 or 700 students, my supervising teacher had no time to supervise; he was planning a conference in the faculty lounge and supervised me *in absentia*. I drew from the knowledge acquired earlier, teaching at elementary, secondary, and college levels, as well as the evaluation education course.

After each bell, students poured into the halls. The principal joined the crowded hallways, tapped students on the shoulder, and called them by name. Students respected him. It was obvious by the looks on their faces when he greeted them by name. In return, they warmly greeted him: "Hi, Sir!" in return.

At an academic conference some years later, I attended a session by Israeli researchers, who observed that the hallway reflected the classroom. This high school was a case in point: the tone of the hallway reflected the behaviours in classrooms. These kids walked the hallways in an easy, calm manner.

My confidence grew. I don't know what I expected from the public high school, but it was a significant departure from what I imagined. These were happy kids. No acting out. In my classes, students responded positively. They appreciated being allowed to make choices—here are three books, pick one. Reading the opening paragraph offered a larger context.

The principal stopped me in the hall and asked, "Mary, would you mind if I observed your class?"

"Of course," I said. I was a bit taken aback, a bit complimented.

The next day, with a soft knock on the door, the principal slipped into an empty seat at the back of the room. He stayed for the entire class and even participated a few times.

As the students left after class, he said: "You sure had their attention. Does your supervising teacher observe you daily?"

"Not really…" I answered reluctantly.

"I will tell him he's to watch you. He will learn more about effective teaching."

The atmosphere, the inclusion, the environment—all these upended my educational understanding, which had been limited to Christian schools. Contrary to accepted, unquestioned beliefs, my public teaching experiences promised to open spaces and expand my worldviews.

With a completed Bachelor of Education, I contemplated the next steps.

"I can't stop now," I said to Wayne.

Wayne agreed that my going back to teaching school was not in the best interest of our family. Everything changed in his schedule every three months. If not teaching, what next?

"Keep going," Wayne said. "You know it works. We'll adjust as we go."

Several professors encouraged me to pursue an MA in Language Education. My reflections about teaching, even at this stage of my life, continued to evolve and change. I had a choice. I did not have to teach or work or bring in a pay cheque like my siblings. Wayne, established in his career, made it possible for me to continue and backed me fully.

Returning to my Roots
Spring 1979

Wayne, whose spontaneous delight in flying continued unabated, could not believe his good fortune. When we sat down to talk that evening after the kids were in bed, stories of flying to Schiphol Airport and Amsterdam poured out.

As a DC-10 First Officer, Captains invited him along to see the sights in Amsterdam: Schiphol. Uitsmijter (fried egg, ham and Gouda cheese). The big markets. Broodje van Kootje, prostitution sold at picture windows, pot puffs wafting on to the streets from some restaurants, De Vijf Vliegen (Five Flies) restaurant, Indonesian food (Nasi Goreng).

Wayne said, "Let's go on a Dutch holiday. You need to see it, to get a view of your birthplace. You will enjoy what you see and eat!" I agreed, and it would be my first time back in twenty-six years. I was eight when we left. Gratefully, Wayne's mother offered to stay with the children in our home.

The sun shone brightly as the plane descended into Amsterdam. Row upon row of tulips painted in brilliant reds, yellows, whites, and orange tulips filled the landscape. Postcard images could not fully capture that astounding view – tulips bloomed everywhere.

Wayne and I walked and talked. I was profoundly moved, particularly when I visited my three aunts, sisters to Pa, who lived in the same seniors' home. We had talks and tea.

One said, "You look exactly like your Pa."

"I wish," I said to myself, but "Thank you," I said to her.

My Aunt in Stroe invited us to stay for midday dinner. My cousin was home; we'd never met but had the most wonderful conversation. Feelings stirred; unwarranted resistance faded.

We walked around downtown Baarn, the place of my birth, where the market was filled with stalls of fruit, vegetables, meat, licorice candies, clothes, and flowers. We crossed bridges and found my real school, our church, and the house on Heuveloordtstraat.

To my utter delight, I visited with my childhood neighbour, Mrs. Surksum, who warmly welcomed me in, made a cup of tea and told me stories about her family. My friend Willie had died tragically young, and Mrs. V. was now all alone in her house. I gave her a warm, long hug when I had to leave. Lots of memories were revived.

We drove through the countryside, ditches and canals on either side—black-and-white cows and white sheep in the fields. We visited Zeeland (Sea Land), crossing over the the Haringvliet Water Works. Water endangered the country and needed to be reliably controlled. Canals everywhere. The country is known for its mathematical prowess, apparently because of the water issues.

Every time we stopped for gas or directions or a bite to eat, Wayne kept urging me: "Speak Dutch."

To him, I sounded like a native, though it had been over twenty years since I spoke Dutch. Wayne could not speak Dutch, so anything not English amazed him.

"You still speak Dutch? I can understand, but it's quite old-fashioned," the Dutch told me.

Of course. That made sense. Language changes. Radically, though not necessarily what was dropped but what was added. Think technology, for instance.

I gained a new appreciation for the land, the spaces, and culture, and a reviving awareness of my roots, which had been suppressed for a long time. For so long, my Dutch identity had been a source of shame and embarrassment. Now, we wandered the streets in Amsterdam and crossed the square with a palace home to Queen Beatrix. Bold organ music invited us into a free concert in the church in Amsterdam Square. A visit to Het Bosje Van Ijsendijk brought back memories of Anne in the pond and a speculaas windmill cookie. We admired Drakenstijn in Laage Vuursche (very close to Baarn), where Princess Beatrix raised her family. We stayed in a classic Dutch hotel with no elevator and narrow, curvy stairs. Great street food (small puff pancakes called *poffertjes*). Almost too much to take in.

Home again to my Canadian reality. Upon arrival home, Wayne's mother said, "The kids were great, but Kent wet the bed every night when you were gone."

Puzzled, I asked him, "What's going on, Kent?"

He put his head down, shifted his feet, and pursed his lips. Kent was so vulnerable. Finally, he could no longer hold it back and blurted out: "Miss Pat hits me. She slaps me hard at recess and noontime when I am slow getting my work done. She does it when the kids are all outside. She said, 'If you tell your mother, I will. . .'

The dam burst. I pleaded with God and pleaded with Wayne. "Make this stop. I am not sending them back to that school."

Why did I not approach the teacher directly? If we stayed, Kent, I was sure, would pay with more abuse. I wanted them out.

In hindsight, I realize we should not only have left the school immediately but reported this abuse to the police.

Chapter Twenty-Three

The School Problem
1980 - 1984

"I don't know if *you* want to stay here, but the kids and I will be gone in September," I told Wayne with anger and certainty. Wayne resisted any change. I resisted his resistance.

I DID NOT INVESTIGATE OPTIONS OR ALTERNATIVE PUBLIC SCHOOLS IN Surrey. I called only the Christian School in Surrey. Tony, the principal, agreed to register the kids. Stuck in a way of thinking, a way of believing that Christian schools were a non-negotiable requirement for Reformed Christian living, I caved.

Why, I ask now, did I not leave the system? Like a cult member, I felt forbidden to challenge, question, or seek alternatives such as a good public school. I should, of course, have left the flock. I was an outlier. I felt helpless, not ready to make out of the box decisions. I thought I was stronger.

"WHAT DO YOU NEED IN THIS HOUSE? MAKE ME A LIST OF WHAT YOU and the kids need," Wayne instructed me.

A kitchen bar, I wrote, where the kids could sit so we could talk and eat snacks. The list grew: An office with a built-in desk, a chair, and shelves for books. A room for the piano (Tracey) and drums (Kent). A basketball hoop, outside, of course.

Wayne returned with a striking drawing of a modern home.

THE KIDS ATTENDED CHRISTIAN SCHOOL: TRACEY, NOW IN GRADE 7; Kent, in Grade 4; and Kurt, in Grade 2. Tracey jumped in, excited to meet new friends. Tony, the principal, was her Grade 7 teacher. He loved kids, and they loved him. He had eight kids of his own.

My concern again was for Kent, who said little or nothing about his teacher, a humourless, mean-spirited woman. I was suspicious of teachers with no sense of humour. They took themselves entirely too seriously

Very bright, a reader long before entering school, Kent did his work and completed his assignments. He loved Bible stories and listened carefully as his teacher read one aloud. "Retell the story you heard in your bible class notebook," she told the class. Kent immediately went to work.

The end of the world has come to Judah
(Excerpt as written by Kent, unedited)

For Judah, it's the end of the world. Neco, the pharah of Egpt attacked Judah one day while the war was on against Media and Syria against Assyria.

It wasn't Neco's fault. All he wanted to do was to get past Judah so he could help Assyria fight against Media and Syria.. . .

It all happened this way. . . .

On the way there, scouts reported that Josiah's troops were blocking the way. Neco scoffed when he hears this news. "What's the poor man doing? Trying to commit suercide? Ha!" then Neco became more serious. "Send some messengers," he gruffly said. "Tell Josiah to move his troops by morning or they die." The messengers went to Josiah and reported the message. But the reply from Josiah did not suit Neco. "We shall keep our ground," said Josiah. Neco sent two more messages. They both responded to by the same stubborn answer, "You shall not pass."

Finally, Neco sent 1 more message saying, "Move your men Josiah, because I am coming through." Josiah just sent back his same old stubborn answer: "You shall not pass. So there was a great battle in the morning. And by nightfall, Josiah was dead.

He handed it in. Some years later, packing for a house move, I discovered this retelling in a box. I read. I became angry when I saw an x over each "error" in spelling. The teacher's comment read, *"Too bad you didn't finish this, Kent. 4/10.*

I cried.

SOMETIME LATER, I READ THE STORY ALOUD TO KENT. "WOW! DID I get an A+?" Need I say more?

As I distributed the clean essay in a workshop to the principals, they began their work of reading and marking. "This essay was written by a nine-year-old Grade 4 student; I began the workshop for principals interested in evaluation for their teachers. The teacher asked the class to retell a Bible story she read to them." I distributed the essay and added: "Think about the evaluation process. How would you instruct your teachers to evaluate this piece?"

I watched as one principal beside me circled every spelling error and put a giant, red C- on the top. If this persisted, I knew I would get emotional. An idea hit at the right moment. I asked them to quietly reflect on what they had read and evaluated. The same words and very different evaluations.

"What does this mean?" I asked.

Awkward silence.

I led a brief discussion on the purpose of the writing (a retelling), which was done in class (not homework), collected, and marked as a first draft. How is it possible that the same words and the same instruction led to such a range of grades? Should writing a retelling in class get a grade at all? Instead, I chose to have the principals around the large table read their grades and comments aloud. It began with a C-, right beside me. A hush settled in the room. It was awkward. Grades ranged from A to D+; only two principals wrote any comments; the two were women.

The next step would have been for the principals to try the same exercise and discuss the role and meaning behind each of the marks. But this was a workshop, and in education, that meant a one-off. Lost opportunity.

CONSTRUCTION ON OUR HOUSE BEGAN WHILE WE LIVED IN A SMALL, rented place close to Surrey Christian School. Kurt often went to the huge backyard and threw balls, without fail, in the direction of a picture window. Repeatedly, I hollered out: "Kurt, turn the other way with the ball. You'll break a window."

Done. Broken window. With a sigh implying, "I told you so," I called the glass repair shop. Someone came that day. The repairman removed the broken window and showed it to me. "This window is loose and unsecured. Someone slipped it in the slot and just left it."

Great. I was home with the kids in a strange neighbourhood. Hoped no one watched or saw.

Some months later, a neighbourhood cat got trapped in the house. Try as we might – opening doors and windows – the cat evaded us. It could be found nowhere in the house. Finally, we assumed it found a way out and was no longer in the house.

Wrong. In the middle of the night, the howls of a trapped cat interrupted our sleep. We jumped out of bed and ran to see. The cat had apparently tried to get out the living room window and, when unsuccessful, clung to the drapes with his nails on the strips of cloth. Tracey ran to open the front door and put up a human barricade. The cat, trapped with no other place to go, saw the front door and screamed out of the house.

FRIEND AND PRINCIPAL JOHN M. (WHO TOOK ME TO THE PARTY WHERE I met Wayne) asked me to do a three-month replacement at his high school for a teacher on leave. A class, mostly boys, were unable or unwilling to take French and assigned drama instead. Probably wanting to make things easy for me, the regular teacher had left instructions to assign a chapter and ask students to make notes and answer the chapter questions.

Motivation sank, including mine. I didn't blame the students. It was easy but not relevant enough to be remotely interesting to them. Blubbering, mumbling, "I'll be back soon." I left in a panic and walked to John's office and knocked, still wiping away the tears.

John opened the door. One look at my tear-stained face, and tears appeared in his own eyes. He extended his arms and offered a big hug. We sat and talked and determined a few other strategies to motivate some helpful learning for the students and me. I have few memories of that teaching job, but I will never forget John, a principal who cared and the difference that made.

Walt Disney moves in
Summer, 1986

D *ing, dong.*
    I jogged down the hall and opened the door to two casually dressed, smiling people. "We are location managers looking for a site to make a movie, and we're interested in your house," one said. Outrageous, I thought. "Let me check with my husband," I said.

Wayne didn't trust the request. A recent robbery across the street involved two men coming to the door selling paintings. They returned when no one was home until Jo returned from the grocery store. In the driveway, she called the police. In their walkabout, Jo was sickened – the intruders had urinated and defecated on the walls and floors before flying out the deck doors at the back.

Back to the movie set request. A police officer friend, Bill, offered to check the location managers' claim. To our complete surprise, he said: "It's legit! It's the Walt Disney Corporation! The working title is *Hero in the Family*. Lucky you!"

In a formal meeting, we listened to the process of filming. We signed the agreement. Soon a large convoy of movie-support vehicles including motor homes, dressing rooms, film star quarters, canteen and portable bathrooms filled a large bare lot behind our house.

We moved out of our house and into a large motorhome in the middle of the movie equipment. We turned down the offer of a hotel room since the entire process would be a powerful learning experience for Wayne, me, and our three kids aged 16, 13, and 11. Instead, we accepted the offer of a motorhome that stood alongside three more on our property: the others served as a kitchen, a viewing room (where we could all watch them review the day's filming), and a respite motorhome for relaxing and napping. We often ate with the crew and actors, enjoying phenomenal menus.

The following day, the cast and crew arrived *en masse*. The dismantling of our house began. The house became a movie set: different carpet, doorknobs, lighting, paint on the walls, furniture. A computer on the kitchen counter (this is 1986). Our garage now held a candy-apple red Corvette.

Behind the house, using three massive branches in a tree, they built a tree house complete with a spacious veranda, side windows, and a long ladder leading to the front door. Next, two large dark-haired chimps arrived for the show. They wore diapers in the house and exercised daily on our trampoline. The tree house, complete with a deck and stairs into the room, had ample room for the chimps who lived and slept there. In summer, with leaves on the trees, the tree house took on magical proportions.

The crew and actors explored their new space: Annabeth Gish starred, and Jason Priestly was a stand-in who later starred in *Beverly Hills, 90210*. Tracey met Annabeth (also 16) and invited her into her bedroom in the house.

That evening, several people recommended a new movie starring Annabeth Gish. Tracey and I went to see a movie entitled *Desert Bloom*. I cried throughout the movie. Can you imagine? You watch a show in a theatre and then invite the star into your room – all in one day. It was a dream.

Tracey's response? "I will never sit next to you in a movie ever again!"

All three kids signed up as extras, and Kurt took a special role as stand-in for the chimps, whenever they could not assume the skill required, such as sitting in the Corvette to look like he was driving, wearing a spectacular chimp head, or writing in white foam on the hood.

"Perfect," I said. "Couldn't have found a better substitute."

Every filming day, friends and neighbours came to watch, standing in small groups around the activity. The newspaper interviewed Wayne and me. The next day, the front page of the Vancouver *Sun* detailed and described the movie in a full front-page article. It was a spectacle.

By the end of the month, our outdoor space consisted of a bald one-acre no-lawn area. Feet had wiped out all the grass. The movie crew and motorhomes packed up. The photos taken before the conversion to movie set allowed the location managers to magically re-transform every room in the house to look just as it did before. Walls painted, knobs returned to cupboard doors, carpets re-laid; they reseeded the grass and within a week a new lawn sprouted around the house.

When they were about to chop down the tree house, our kids begged them to leave it. We agreed and bought insurance to keep it intact. The kids often went up on the ladder to lounge on foam in mattresses in it. One morning, after everything had been cleaned up, I thanked Tracey for making her bed. With a scowl, she told me, "I slept in the tree house." Good thing we kept it. I never found out what had prompted her to sleep outside, high in the trees.

I smiled at the mileage the kids gleaned from that movie-making experience. A writing assignment? The movie came in handy. Each told a different, individual story of the experience over many courses and assignments.

FALL ARRIVED AND WITH THINGS SETTLED – AT LEAST AS FAR AS SCHOOL and activities and my classes went – I called my sister Tina in Ontario to come for a visit. Within a day, she called back: "Alice wants to come along."

I said weakly, "Really?" I wanted to say, "no, just you," but I didn't.

Tina's voice took on a strained edge. "I have to go and see my other sister, too." I never said she could not see our sister Anne. Despite my disappointment, Tina and Alice arrived. I welcomed them. After two days, I drove them to Anne's house in Chilliwack.

Upon their return a few days later, Alice told me about her wonderful sister, Anne. Did I want to see pictures? Daily, Alice repeated and repeated: "We're getting a coffee shop in Dunnville, you know?"

"Yes, I know. You've told me repeatedly at least five or six times a day." No, of course I didn't say that. After they left, a letter arrived, a white paper neatly folded. A brief note scribed in Tina's beautiful handwriting, and a cheque that covered the entire airfare I sent her. Was this my sister Tina? After their recent move to a far more traditional church in a new denomination, Tina had bent to John's wishes for religious purity. I would not be counted as pure. Tina lost every friend she had; they could not speak to each other. John, her husband, forbade her from speaking to me.

I deposited the cheque (I should not have) but did not respond to the letter. That became my way with my family. Let them do and say what they want. I'll ignore it – and them. It didn't work, but they didn't know that.

Chapter Twenty-Four

ᔣ

UBC Graduate School
1986

Excited, I hear the voice in my head repeat, "You are in graduate school…"

I applied to the MA program in Language Education at UBC. Outstanding teaching and learning had motivated me to read more and learn how to conduct research. Intensely curious, I wanted to move beyond what into *why* and develop critical questions for research inquiry. Offer accepted.

One new course was entitled, *Writing in Schools*. The description read: "Students will write in every class and for assignments." One look and one decision: not me. When other courses failed to fit into my schedule or my interest, I reconsidered. Plucking up my courage, I met with the professor who assured me of exploring new ways of using writing in the classroom. Reluctantly, I signed up.

The surprise? Writing in unstructured first-thought forms became less onerous. We exchanged and discussed our writing. The more I wrote, the less anxious I became. The more I read and discussed other people's writing, the more I saw that we all have bumpy beginnings. The more I read, the more I learned about my writing and my thinking. Drafting text opened the mind, connected to, and created new knowledge. The course that had seemed so daunting and out of reach became a critical tool for learning in every subject area. As sometimes happens, the course I resisted and almost did not take proved most influential, transformative.

WITHOUT FAIL, WAYNE'S STEADY HAND CONTINUED TO FULFILL HIS AT-home day promises. He closed his one-man building business to carry out home duties, always with confidence and skill and without complaint. His prediction that new environments, new challenges, and people would usher my return from the "slough of despond" (Bunyan) came true. He nailed it. I loved him then, as I love him now.

Back in the English Department, I took a new course with Andrea L. in Psycholinguistics. The course brought startlingly new views on reading and teaching literature. She introduced me to Louise Rosenblatt (*Literature as Exploration*), who undertook research built on principles of reading response theory, beginning with student knowledge, writing to articulate understanding. An epiphany: personal reading informs pedagogical models for teaching literature. Writing bridged reading and learning. Talking engaged readers and exposed their changing views. Using reading, writing, talking, and listening, particularly in small groups, enriched both reading and understanding.

Writing as a learning tool provided a way to document, consider, and cultivate meaning as the reading developed. I asked myself, why did I not know this sooner? I understood it instinctively, but had made no connections professionally, pedagogically, or in teaching, had not connected personal reading with school reading. As a reader, I could attest to its power of reading, as Rosenblatt proposed, from the brain out, not the page, as evidenced by the unique interpretations and understanding we gain, despite reading the same text.

"This doesn't work," my supervisor commented as she examined my M.A. thesis and the data analysis using simple percentages.

"Can you clarify?" I asked, confused.

"You can't calculate percentages this way."

"I will get to it as soon as possible."

Unable to muster up the courage to challenge her assumptions, I sat in front of my Mac computer and found the thesis analysis in a folder. The small storage capacity of those first small Macs concerned me. Could I fit another data bank and analysis into the Mac? I deleted the entire first analysis of the percentage data. Mistake.

With the second round of analysis complete, writing resumed. I finished. Copy made. Greatly relieved, I delivered the revised thesis to Wendy's house. Ten weeks later, the copy remained unread.

Meanwhile, having expected that I'd finish the MA on time, I applied to enter the PhD program at Simon Fraser University. Despite the unfinished MA thesis, Simon Fraser accepted my application with no additional requirements. Classes began. My PhD was launched.

M eanwhile, my MA supervisor still had not read my thesis. I fretted. Would I be dismissed from SFU? Would my acceptance be postponed, wasting a semester or two of precious time? Would I need to pay for two semesters simultaneously?

The Chair of SFU Graduate Studies listened to my concerns and assured me I could forego completing the MA and progress in my PhD program.

"I am Dutch," I told him. "I can't leave all the work I did in limbo. I'll finish."

When Wendy returned my thesis – after eleven weeks of waiting – she approved.

Dr. B. joined Wendy and me for a final committee meeting. "Great work, Mary, but I'm a little puzzled. Why did you not use 100 as the base for the percentages in your data analysis?" I sat immobile in my seat, staring ahead, wondering how to respond, waiting for Dr. S.

Wendy said, "Thanks, Syd, I agree."

I stayed silent.

Start from scratch, Mary, I told myself. Just do it. Calculations flew off the keyboard. I counted, collected, gathered, and divided, until the work was done, and the changes made in the analyses and interpretations. I dropped off copies to Wendy and Syd and hoped for the best. This backtracking certainly felt right.

Wendy and Syd agreed and arranged for my oral exam.

"How should I prepare?" I asked.

"No need to write anything down. Just tell us about your work," Dr. S. said. I knew enough not to follow through on that suggestion. I created a cryptic written presentation in point form that gave me some control over the presentation. I would not speak spontaneously; I would speak from the text.

The oral proceeded. The committee applauded and congratulated me. Done. A completed MA! I was delighted that I'd pressed on and not abandoned the work.

SFU EDUCATION MARKED A CHANGE IN THE CULTURE OF GRADUATE education. A welcoming, relaxed environment. My advisor provided information on timelines and support networks. He explained the required four-hour courses, two in philosophy, two in educational theory. I worried about the level of the courses, only having taken one course in educational philosophy at Calvin and that focused on Calvinism and Christian philosophical influences. I was prepared to spend the time, work hard, start early.

Both courses assigned a final paper on a subject of our choice. I chose to examine the philosophical grounding of Christian education. Now I write this in disbelief – with all my struggles, even moving to try other Christian schools, I persisted. I still wrestled with the questions. I still felt the need to demonstrate my ability to think and reason. Should I have taken the devil's advocate position to disassemble my naïve thoughts? I might have challenged myself. I knew full well my children's education lacked more than it offered.

Working two semesters, flat out, I completed the four required courses and registered for the qualifying exam. Things were fresh in my mind. I had just completed the last courses. I read, wrote, and handed in the qualifying exam.

Some months later, a formal letter arrived: "Pass." Yahoo. Worth the wait. Time to get serious with a proposal for study. The real research journey began.

Early in the first semester of Year One, Meguido, a faculty acquaintance, stopped by the student office.

"There's a call for an instructor to teach a writing pedagogy course here, Mary. You should apply. I'll support you – you'll be great."

I got the appointment as a sessional instructor and was

successful. Highly positive student responses led to renewed sessional work every semester. Classes filled and overflowed to over thirty students, which meant having a Teaching Assistant. I valued teaching adults. I was home; I belonged.

SFU PhD
1987 - 1994

W riting a research proposal required a faculty supervisor. Jaap Tuinman, the Dean, and Dutch like me, accepted the role. I took charge. The delays of my MA made clear the need for a supervisor who agreed to regular meetings. My monthly reports included a detailed account of our last meeting, research progress, and plans for the next month. Jaap proudly called it the MOS system: *Mary's operational system.* It worked.

My PhD committee functioned smoothly as a team. Jaap as supervisor, and Meguido Z., and Patrick D. from McGill contributed where needed. As Dean and supervisor, Jaap offered the services of a tech/video expert for the research, videotaping in six secondary schools for the full year of my research. An enthusiastic, smart, and skilled videographer, Linda attended every research session in the classrooms and with the teachers.

In the videotaped school-based research, Linda filmed, edited, and created visual clips showing students engaging in reading and discussions. She documented the teachers in their professional learning group. Together, we examined all the data to identify video clips for the dissertation, conference presentations, and clips for my oral defense. Visual aspects of the research over the course of a year, along with professional learning sessions: from real to reel.

PhD COMPLETED. I HAVE NO WORDS FOR THE RICH REALITY OF THAT successful completion. I walked around with my head in a cloud, smiled spontaneously. I sang and danced wherever I went in the house. I was 47 years old, and I finished my PhD.

Graduation took place on Simon Fraser's mountaintop outdoor concourse. Education students lined up outside the education building, starting with the two PhDs, Wendy and me, in brilliant red gowns with royal blue velvet hoods and doctorate caps. Resplendent, we led the long line of graduates descending the massive cement steps to the outdoor Academic Quadrangle as Simon Fraser's award-winning pipe band played "Amazing Grace." The rolling fog covered the massive stone steps, creating a surreal scene. The hair on my arms stood up and my heart swelled near to bursting. Tears rolled down my cheeks as the music filled the billowing mist. A gripping and emotional moment. Amazing grace, indeed.

After spending thirteen years on my return to university, there was no prospect of a local university position in sight. My youngest son was still in high school; Wayne was still flying. I worked out a plan and made an appointment with Jaap.

I began, "Since I am unable to move for an academic position right now with my youngest son still home, I think it would be beneficial to both of us if you offered me a full-time contract here. I could teach six courses a year. You could trust the courses were extremely well delivered and save yourself finding five additional sessional instructors."

"Agreed!" he beamed. He took out a contract then and there, filled it in, signed it.

I signed it back. I would teach six courses over three semesters and earn $45,000 per year, with annual renewals pending appointment of a Language Education tenure-track professor.

Jaap welcomed and congratulated me. I walked down the hall, pumping my fist. I couldn't wait to tell Wayne, our kids, friends, and colleagues. Shout it out!

AFTER CLASS ONE EVENING, JAN, A TEACHING ASSISTANT, PROPOSED: "I know a publisher that will let us write a book for teachers using reading logs in the classroom." Her remarkable knowledge, pedagogy, and interest in and care for students inspired me. I watched and learned; she watched and learned. Jan had already published two books with a former colleague in Toronto. I had never written, let alone published, a book, so I welcomed the opportunity to begin with Jan and focus on teacher practice.

After I handed her the first draft of the book, Jan gave it back with this observation: "Mary, I couldn't wait to read this book – but I couldn't find you. You were missing in action."

Back to the drawing board. Rethinking – making the narratives come to life – starting over. It reminded me of the MA data analysis.

"Tell teaching and learning stories," Jan suggested.

That worked. *Reading Response Logs: Inviting student to explore, short stories, plays, poetry and more,* got published.

Chapter Twenty-Five

Sagas and Stories
1990 - 1991

About every three months, I flew from Vancouver to Toronto, rented a car, and drove to Shalom, a Christian Seniors home for a weekend visit with Moe who had now been a widow for two years after my stepfather died unexpectedly. The trip involved fear, uncertainty, reluctance, and exhaustion. How would Moe respond when I walked into her room?

She greeted me not with, "Thanks for coming," or "How are you?" but with: "When are you going home?"

In our weekly calls from home, without fail, however, she started every conversation with: "When are you getting your PhD?" Moe had little else to ask, and I probably could not have explained my life in ways she would understand. I left home thirty years before. My life continued outside and beyond Moe. In a different world, I did not have enough Dutch vocabulary to explain my academic life, not that she would be interested.

The second last time I visited, my sister Leny accompanied me.

In the room, we chatted. Moe sat in a dull yellow velveteen chair smelling of urine, staring out the window to the gardens.

Without warning, Moe said clearly, "I love you both."

"Moe," I exclaimed. "I have never heard you say that. Thank you. I love you, too!"

I didn't, really.

Years later, when I asked her about it, Leny shrugged her shoulders. "I don't remember that at all." I was startled. Forget such amazing words? I treasured them. Moe had expressed her feelings in that moment – it probably took everything she had to utter those words. She did it.

In the last visit, as it turned out, I fretted and fumed as I flew to Toronto. The weekends were filled with awkward silences, until that one time, that only time. I reluctantly lined up for a rental a car.

Leaving Pearson Airport, lightning struck my thinking, an *aha* popped up! It seemed so obvious. I was ashamed I had not thought of it earlier. I walked into the room: "Moe," I said, "We are each writing our 40th anniversary of immigration and putting them together in a booklet. Why don't you tell me some immigration stories? I want to know more."

She perked up, her interest sparked. I took out a yellow pad and a pen and poised, ready, and let Moe talk. "One day Pa came home and announced: 'We are immigrating to Australia!' 'No, no no,' I said, 'Too far away. I am not doing that. We are immigrating to Canada.'"

Stories poured out. Sometimes she stopped with, "Now, that's enough." But no sooner said then off she went again: "We needed medical exams, so we went to Amersfoort, all on bikes." Moe rested momentarily, took a deep breath. Another story.

"We had a *kist* (a moving crate the size of a single garage), but even that did not have enough room for my organ. I made up my mind. It would hurt, but it came with the immigration move. Pa stood looking at the *kist* taking up most of the lane and said, "As soon as we get to Canada, we will find an organ for you."

He was right. One sunny Sunday at church in Fenwick, Moe

overheard someone saying she had an organ for sale. "I could sure use that organ, I thought," she told me. "Only $12, the lady said: so next morning everyone came down the stairs in their pajamas all singing! Family singing continued with my $12 pump organ."

The magic of the storytelling, of familiar shared activities, let the words pour out with ease. It provided an opening to tell her stories. Even as she tired, and said, "Enough," all it took was a little waiting for another story to emerge. I filled many yellow lined pages by hand and later transcribed them for our 40th anniversary immigration stories and leaving the Netherlands.

When my booklet arrived in the mail, I read every word. Each told a story from a personal perspective and angle. The differences and quality of the writing amazed me. When I got to the end, I missed Moe's story. I called Anne, and said, "Thanks for putting the stories together. Amazing you managed to get everyone on board, but one thing: I missed Moe's stories that I included along with mine. What happened?"

"She's dead," Anne responded, dismissively.

I was speechless. Are there even words I could have used?

A FEW WEEKS BEFORE, MOE ENTERED THE HOSPITAL; BY CHANCE, ALICE walked into the room soon after, and to her great shock, discovered Moe had passed. A mere six weeks after I was awarded my PhD, it seemed, Moe waved her Mary trophy around to the others in the senior home for the last time. She did it. It was enough.

Wayne and I flew out for the funeral, arriving with only minutes to spare. We rushed into the church and found the family gathered in the basement before moving together into the sanctuary. Brother Hugh prayed. We filed up the stairs to the front of the church.

"Tina, can we open the coffin so I can say good-bye to Moe?"

"Of course," she said.

Together, we lifted the heavy lid, but immediately heard steps running down the church aisle.

"Stop," the funeral director said as loudly as he dared. "You can't open the coffin!"

As I continued to prop open the lid I responded, "We just arrived. I was not here when my mother died. I have to say goodbye."

He turned a sharp left and returned to his spot at the back of the church.

The tears I cried in the funeral service only indirectly focused on Moe: familiar hymns she played on the organ, some Dutch, most in English. Standing there, my heart felt hard. My relationship with Moe was unfinished. On the other hand, I felt relieved. Visits to Ontario would be limited, certainly fewer. My picture would come down from the wall in Moe's house. Thankfully, my role as trophy ended.

At the restaurant with my family, I felt out of place, detached, unwelcome. I could not follow Ann Landers, who advised, "Remember who owns the problem." I was just insecure enough, just vulnerable enough, to take it personally, to look through a fog instead of digging to clarify the meaning.

Though I graduated with my PhD only three weeks before, no one mentioned it. No congratulations, no questions. The outlier still. I stood by on the fringes and even that seemed too close for comfort.

"Remember who owns the problem," Wayne reminded me.

WAYNE'S WORLD TRANSFORMED MY LIFE, AND IT CONTRIBUTED TO WHAT happened next in powerful ways.

My family had an altogether different tactic. They dished out fear to anyone unable to accept the party line – and I was the example.

After years of not speaking, relatively new to Toronto, I decided that on a trip to Michigan to see the kids, I should drop off a box of books for Jane, my brother's wife, recuperating from breast cancer.

A few book deliveries later, Hugh invited us in for coffee, then lunch – then to his summer place, where most of the family gathered every August for coffee and lunch by a literal babbling brook. Storytelling and singing burst forth.

By mid-afternoon, I made my way out to my car where John stood by himself. Seeing me walk up the grass, he stiffened and pulled his hands behind his back. When I reached out to hug him, he turned away.

Puzzled, I asked: "What's up?"

He mumbled: "You left your husband. I can't touch you. I would defile myself."

My mouth dropped. My hands shook as I tried to open the car door with my key.

Leaving my husband? Who said anything about that? Where did that come from?

On the way home, salty tears and angry internal conversations filled the drive time. *I left my husband*? I yelled. I threw my hands up in the air in disgust, still huffing and puffing when I arrived home.

Focus on the good things, I reminded myself. Remember who owns the problem. I was taking this far too personally. Why should I care what he thought? The fact is, I did care. I wanted to celebrate my new life. Nobody asked. Yet, I lived with the conviction that I was meant to be called to be in this place. Too many quirky coincidences.

THE HEALING PROCESS BEGAN WHEN I STARTED SENDING TINA CDS OF Dutch male choirs. She enjoyed them, reveled in them. She whistled along. Each time I bought one for myself, I bought one for her, and sent it along with a short sticky note, "Enjoy."

On CBC Radio One I heard Gaelic music. The announcer said, "If I could have only one song in the world I would play every day, it would be *Gair Na Gairbe* from Shaun Davey's *The Pilgrim*.

I called every possible source until I found a music store in a barn that focused exclusively on Gaelic music. I immediately ordered two copies and asked Tina if I could come for a visit. On my arrival, she stood by the entrance, outside. She spied me coming and ran alongside the car to direct me to a guest parking spot. We embraced, and I followed her into the building and up the stairs, down the hall to the apartment entry door. She welcomed me in and made faces, pointing to John, who was now sick.

"Hi John. Don't get up." I asked Tina, "How about lunch at Niagara on the Lake?"

She couldn't get to her jacket fast enough. "My favourite town. Let's go."

Tina had altered since I last saw her. She now wore men's pants, men's plaid shirts, very short hair. What was she trying to say? Was she sending a message?

When John passed away, she got rid of every piece of male clothing and replaced them with blouses and dress pants. I never asked her about that.

Time on her own in the church-run apartment building became increasingly challenging for Tina. My niece campaigned that it was time to go to a senior home, and she finally relented. The place was new, beautiful, but clinical.

Shortly after, a room in a Mennonite seniors home opened, and Tina moved there. For most residents came from a Mennonite background and knew many residents there. Tina withered. An extrovert, she wanted desperately to go to Shalom Senior Residence, where Moe lived for a few years, the first home built by the Christian Reformed church.

On the first visit, it was plain to see why; Tina was home. I heard the laughter. The support workers enjoyed her storytelling, her love of music. We sat down together to watch *Nederland Zingt* (The Netherlands Sings), the powerful performance we had enjoyed in the Netherlands for my birthday in 2008. My frequent visits involved drives along Lakeshore Road to Niagara on the Lake, passing many familiar sights: fruit farms, orchards, vineyards. We remembered the names of church members who lived along the road.

I treasured the visits; I did not love the drive. We enjoyed lunches, often eaten outside, beginning and ending with thick, foamy lattés. We'd take a sidewalk tour down one side of the street, cross and go back in the other direction. We'd stop at the Shaw Theatre to check out the plays. It was a highlight for her and for me. We were sisters.

Around this time, Tina faced the frightening diagnosis of Alzheimer's disease. She rarely complained. She joined an Alzheimer patient group and asked me to be her partner at lunches and programs. I tried to accommodate her.

After the second time, however, she no longer wanted to go. Generally patient with changes, this got the best of her. As I approached her door in the seniors home one day, I found Tina in the hall with a support worker. She saw me coming and burst into tears. "I forgot you were coming. I forgot completely," she said softly.

The case worker put her arm around Tina.

"I'm here, and so glad to see you," I said.

ON MY FIRST VISIT WITH WAYNE, WE FOUND TINA IN A CHAIR. Unprompted, spontaneously, she began a story about our Pa.

"During the war," she said, "we were out of food at home and Pa found a wheelbarrow to carry once-used coal. Early in the morning, Pa, Margaret, and I left and walked until we got into a farm area. We were getting hungry so Pa said, 'Go to this farmhouse and ask if they will give you a sandwich' – which we did. One each, but nothing for Pa, so I said to Margaret: 'Give me your coat and you take my glasses, so they won't recognize us, and we'll get another one.' It worked! Much later, we talked about fooling the farmer's wife – which we agreed we didn't."

"In the late evening, we arrived at our Oom Henk and Tante

Cor's place. We had walked and pushed the handcart over 40 kilometers! We had supper and went straight to bed – one bed for all three of us. Instead of lying from headboard to footboard, we lay across the bed. No sleep at all, of course, but in the morning, we loaded up the cart with wheat. I think we had breakfast, and maybe some food for on the way back."

"Of course, the way back seemed a lot longer than the way up! Margaret was ten, and got tired, so she got to ride on the wheat. When we got within about 15 km of our house, we had to go on the dike, since our earlier trip it had flooded when the Germans blew up a major dike connected to the one we were walking on. The water was so cold – it was February. Margaret wore only a pair of light sandals, so Pa said she could sit on the handcart. I was a bit upset at first, but then I thought about her being the youngest, and she had been on a long, long walk. We arrived home around 7 p.m., cold, wet, and happy to be back. Pa immediately took the wheat to the baker, who used it to bake bread for us and other people."

People immigrating from one country to another carry with them a culture frozen in perpetuity: celebrations, standards, taboos, expectations. When we left the Netherlands, men and women smoked, birthday celebrations consisted of family and friends stopping by for coffee and *gebakje* throughout the day, Sinterklaas brought presents (though not to all children, I learned) and everyone ate *oliebollen* on New Year's.

Canadians like me, whose families lived some fifty extra years in the Netherlands, including five years of German occupation during World War II, arrived with a starkly different worldview that included a deep interest in Calvinism, theology and the claim that "every square inch" belongs to God.

Understandably, the longer immigrants were away from the Netherlands (or other countries), the more they adapted and assimilated into Canada. Sinterklaas on December 5th became Santa Claus on December 25th. The pragmatic Dutch merged with Canadians. They did not live in separate communities like

American church members. The Netherlands remained as it stood when they waved goodbye from the immigrant ships. Intolerance and disdain grew for the Netherlandic Dutch, who, according to the critics, became far too liberal, leaving the faith. I heard it so frequently, so convincingly, I believed it.

Changes
1995 - 1996

The view from my home office included a verdant front garden in full bloom, including what the kids called the strangely twisting Dr. Seuss tree. When the phone rang on my L-shaped desk, I grumbled to myself at the interruption but picked it up.

"I don't have much time, Mary," the voice said. "I wonder if you could meet with a committee here in Toronto to interview for the Language Education position. I see you have been working very hard this year."

Irked by this brusque condescension, I stayed uncharacteristically calm: "Yes, Dennis, I'm sure we can arrange that."

"We need two days for the interviews," he continued. "We are transitioning to merge with the Ontario Institute for Studies in Education, so you would interview with the Faculty of Education, University of Toronto (FEUT) the first day, and at OISE/UT the second day. I'll forward the interview schedule."

How would I prepare? I panicked, unable to think of any questions. I might provide brilliant answers, but usually some ways after the fact. "Ah, yes! It's Dewey." This constituted a critical event for a tenure-track career. I lived in Vancouver (not Toronto). I was fifty-two years old; OISE was a living library with a famous faculty. I had not yet held a tenure-track position. Chin in hand, after a thoughtful moment, another Dennis came to mind, a colleague who turned down a U of T offer the year before and accepted a position at Simon Fraser – ending my contract position. Dennis confirmed what I had learned.

Work began immediately to prepare. I scribbled keywords and got ready to state what I knew and needed to know. I added questions to explore. My writing continued. I read and reread, adding comments in the margins.

We arrived in Toronto a few days before the interviews to connect with Tony and Sue. We decided to attend church in Toronto, one renowned in the denomination for its activism. The first church to have women in office, the first female pastor. The welcome there was unlike anything I had experienced. Several women volunteered to gather in a room close by before and during my interview.

Interviews began at FEUT in the traditional format, with committees and faculty groups from 8 in the morning (5 a.m. Vancouver time!).

The interviews went well, with positive responses to my descriptions and explanations. A long dinner with Anne, the Associate Dean, ended at 10 Toronto time. I collapsed into bed. At least Wayne was there waiting in the hotel.

Understandably, my research program received the most attention during the interview the following day at OISE. I prepared visuals to describe the studies, used video tape clips of teacher and student discussions around the study of literature in K-12 schools. Meeting with various groups and individuals ended by 2. Wayne and I went directly to the airport. Probably for the first and only time in my life, I slept on the airplane from Toronto to Vancouver.

NOT EVERYONE RESPONDED TO MY NEWS WITH ENTHUSIASM — admittedly, I did not seek their consent. The most challenging remarks came from church people in British Columbia. Almost to a person, they asked, "Are you coming home on the weekends?"

"From Toronto to Vancouver? With Wayne gone all or part of every weekend?"

Head shaking was common.

No one asked: "Is Wayne home on the weekends?"

A week later, at the National Council of Teachers of English

(NCTE) in Chicago, as I sat around a table with other academics, an urgent call came from Wayne.

"Somebody from the University of Toronto is desperately trying to get hold of you," he said shakily. "You'd better return the call."

"I'll do it right away. I'll let you know. Thanks!"

I walked back to my room just in time to hear my phone ring.

"Hi, Mary. Anne here from the Faculty of Education at the University of Toronto. We are eager to talk to you about an offer for the Language Education position."

I don't know why, but I responded, "Many decisions are to be made. I'll discuss this with my husband and get back to you. Can it wait a few days?"

"Of course. I'll give you the Dean's number, where he can be reached in California."

I called Wayne and we agreed that I would accept the offer. Dean Fullan and I spoke the following day. We agreed to meet.

At OISE, sitting on a bench in an unoccupied room by the elevators, Dean Fullan formally offered me the position, explained the parameters, suggested a salary. He explained the courses, research funding, and the shift from FEUT to OISE that would happen a year after my arrival. I agreed, accepted the offer, and signed the contract.

My heart leapt. Intense discussions with Wayne and the kids followed. "Great, mom!" "What could be better?" "You'll be a lot closer to us." Wayne said: "I can book as many flights as I can to Toronto. Can you come home for the times you are not teaching?"

The timing worked. Being on my own became a gift – thanks, Wayne! My appointment at a university pushed me to establish my own identity. For years I'd been the pilot's wife, the student. I was still the pilot's wife, but now also a faculty member in a prestigious institution. Starting my academic career at age fifty-two required time, silences, and spaces. I had a lot of catching up to do.

Commuting from Toronto to Vancouver was not an option for Wayne. "That," he observed, "would be too much."

I agreed. And I needed the time. Feeling considerable pressure to catch up not so much teaching practice but research and publications, we decided I'd find a small apartment. Wayne would stay in White Rock for the time being.

"Let's try this for a year and see what happens. I'll book as many flights as I can into Toronto – and you'll be home here for the breaks. If it works, we'll proceed with permanent arrangements. Kent can also stay in the house for now."

I mused, "Good thing I married a pilot."

Basking in the gift and glory of a very special life-changing moment – a tenure-track appointment as Assistant Professor at the University of Toronto – I was in awe and wonder. Like the zenith point captured in Robert Frost's poem, "The Road not Taken," I made choices: this door or that one? The road metaphor has limits, since a road ends. I haven't reached the end of a road yet, or even always chosen the right one. Benevolent interveners have been instruments for my change, development, and growth. The timing uncannily on target.

MY CONVICTIONS STRENGTHENED. I HAD NO DOUBTS ABOUT THE GIFT, although I might have doubted that I could live up to the expectations. Moving cross country was a major undertaking, even with family support. Packing and preparing, saying goodbye to friends, finding an apartment in Toronto, connecting with a few Ontario friends, particularly Tony and Sue: all of it fell into place.

For the first few years, I taught pre-service (teacher training) at U of T, and at the Graduate school at OISE. Research grant applications, the research itself, publications in peer-reviewed journals and academic books, proposals for conferences, preparing and attending conferences: it was a whirlwind. Publications and annual reviews were a mainstay, primarily at the large universities ("publish or perish").

My transition to living in Toronto happened in a few months; Wayne's transition to Toronto took four years. Most people felt sorry for us being separated – but were we, really? I knew absence from years of living with his pilot schedule, and the uncertainty of a regulated home life, "here today; gone to Maui."

Living in a small apartment downtown, right across the street from the Faculty of Education, allowed me to forge ahead in the diverse aspects of my new life. This was the day, once again that changed everything: my life, environment, career, social connections, colleagues, church, a new city. In a good story, this point would be the climax, the high point. I unsettled my roots and rose above the challenges faced by most post-war Dutch immigrant women, certainly ones I knew. Wayne's saving grace and my passion for my work opened the doors leading to this moment.

Being an immigrant had made its mark. In the largest church in the denomination in St. Catharines with 1800 members, I became the first woman to graduate from university. I felt carefully and wondrously prepared for this part of my new career, I could say, because I immigrated.

My corner office on the third floor had a fresh coat of paint and a view of Bloor Street out the large windows. Friendly staff eagerly supported my transition: Mary in the Dean's office; Joanne in the FEUT office... a strong endorsement for my new career ("unanimous," David told me).

Still, this Dutch immigrant woman walked along Bloor Street, repeating to herself, "You are an imposter. If they knew how dumb you really are, they never would have appointed you." Thankfully, that didn't last long. I just didn't have time to dwell on it.

Academic schedules and ready access to flights left times to return to White Rock. This ideal, unexpected opportunity proved rich in learning, teaching, and contributing to my field through conferences, research, and publications. The value of time on my own cannot be overestimated. I made progress, an essential ingredient for playing catch-up. I had time to read, prepare, keep office hours, prepare research-based conference proposals, conduct a study, finish my first book, and to write for journals and books. No television probably helped.

Two or three times a month, Wayne's schedule brought him to Toronto overnight. He would call from Pearson airport: "Just landed. Should be at the hotel in 30, 40 minutes," and I would joyfully hop into my car. Each time, as he stood by the hotel doorway with colleagues, I drove up in my bold little turquoise car; Wayne waved to the crew and walked to the passenger side of the car. A quick kiss on my cheek and we headed back to my apartment. Oh, the looks we got. We laughed aloud each time.

Soon after I arrived, I invited some colleagues and a new Toronto friend to form a book club. They all accepted. At our first meeting, I made a large pot of soup and bought fresh bread and filled the coffee table with books. We ate, browsed, compared, and chose a book to read. A month later, we gathered again at my apartment for supper and animated talk.

Toronto was a world apart for me. I attended readings, movies, church, the Toronto International Film Festival, Word on the Street. During the Toronto Film Festival, as Sue and I walked down an alley, we watched Tom Cruise climb out of a limo. He barely reached above the car. Sue and I looked at each other and snickered. The big star was a little man.

Now, in his first year at Calvin and with his usual style, Kurt surrounded himself with new friends. He rounded up for many weekend visits to the big city. Equipped with sleeping bags and pillows, they claimed their spaces along the wall of my apartment.

I asked, "How are you doing, Kurt? How is it all going?"

"Just remember, Mary," (that first name familiarity began at sixteen) "Cs get degrees."

I could hardly contest his stance. I had lived by the same standard, though I'd hoped my kids would follow Wayne, not me, regarding motivation and dedication. I hoped in vain.

Kurt and his crew arrived late Friday afternoon, dropped their stuff, and went off to a pub where he had his fill of beer, no doubt. At least he wasn't driving. At the pub, he bundled up a small

Christmas tree with tiny red balls and coloured lights and tucked it under his jacket. When he got back, he set it on a credenza and plugged it in, and the little lights began to blink.

"Where on earth did you get that?"

He said, "I can't have Mother Mary without a Christmas tree! I took it from the bar."

I couldn't help it. I laughed and shook my head.

FOUR YEARS LATER, WAYNE RECEIVED THE LONG-AWAITED OPENING FOR a Canadian Airlines base position in Toronto. When I say "Wayne stayed in White Rock, BC for four years," people always say, "I'm sorry. That must have been hard."

No, it was a wonderful thing. I'd been carefully trained over the years. A pilot makes a career of absences. Wayne frequently came to Toronto for stopovers, and I had holidays and non-teaching times. I could fly cheaply. To me, a gift.

Family members ignored my move to Toronto. No one called. That felt otherworldly.

In my first summer after Year One, brother Jack was about to leave for Ontario to see and say goodbye to our siblings. He was terminally ill.

I pleaded: "Our Ontario family has been very difficult. Please don't discuss my situation. I don't need any more manufactured stories that I left Wayne."

He paused at the other end of the line, then spoke his final haunting words: "You made your bed. You lie in it." Click.

I'm sorry our relationship ended that way. In some ways, I can't blame my family. They went straight to work after school, and every week, put their pay on the table. I did not. Most never forgave me. Moe did once say, "I paid for Calvin because for four years, you did not work and pay me. That was four years of no income, which equals a large contribution to your education at Calvin."

Sure, right, Moe?

My academic life proceeded: teaching four courses a year; research, writing and service. At the intervals, I received tenure, promotion to Associate Professor and ultimately, Full Professor. I worked hard, committed to research focused on teaching and teacher learning in social networks.

"You worked so hard," people often told me.

"Most people work hard," I'd say, "and they don't necessarily land where I did."

I saw no flash of light like the apostle Paul on the road to Damascus, but day by day, event by event, choice by choice, the narrative of my new life built. I didn't turn down an open door that could lead to something more, something new, something that moved me forward, some mistake that needed fixing.

Deeply grounded in gratitude, I celebrate the honour of my life.

Chapter Twenty-Six

Identity
2008 - 2009

Plans and proposal prepared and accepted: my full year sabbatical from OISE for 2008-2009 drew closer. Dutch colleagues at conferences had encouraged me to consider coming to the Netherlands. My interest in my Dutch identity spiked – I wanted to hear the language. My speaking lacked currency; it had been fifty-seven years since I left the Netherlands. Language changes as times change.

On the streets of Toronto, I sometimes overheard a Dutch conversation, and passed up no opportunity to stop, ask, find connections. Each time, a joyful reunion of my Dutch and Canadian selves lifted my spirits.

International academic conferences provided context for tuning my ears to Dutch. Once in the UK, walking down the hallway to another presentation, I stopped.

"Are you speaking Dutch?" I asked the small group of people.

"Yes. Dutch. Do you speak Dutch?"

"Not very well, I'm afraid."

After brief introductions, our conversation continued over dinner. I spoke English; they spoke Dutch so rapidly I couldn't follow, though I did not confess my Dutch language inadequacy. The language rushed past my capacity to take it in. Colleagues and friends called my language old fashioned Dutch. My vocabulary had not caught up. The words I used belonged to another era. I wanted to communicate in Dutch, but I had a lot of catching up to do.

When the conversation turned to starting a new international journal for language and literature, Gert and Tanya from the University of Amsterdam asked: "Would you be interested in joining as co-editor?"

Excited and honoured, I agreed. Revisions and editing became my responsibility; Gert took on the business and contacts and planning a bi-annual conference. We worked as co-editors for the next twelve years. The work required in-person meetings annually. Gert introduced me to many Dutch language education experts. My Dutch colleagues became friends, co-researchers, and writers, and nourished the Dutch parts of my life and history.

Interactions at conferences led to invitations to speak, email, and times to write together. The Dean at ICLON (Graduate Education) offered me an eight-month stay at the University of Leiden's Centre for Teacher Learning and Development. It would mesh seamlessly with my research. I would work with doctoral students and collaborate on a book on *Teacher Learning that Matters: International Perspectives*. With a SSHRC project underway and a book to write with Klaas Van Veen, I joyfully accepted the offer.

Little packages and communications arrived from the university: a CD read-aloud version of a popular Dutch book, comedians, music. I listened intently. The novel, *A Brilliant Flaw*, (*Een Schitterend Gebrek*) severely challenged my capacity to read Dutch. I became an immigrant again: new to the current language, new to the culture, new to Dutch university life.

"Wait till you're in Leiden," Wayne suggested. "Ask for advice from Dutch speakers."

"I'll try."

From Toronto to Schiphol, Amsterdam (Wayne's favourite airport), we took the train to Leiden. The organized Dutch planned my stay in meticulous detail, securing me a fully furnished place, with a bike, in central Leiden. To my delight, it was a two-bedroom unit with kitchen, bath, living and dining room – even plants. I filled the drawers, checked out the kitchen equipment, saw the windmill through the front window, watered the plants.

Walking across the bridge, we encountered an amazing scene: hundreds of bicycles stored in a bike parking lot. How would anyone ever find their bike if they parked there? Fortunately, I did not need that parking, since the ICLON building was close to the classic train station, red-brick, square, with massive arched windows. A fish truck stood on the square along with views of the buses, a grocery store, and more racks and racks of standard Dutch look-alike bikes.

We explored Leiden and familiarized ourselves with the canals that met in the centre of the city, bridges, the restaurants, Haarlemmerstraat (the shopping street) filled with small shops. No bicycles, cars, trucks, or deliveries after 10 a.m. Parents walking their children always seemed to be involved in conversations. At that time, there were no cell phones in sight, nor many strollers, either. Children walked or rode in the basket in front of the bike or rode a small bike by themselves alongside their parents.

The sign on a Delft blue square noted the 100th anniversary of *De Pannenkoek Huis* (the pancake house), serving enormous Dutch pancakes set on a platter, too big for a plate. Even then, the pancake fell over the edges. More like French crepes than Canadian pancakes, *pannenkoeken* come with myriad fillings, both sweet or savory.

Too soon, Wayne headed back to the airport. I was on my own, anxious, nervous to be at the university in Leiden.

But stress and tension melted in the warm, welcoming

atmosphere. I relaxed. Each day, I cycled to Central Station, paying close attention to traffic lights (little bicycles) and other (more skilled cyclists) speeding on the bicycle paths. I walked the bicycle through the crowds to the back door, climbed back on the bike, and parked on the rack next to the ICLON building.

The Education building had opened after a total interior renovation. Grand, masterful steps to the entry, like Tara in *Gone with the Wind*, welcomed us. Mosaics on the walls of the mezzanine overlooked the entry. Each floor had new, wide hallways, big live plants in every corner. Faculty, PhD students, and staff had only been in the building one week.

Openly and generously, they welcomed me. Office staff proudly pointed to my name on a nearby door. Entering, I found business cards on an executive-size oval table, magnetic walls, posters to hang with ICLON circle magnets. The desk drawer was filled with supplies. Having the only Mac computer on the floor, I was assigned computer support.

My first morning at the office, I sat at the large table, door ajar, hearing the buzz of people walking and talking, speaking Dutch. I became very emotional, tears welling. Softly, I shut the door, and broke down, head in hands.

Tears wouldn't stop dribbling down my blouse, blotching the fabric. Why was I crying? Happy tears? Where were the Kleenex? Reclamation proved more visceral than I had expected. I was home, not as an immigrant kid but as a reconstituting citizen.

In the first week, I listened as colleagues shared research on teaching and learning. I attended my first meeting. I headed to the Dean's office to discuss my role with colleagues and the department – that meeting left me wondering if I still understood Dutch. Why couldn't I follow? Why did they talk so fast? It seemed a new language entirely. Even assuming I could speak some Dutch, the academic language was entirely new territory.

I determined to learn more of this updated Dutch, to make sense and, more important, to make meaning. I was aware, though, that I was not fooling anyone – least of all myself.

Sabbatical University of Leiden
2008 - 2009

O nce a few words left my mouth my Dutch colleagues recognized my limited, old-fashioned Dutch, tinged with an awkward Canadian accent. Listeners switched to English without a pause, saying, "I like to practice my English."

"Could you say that in Dutch?" I countered. "I like to practice my Dutch."

Lots of bumps along the way. Language is a moving phenomenon; new vocabulary, staying current with the times (think technology) and forward-moving culture. Language expresses culture and changing culture produces new language.

Standing in the hall with a small group of colleagues, I innocently used a wrong word, suggesting strong sexual overtones. Spontaneous laughter exploded.

"What did I say? What did I just say?"

Several spoke at once – I wanted to shrink away, but only briefly. The Dutch have a "no bullshit" approach to life. Get on with it. Work harder. Work on your pronunciation. I began by sharpening my listening skills.

Discussions with the Dean and my colleagues included collaborative writing on a book chapter (published) and a book on international perspectives on teacher learning (published). I collaborated on a study for pre-service teachers focused on English education. I met with PhD students on their thesis writing – all in English. I attended meetings of all sorts, did presentations on my research, attended oral exams, and served as external examiner both at Leiden and other universities. Days were filled to overflowing with work, meetings, reading, and plans for more work.

Surrounded by Dutch and straining to understand made for

hard work and, sometimes, exhaustion. *A Brilliant Flaw (Een Schitterend Gebrek)*, the story of Casanova and the young girl he loved – I'd planned to take the time in the Netherlands for deep listening. When even listening failed, I asked a doctoral student for a copy of the book.

I opened the book, turned on the CD, but to my great disappointment, still could not follow the narrative. Determined, I planned to read at least 30 minutes in bed. Just read.

Every night I finished the day in bed, reading, engaging in rapt attention to the story. By the end, Casanova mesmerized me. Initially, I probably understood a little more than half of what I read. That percentage grew. Others brought and recommended books like *The Undutchables*, a hilarious and delightful book on the Dutch. A colleague gave me a book on the history of Baarn, my hometown. As my reading ability grew, I read articles and chapters by colleagues. Being grounded in the university culture improved my listening, particularly academic Dutch. The fact that I now understood Dutch delighted me, my colleagues, and their students.

Oral speech remained challenging. When young children spoke animatedly on the street, I thought, "I wish I could speak Dutch like that." On the other hand, I could now sit in a meeting about complex educational issues and say, "I understand." That made it possible for me not only to support PhD student dissertation writing in English but also, to my amazement and joy, to serve as a PhD external examiner around the Netherlands. It quickened my spirits to follow responses and questions. I belonged here. I was at home.

After a presentation on my research on teacher book clubs, a group of Leiden PhD students approached me, wanting to start a book club. Eagerly, I agreed, and we hammered out a quick outline for creating a book club.

Saturdays were market days. A sight to behold. Booths on either side of the walk filled the square. Shops, coffee shops, restaurants lined the canal on either side. This market was set up in themes:

fish, fruit and vegetables, flowers, chocolates, candies, cheese, leather goods, clothes, linens – all meticulously displayed. The lively atmosphere, the chatter, students bending back their heads and slipping a raw herring in their mouths and down their throats. Deep-fried fish on sticks or in Styrofoam containers – I never missed the Saturday market, or the purchase of the fantastic hand-tied flowers, including many I had never seen before.

A colleague at ICLON recommended going to De Hooglandse Kerk. I'll try it once, I thought. Could I even understand Dutch church language?

One Sunday morning I walked my bike through the Haarlemmer Straat (no bike riding was allowed on the weekend on the shopping street). I turned the corner, crossed the bridge, and found a massive 15th century Gothic structure. The congregation met in a smaller open area. The organ stood in the space high above the parishioners; the organist climbed the stairs, sat down and music wafted and danced in the air. I understood the sermons, perhaps because the preacher's language resonated with my Dutch heritage. Religious language does not change much, I figured. I returned weekly.

Early in my stay, cycling home after a day at the office, two clear voices singing surprised me. I stopped and stepped off my bike to see a mom and her son, maybe twelve years old, cycling close beside each other. The mom's arm was wrapped around her son's shoulders. They continued, and I followed until I had to turn to my apartment. I veered to the side of the road and stepped off my bike again to listen to the last of the music. I etched the image into my memory. Imagine this in Toronto, where bikes were a relatively recent phenomenon on city streets and bike paths had only now appeared. Singing? Together? Out loud? Not likely. But oh, the joy.

Wilma, my college roommate, visited me in the Netherlands during her sabbatical from the Rochester Institute of Technology, where she served as head of languages. Also a Dutch immigrant, we spent time together in Leiden, the coffee shops, took long walks, and ate in the famous restaurant serving *pannenkoeken* for one hundred years. We talked and laughed. "Could we ever have imagined this when we struggled through our Calvin times?"

Wilma and I had rarely spoken about our immigration experiences. She immigrated to the US at 16, my older siblings ages. She knew more about the Netherlands. She grew up by accommodating and adjusting to the majority of Dutch Christians in New Jersey.

Wilma agreed to join me to surprise the members of the book club. Down a gloomy street with soft yellow streetlights, we located the house number, knocked on the door and waited a moment or two.

When the host opened the door, her face lit up.

I put my finger to my lips, "Shh."

Wilma and I followed Ciska into the house, and shouts of surprise and welcome erupted from the living room. "Welcome," Tamara said, "to the Mary Kooy Book Club!"

The raucous welcome by at least a dozen women who sat around the table with a copy of the book under discussion delighted me. Wine glasses filled, Wilma and I watched and mostly listened to the discussion, told stories prompted by the book, then bade them all a good night and walked back to the train.

Work at ICLON moved ahead. Collaborative work on a chapter on language education in the Netherlands was my first assignment. My colleague's English was as limited as my Dutch, but we did it – together. I read enough Dutch to manage the translation of his parts to English. The Dean, editor of *The International Encyclopedia of Education* (3rd Edition), read the chapter and was unimpressed. He made suggestions, offered other chapters to review, and set a deadline.

We set to work, improved much, and completed on time. The new version brought extended and effusive approval.

Wayne came once a month, for a week, and brought my sister Tina to Leiden to celebrate my 65th birthday.

I worried about the trip. Wayne often forgot that airports, so familiar to him, were unfamiliar to others. He who never walked; always ran, and Tina, who never ran if she could walk, might face a dilemma in the airports. Could she keep up with Wayne? Thankfully, they arrived.

Oh, what a day! Together, we travelled to Baarn (my birthplace), Boskoop (her birthplace), and other spots along the way. She became a lighthearted, joyful presence and superior guide. The day she led us through Boskoop, we put in 20,000 steps – no small feat, as she was 78 years old.

"The book and this trip," she repeated throughout the visit, "are the best things that have happened in my life. When I came with John, all we did was stay with his relatives. I have experienced nothing like this."

I knew she meant it. She radiated happiness.

While I cooked, Tina walked back into the living room and proudly, face beaming, presented me a sacred icon: her book for my 65th birthday. We sat close together paging through the entire beautiful book, laughing, crying, remembering the pictures, particularly those of the liberation after World War II. Here we were, sisters with a thirteen-year age gap, sharing and looking at the text and the photos Tina had saved across the years, packing them for immigration to Canada and years beyond.

As a tour guide, Tina invited us to see the Boskoop where she was born, and my family lived until 1942. She recalled the swing set in the park; she took us to our Opa's house, her school, the town. She showed us the canal where her friend fell in. As Tina told it, she hollered: "My friend is in the canal. Help!" Two men dove in and rescued her friend. The men praised Tina and took them to a local house where they were given dry dresses and socks.

On 3 October, Leiden celebrated Leidse Ontzet, an official city holiday. Celebrations began early in the morning with a service in the massive church. A choir sang. The story of chasing out the

Spaniards and liberating the city of Leiden from Spanish rule in the 15th century gripped the audience. Small wonder everyone was familiar with the story told and retold annually. The reward for the rescuers? Leiden University, the first university in the Netherlands, was established in 1575.

At the end, the audience sang the national anthem, *Wilhelmus van Nassouwe*. Tina knew all the words – I did too, given they were printed in the program. She zipped her lips at the line, *'ben ik van Duitsen bloed'* (I am of German blood). She would not and could not sing those words, suggesting she was of German blood.

Festivities included stands with Dutch food such as *oliebollen*, for instance, literally translated, means "oil balls," which does not, at least to me, sound too tantalizing. I assure you, they are. Nevertheless, the Dutch word has much more appeal and taste.

Droves of people in the laneways among the stalls enriched the celebration. At the dinner hour, citizens of Leiden lined up for a basket of fresh white bread and raw herring, the food left in the vats to feed the Spaniards chased out by the citizens.

In the dark, on our way home, we rehearsed, over and over, the delights of the day. We indulged in the fragrances of baking and frying, the traditional foods I had mostly forgotten. We stayed until dusk, linked arms and waltzed home.

With the needed groceries in hand, I prepared the pan for *Hutspot* – chunks of onion, potatoes, and carrots that cooked till soft while rings of smoked meat boiled. The vegetables, drained and mashed, were crowned with chunks of smoked meat.

"On my birthday, we are going to Nederland Zingt," I announced.

"Nederland Zingt?" Tina whooped and hollered and danced around the room.

"No seat reservations," I said, when the day arrived. "Let's go early."

We arrived at the grand church, lofty ceilings, choirs gathering, organ playing. Taking seats in the third row from the front, facing the choirs, was a holy moment. Tina sang her heart out with each song, invited to join the choirs or not.

She talked non-stop about the wonder of it all, her favourite songs, the powerful choral singing. Her voice rang out on Leiden's dark streets. The joy of watching her brought me back to singing at home with Moe at the organ and the voices ringing each day after supper. Alison Krause, the songwriter, captures the impact of music on Moe and Tina: "*If there was no music, I don't know how I'd get through.*" Music resonated in all parts of Tina's life. "I'd take Moe again," she'd say, "because she gave me music." An outstanding legacy.

A week or so later, I received a letter from Tina saying "thank you" for her experiences. At home, she distributed hard copies of her book to her own families (five children). She ordered about fifty more soft cover books, and within a week, they sold out to her neighbours. A good thing, too, since not one of our siblings bought or read a copy. Not one.

Now that I had attended four or five oral exams, the Dean invited me to be an external examiner. Wayne brought my SFU robe, candy-apple red with royal blue velvet hood and tam (SFU). At the earlier oral exam I attended, I noted faculty wore only black robes.

"Could I just order a black robe?" I asked.

"No. You are the first English-speaking Dutch-born person living in Canada participating as an external examiner. I ask you to wear your academic robe, so everyone catches the international flavour of the defense."

With trepidation, I conceded. After an oral committee meeting to discuss protocols and procedures, the faculty lined up behind the beadle. Entering the room, I heard a gasp from the audience. The beadle took the ornamental staff and stamped it on the floor, saying, "*Hora est*" (the time has come)." We filed into our reserved places on the benches on the side.

Typically, about one hundred people sit in the audience for the PhD oral exam. I learned two important things: first, candidates must have successfully published the dissertation *before* the oral exam. Second, only external examiners asked questions. Completely sensible. Two attendants (paranymphs, friends of the candidate) came onto the stage. They helped, planned, invited, and organized and managed the event. Like a wedding, attendees enjoyed snacks and drinks and congratulations all around. Later, the restaurant was reserved for the guests' dinner, with gifts of personal poems and songs written for the occasion. Brilliant. A masterful and distinctive celebration of a critical event. Every important occasion or day required celebration.

We have to celebrate. If we don't celebrate, our only memories will be of funerals. We have to go to funerals. We don't have to celebrate.

I have never forgotten. I am Dutch. I celebrate.

The ongoing transformation from a semi-Canadian to reclaiming my Dutch citizenship re-situated my feet in two cultures. A dual identity. Will identifying with two cultures bring about a unified self? Why do I feel lighter, more balanced as I leave behind the shame of my Dutchie status as a girl?

That began, I think, with my first trip back to the Netherlands with Wayne and was crowned by the sabbatical at Leiden University.

THE SABBATICAL ENDED. OVER AND OVER, I REHEARSED THE inconceivable life moments. The joy of growing and knowing: I am Canadian, and I am Dutch.

I listened to lively music as I cleaned the apartment, packed suitcases, washed the bike, left a few groceries for the owner. Wayne came to help with the final move. Time to say farewell to the faculty and the staff. Painful.

"I could live here," Wayne said.

"Me, too."

"Even leaving the kids and grandkids?"

"Right. That wouldn't work."

My homecoming offered a powerful sense of belonging. My parting gift? Not one *or* the other; not even one *and* the other. Straddling two divides and not toppling over in one direction or the other is welcomed. I am at home here. I belong. I belong in Canada, too. I am a reclamation project.

Feet firmly planted, I prepared to move on back to Canada.

Teaching And Learning
2015

S itting on the deck in our Toronto backyard checking my email, one arrived that, completely unexpectedly, made my eyes widen and spiked my curiosity.

I read:

> "Did you teach English in BC at FVCHS in 1984?"

Bolting upright, my eyes widened, tears fell. Without hesitation, I responded to the email:

> "Yes; I did!!"

I asked:

> "In 1984 [1985], did you write an incredible reading log on Cry the Beloved Country?"

> "Of course, I remember you, Ed. Indeed, what are you up to? Would love to hear."

And our conversation began…

"Wow! Love the internet! Track someone
down after 28 years. I was talking to a
friend on the weekend about my school
experience as she is a teacher. I explained
my Grade 12 English class and what
happened, and she says: Was that Mary
Kooy? Apparently, she knows you. Small
world. . . Every student has one teacher
they always remember and makes a lasting
impression, and you were that teacher for
me. THANKS."

Ed responded to my query about his life since he was my
student. He began:

"This letter has been 28 years in the making."

His heart spilled out on the pages. My heart jumped in my
chest.

*"I've told this story to my wife a few times and
she tells me to look you up and thank you. So here we
are. Not sure if just a thank you is sufficient. I
figure I should go into detail. Should I write a
simple note or a letter? As you can see, I've opted
for the latter."*

*"Many times, I have thought of you and your
class, my education, attitude back then, and what could
have been or should have been. . .So here are the meat
and potatoes of this letter, my education. In grade
school I was a very active boy whose interest was not
so much in school but playing sports. I think I*

probably had a little ADD and have found out over the years, a bit of dyslexia also."

"As I got to high school my interest dropped more and more every year."

"By the time I got to grade 11-12, I didn't care at all, thought I was wasting my time and just counted the minutes, hours, days, and months till I could get out of school and start life. I thought school was stupid and my attitude and marks reflected that."

"This has always been a big regret of mine and I find myself thinking back to those days. Why did it happen and how could it have been different? Could anything have been done that would have changed the road I was going down? Was it all me? Should I have participated and had a better attitude? Was it my parents who were not as involved and encouraging as they should have been? Or was it the education system that failed? As I've reflected on this. I've always come to the conclusion that it's all of the above."

"As I talked to Sophie last weekend, she says it's the system and not my fault, it was not me. She was very adamant. I'm still not so sure. I can blame my parents and the education system, which has lots to do with it, but ultimately, I am responsible for my decisions. . ."

"My parents did the best they could with the tools they were supplied with and the situations they came from. Not an excuse, but I understand how it happened, encouragement and involvement in children's lives was something they did not receive so it was very hard for them to give it to me. That is something I have had to work on and learn with my own children."

"The school at the time was doing what they deemed right. Looking back there were many flaws. The big glowing flaw was having slotted a student in grade 9 to level C, or non-academic, based on the previous year's teacher's opinion. WOW, why would anyone think that was a good idea? I'd love to know the rationale behind that decision."

"So, all this is background leading up to your class. I came as a kid with a bad attitude, who hated school, had given up at that point and English was my least favorite subject. My mind works with numbers, science, logical and facts. English doesn't really fall under those categories. Now, you stepped in, Mrs. Kooy. I really don't remember much from that class, sorry. I remember you letting me do a book report on a Steven King novel and thinking, this is different. I remember the journal and the 'aha' moment of that novel where I realized the book wasn't about the boy but about Africa. I also remember that you were very excited about it. Another memory was about going to your house with the class and talking to you about your trampoline. Funny the things we remember. Every time I drive by that area you come to mind."

"And of course, I haven't forgotten that you fought for us to write the provincial exam as an A student and not a C student. Not sure what you did in that year, but it was the only class I cared about and tried in and one of the only good memories I have. The irony after all this is that I was one math credit short of graduating. But thanks to you I have my Academic English credit."

"So again, as I reflect, I feel regret at what I could have done and should have done. You planted a seed of a better attitude. I have come to love reading. I have come to appreciate school and what the teachers go through with students like me. I don't think though, it's all on the teachers as my friend says, that is too much pressure and responsibility. As the saying goes, it takes a village to raise a child. I'm still not sure if anything would have helped to get me to like school at the time, dark times for me, but then I remember back to your class a light goes on and a smile on my face as I think, hey anything is possible, and anybody is reachable. So once again thanks. Where were you earlier on?"

The letter speaks to Ed's transformation and mine. I think of my first years of teaching as a "fake" teacher. His questions were my questions. Ed's reflections moved me. How did my transformation develop? How did my teaching become so integral and critical to my shifting identities? Ed confirmed that teaching was always my calling. His powerful testimony touched me deeply.

All I know is that it happened. Many years of annual reviews and student evaluations made this clear. I carefully read student evaluations and incorporated what I could into the revisions of the courses affected. *Educare* means "to draw out," not to pour in, and was often reserved for teachers and the practices they used. For me, it was a call to draw out my students, to give them voice. I received more than I could have given. An embarrassment of riches. I answered the call. No teacher could ask for more.

Homecoming
2015

Immigration, even as an eight-year-old, transformed my life: family, identities, teaching and learning, and spirituality developed and expanded as my worldview grew. The expectations of my birth family to work and bring in money never reached me, or my children. A chasm was between the two. Our children experienced a mother who returned to school in her late 30s.

My MA thesis is dedicated to my children, Tracey, Kent, and Kurt, "who for years endured the question: Is your mother still in school?" These same children had parents who valued education, hard work, and commitment. They followed suit, all in their own ways.

Because I immigrated and was a stranger in Canada, I wanted to belong. I abandoned my Dutch identity, desperate to be fully Canadian. Re-activating my Dutch citizenship made the circle more complete, and returning there for a sabbatical made me whole again, both Dutch and Canadian.

My teaching dreams came and went, strong early on – typical little girl dreams that underwent doubt about being an unlicensed, fake teacher. Transformed again through possibilities and support from Wayne that most people cannot imagine. He led me back to university to pick up where I left off and altered the face of the tragedy of the crushing loss of my best friend. Wayne soared (literally) in his flying career, and I continued my adventure at the university.

WRITING THIS HAS BROUGHT SMILES AND SOMETIMES DEEP SADNESS. MY stance has changed from moment to moment: sometimes liberating; other times, I was tossed into the Slough of Despond. Sometimes I reread humorous parts to Wayne, sometimes I walked away, not ready to dwell in morbidly dark places. The page stayed blank.

Other times writing felt like a smack on the side of the head, a reminder: Stop. Listen up. I sensed that the predictable life I was raised to expect would not satisfy me. Too small, that life. Too narrow. Increasingly daring, risking, and moving from the familiar into the unimagined changed and motivated me. It all happened because I immigrated.

This memoir is not only about loss (though loss happened) or accomplishments, but a testament to, among other things, determination and perseverance, staying the course. For the most part, I travelled without a compass, oddly out of sync with my family. I traveled in trust; I took risks. Not having the wisdom required for critical decision-making, I depended on interventions. Uncannily, at critical points, someone stepped in and opened or closed a door, pointed to new vistas, advocated. Often, naively unaware of implications or impact, I forged ahead.

"More luck than wisdom," Moe would say. Perhaps.

MOE WAS A DAUNTING, PRICKLY PRESENCE IN MY LIFE. WARM MEMORIES do not emerge without concentrated effort. Fear and negativity predominated, rising easily, and a catalogue of the wrongs of my mean mother spill out. With no logical explanation, a critical thought struck me forcefully when my therapist asked: "Did you ever sense that your mother loved you?"

My first impulse: "No."

But the more I wrote, the clearer it became that nothing stood still, not even my mother. In my head I heard, and in my heart I clearly experienced an epiphany: "This is precisely the mother I needed to do what I did."

The mother I needed? The burden I had carried for much of my life fell off my shoulders with a thud. I forgave Moe and even thanked her, mentally and emotionally – but unfortunately, not before she passed. The release proved critical for me. My view of

Moe passed with her. But a new awareness of what it means to forgive, to move on, to be grateful in all circumstances evolves.

I give my mother these final words: "And my darling, what more could you want?" (*En m'n liefie, wat wil je nog meer?*)

That's it, Moe. Thank you.

I identify with *The Message* where Eugene Peterson wrote: "I did not get God's attention by living my life like a saint; God made something out of Mary when she was a nobody."

The words resonated. Mary got a voice. It just so happens my name is Mary. I didn't have to change a word in that quote. It fits. I was a nobody, open to a re-do. I stand in awe at the hope that blossomed.

The poet Mary Oliver asked her readers: "Tell me, what have you done with your one wild and precious life?"

It began with events leading to immigration. Immigration propelled change. It stretched, and I gained, emerging increasingly confident through lived experiences. In the face of "I don't want to end up simply having visited this world," I say, I live life dynamically.

People, particularly immigrant women, sometimes ask about my life. They ask, "How did you get here?" A question I still ask at times.

A little forethought, a sketchy plan, not an easy escape but a hard-fought, glorious circle. I think of God creating a map, complete with directions and purposes unknown to me, yet leaving me stronger, spiritually uplifted by the experiences. Trusting, risking, daring, faith fulfilled and carried me along.

Over the years, my siblings grew increasingly distant. When Tina passed, the last family connections withered. We don't speak to each other, though it's not for lack of effort on my part. I understand why at some levels. I went my own way. I was the lucky one, with the horseshoe up my ass. I can't disagree, but I also know that many families are broken. Mine became toxic. With the help of a therapist, we decided I should walk away, though not without many attempts to connect. It worked with my sister Tina, but not with the others. I learned family from having one, learning what to carry forward and what to leave behind.

The relationships I yearned for came in the form of longstanding friends – who drove me to the party where I met Wayne, came to my wedding, became travel partners – who, by grace, have been my family for fifty-plus years. The very stuff needed to move, to change, to make a difference blossomed in my personal family, my children and grandchildren, who taught me the power of complete acceptance. I vowed to make my family a home of belonging and inclusion. We belong together.

Writing with my sister Tina affected both of us in powerful ways. Like water to a dry plant, it proved to be her ultimate achievement. She wrote in longhand in pencil, on paper. In our work together, she read the words aloud while I was at the keyboard. For the most part, the book was built as she read from her first draft. The emotional experience of putting her book together proved powerfully inspirational and bonded us as siblings. I thanked her for the learning, the sharing through funny, sad, dangerous stories – and I discovered I too had a story to tell.

My sister died unexpectedly a few years ago. I mourned deeply for the one sibling who called me family. My niece asked if I would do the eulogy; of course, I agreed, but I struggled to retell her story, until I hit upon the idea of creating a eulogy using Tina's own words. I quoted directly from her book *A Basket Full of Appels: Baskets full of stories*. She spoke at her own funeral. A final chance to have her tell some of her story.

It was a holy moment. The room filled to the brim. I waited briefly for silence and began to read. The air was charged. Not a cough, not a whisper, not a shuffle, not a sound from the crowd gathered round – utter silence.

On our way back to Toronto, Wayne said: "Rapt attention. Nobody stirred."

My sister would have been proud.

THE POET COUNTEE CULLEN WROTE: "YET DO I MARVEL AT THIS curious thing," Not just, "I marvel," but "*yet* do I marvel – at the *in spite of* in my life." Wonder lingers and diffuses. I play with those words: "Yet do I marvel at this curious thing/ *To make this girl an immigrant and make her sing.*" My singing continues.

At this point in my ongoing journey, I identify as both Dutch and Canadian – not "either/or," not "both/and" but a blend. I can't see where one begins and the other ends. Events and interveners brought me ever closer to an identity that fits, is comfortable, feels happy and accomplished. I am becoming more completely myself. Beyond measure, I am grateful.

About the Author

In 1995, at the age of 52, Mary Appel Kooy received an offer she could not refuse: a tenure-track position at the Ontario Institute for Studies in Education (OISE) of the University of Toronto as an Assistant Professor. Returning to school at 38, she had completed a B.Ed. and an M.A. at the University of British Columbia (UBC) and a PhD at Simon Fraser University. She was ready!

Since she lived in Vancouver, however, this required a significant move. Mary settled in Toronto and eagerly took up her teaching, learning, research, and writing. She conducted research with practicing teachers who were through /in professional communities. Teachers became collaborators and colleagues and wrote a book entitled "Can You Hear Me?"

After 21 years in her dream career, Mary became Professor Emerita. She continues to write, visits her children and grandchildren, and long-standing friends, mostly in BC. Her family celebrates holidays and plans ventures and adventures. With her husband, she takes long morning walks and spends some time in sunny California.

May the traits from which Mary's inspiring story is forged, encourage you to continue to step boldly forward through your own incredible life's Odyssey!

References and Quotes

"The Hound of Heaven" *Poetry.com*. STANDS4 LLC, 2024. Web. 26 Nov. 2024. https://www.poetry.com/poem/13940/the-hound-of-heaven.

Oliver, M. (1972). 13 Best Mary Oliver Poems: Reflective and Inspiring Poetry.

James Wendell Johnson. (1927). *Go Down Death: A Funeral Sermon,* From: *God's Trombones: Seven Negro Sermons in Verse.* Penguin Group Canada, pp. 27 – 29.

The Appel Family. *The Immigration Story: Holland to Canada.* 98 pages. Edited by Anne Appel Norder.

Tina Appel Wynia. (2008). *A Basket Full of Appels: Baskets Full of Stories.* 76 pages. Edited by Mary Appel Kooy.

Raska, Jan. (2020). Immigrant Voices: Diverse Reactions to the Transatlantic Voyage from Europe to Canada's Shores.

Raska, Jan. (2020). *Pier 21: A History.* University of Ottawa Press.

www.ingramcontent.com/pod-product-compliance
Lightning Source LLC
Chambersburg PA
CBHW030352130626
46549CB00004B/1462